CRIMINOLOGICAL
THEORY
IN CONTEXT

SAGE was founded in 1965 by Sara Miller McCune to support the dissemination of usable knowledge by publishing innovative and high-quality research and teaching content. Today, we publish more than 750 journals, including those of more than 300 learned societies, more than 800 new books per year, and a growing range of library products including archives, data, case studies, reports, conference highlights, and video. SAGE remains majority-owned by our founder, and after Sara's lifetime will become owned by a charitable trust that secures our continued independence.

Los Angeles | London | Washington DC | New Delhi | Singapore

CRIMINOLOGICAL THEORY IN CONTEXT

JOHN MARTYN CHAMBERLAIN

Los Angeles | London | New Delhi
Singapore | Washington DC

Los Angeles | London | New Delhi
Singapore | Washington DC

SAGE Publications Ltd
1 Oliver's Yard
55 City Road
London EC1Y 1SP

SAGE Publications Inc.
2455 Teller Road
Thousand Oaks, California 91320

SAGE Publications India Pvt Ltd
B 1/I 1 Mohan Cooperative Industrial Area
Mathura Road
New Delhi 110 044

SAGE Publications Asia-Pacific Pte Ltd
3 Church Street
#10-04 Samsung Hub
Singapore 049483

Editor: Natalie Aguilera
Editorial assistant: James Piper
Production editor: Sarah Cooke
Copyeditor: Jane Fricker
Proofreader: Lynda Watson
Indexer: Judith Lavender
Marketing manager: Sally Ransom
Cover design: Jennifer Crisp
Typeset by: C&M Digitals (P) Ltd, Chennai, India
Printed in Great Britain by Henry Ling Limited at
The Dorset Press, Dorchester, DT1 1HD

MIX
Paper from
responsible sources
FSC
www.fsc.org
FSC™ C013985

Library of Congress Control Number: 2014942886

British Library Cataloguing in Publication data

A catalogue record for this book is available from
the British Library

ISBN 978-1-44626-986-2
ISBN 978-1-44626-987-9 (pbk)

At SAGE we take sustainability seriously. Most of our products are printed in the UK using FSC papers and boards.
When we print overseas we ensure sustainable papers are used as measured by the Egmont grading system.
We undertake an annual audit to monitor our sustainability.

DEDICATION

For my daughter Freyja,

for reminding me about classical and operant conditioning.

For my family,

Freda, Irene, Shelly, Gemma, Harvey, Sasha, Cody, Andy, Richard and Geoffrey.

And for Jane,

because she said yes...

BRIEF CONTENTS

CONTENTS

PURPOSE AND STRUCTURE OF THIS BOOK

This book offers the reader a concise but authoritative overview of criminological theory, including classical, biological, psychological and sociological approaches, an analysis of the strengths and weaknesses of each theory discussed, as well as recommendations for further reading and self-study. The idea of completing a theoretical course in criminology as part of their studies may well be attractive to students. But it can nevertheless be quite a daunting exercise to complete and indeed cause them to become anxious about their ability to make their way through what at times can be quite complex and esoteric learning material. This book seeks to make this process a little easier for the first-time student in particular through outlining in a clear and concise manner the main features of different theoretical approaches to the problem of crime against the background of their emergence within the development of criminology as an academic discipline. Hence it has two key aims:

1. To provide an introduction to different types of criminological theory as well as to place this discussion within the context of the historical development of criminology as an academic discipline.
2. To outline key features of the theories discussed and provide guidance and further readings to help students plan a research project.

The following chapters are structured in such a way as to fulfil these aims. Chapter 2, 'Classical Criminology and Contemporary Rational Choice Theory', begins our journey into the realm of criminological theory by examining how criminal behaviour is the result of a person exerting their free will and weighing up the costs and benefits of pursuing a line of action. This view of crime emphasises that its causes lie in our ability to choose how to act. The chapter discusses how the emergence of the Classical criminological view of crime and 'the criminal' was the result of a gradual shift away from religious interpretations of human nature and the natural world. This, in turn, was bound up with the growth of modern science and liberal-democratic politics from the eighteenth century onwards.

Chapter 3 focuses on *Biological criminology* and how medicalised explanations and solutions to the problem of crime have changed and developed over the last two centuries. The chapter covers approaches which focus on physical difference, genetics and biochemistry, diet and nutrition, in shaping how criminologists understand the causes of criminal behaviour. In doing so, the chapter highlights the importance of the interaction of environmental and genetic factors in shaping human behaviour, as well as how Psychological and Sociological criminologists criticise Biological criminologists for neglecting the role of cognitive and socio-cultural factors.

Chapter 4 builds on the previous two chapters and explores *Psychological criminology*. It focuses on personality and cognitive development as well as psychosocial learning theories in the form of social learning and differential association theory. It also considers the contribution of research into violent and sex offenders to understanding the causes of crime. The chapter highlights how, like Classical criminology and Biological criminology, Psychological forms of criminology locate the causes of crime inside the individual. Although rather than emphasising free will and genetics, it is argued that our actions are to some extent determined by our psychological makeup and learned behaviour.

In Chapter 5, 'Strain Theory, Social Disorganisation Theory and Labelling Theory', we move towards a more sociological focus looking at explanations for crime which highlight the role of social change and anomie, the organisation of city spaces and urban environments, along stereotyping and labelling, in promoting antisocial deviant and criminal behaviour.

Chapter 6, 'Critical Criminology, Part 1: Marxist, Peacemaking and Realist Theories of Crime', introduces Critical forms of criminology, which collectively critique earlier forms of criminology (both sociological and otherwise) for advocating a positivist value-free form of criminology and failing to acknowledge the role of class, race and gender in shaping both definitions of crime and law and the likelihood that an individual will be labelled deviant and criminal. The chapter focuses on explanations for crime based on economic and social inequality as expressed in and through the class system.

Chapter 7, 'Critical Criminology, Part 2: Feminist and Cultural Criminology', builds on the contents of Chapter 6 and explores how criminologists came to recognise the importance of adopting a more critical stance towards traditional explanations of the causes of crime which by and large ignored the role of gender and race and ethnicity, in addition to class, when it came understanding why crime happens and what the solution to it should be. It also highlights sociological subcultural theory, which is concerned with exploring the role of youth and alternative subcultures in relation to crime, as well as the emergence more lately of Cultural criminology. This emphasises the role played by human emotions and thrill seeking behaviour in crime.

Chapter 8 details the emergence of *Life Course criminology* against the background of the emergence of postmodernism within contemporary Critical criminological perspectives discussed in previous chapters. Life Course criminology examines the criminal career in the context of life pathways, stages, events and turning points, all of which are embedded in social institutions such as education, work, family, and of course, the penal system.

Finally, in Chapter 9, 'Reflecting on Theories of Crime, Theories of Human Nature', we look at current trends and developments in western societies and criminal justice systems and in doing so it is noted that criminologists have increasingly argued over the last three decades that governing elites are promoting a more popularist and punitive approach to crime prevention and control which is based on population surveillance, profiling and risk appraisal. This is targeted at social groups and individuals held to present more of a potential threat to public safety, such as people from inner-city estates which possess high levels of social deprivation, lower than average life expectancy, as well as greater intergenerational unemployment and welfare dependency. Here the chapter brings together several key themes and issues from previous chapters to explore the study of crime in the age of the enterprising, risky citizen-subject.

KEY SUMMARY POINTS, SELF-STUDY TASKS, REVIEW ACTIVITIES AND FURTHER READINGS

Each chapter has study boxes which contain key summary points, further readings, as well as chapter review activities in the form of self-study activity.

Key summary points are provided throughout the book for you to understand key issues and points as well as how the theories outlined relate to one another.

Further readings are provided to act as resources and help the reader examine a topic or issue in greater detail. Not all the further readings are book-based, some useful website references are also provided.

Self-study tasks are provided at the end of each chapter to help you to consolidate your learning by further exploring and reflecting on the ideas, issues and questions discussed in each chapter.

1 STUDYING CRIMINAL LIFE

CHAPTER OVERVIEW

Chapter 1 outlines the aims and objectives of this book and introduces some of the key ideas and questions relevant to the study of crime which will be explored in more detail in subsequent chapters. It begins by discussing how criminologists find it useful to view crime and deviance as labels society attaches to particular human behaviours deemed to be socially or morally unacceptable and as a result are held to be deserving of, at the very least, stigmatisation and disapproval,

(Continued)

(Continued)

at most, punishment and retribution. These labels can, and often do, change depending on which country or point in time in human history we are concerned with. For example, homosexuality was viewed as crime in the United Kingdom until 1967 when the Sexual Offences Act was passed by the British Labour government under Prime Minister Harold Wilson.

The chapter then asks if crime is a problem we should seek to solve in all circumstances. Modern scientific, technological and medical advances bring to the fore that in some cases solving the problem of crime has come to involve intervening medically and using a mixture of drug therapies and other treatments, including on occasion surgery, to change an individual's biological and psychological makeup, with a view to curtailing emotional and cognitive states associated with certain behaviours. Does society really possess the right to intervene in individual human behaviour in this way? Or are certain acts, such as paedophilia, so harmful to others that they provide justification enough for us to do so?

Here the chapter highlights how although we may instinctively feel that this is indeed the case, particularly when it comes to protecting the most vulnerable members of society from harm, the labelling of deviant and criminal behaviour is nevertheless a value-laden activity and can reflect the entrenched interests of certain sections of society. The history of human rights activism and political dissent, such as the suffragette and civil rights movements, readily attests to this state of affairs. Criminologists, therefore, tend to argue for the need to place limitations on the power of those in authority to monitor and constrain human behaviour. Systems of checks and balances need to be in place to ensure that when society intervenes in human behaviour it does so in a transparent and accountable manner and with good justification. Later chapters return to this and a range of other pertinent issues and debates as the different theories of crime and their consequences for managing the problem of crime are outlined and discussed.

The chapter then turns to outline how the causes of crime can be said to have been theorised by criminologists in two key ways. Sometimes deviant and criminal behaviours are held to be the result of characteristics which belong to an individual, such as their biology, their psychology, or their free will and ability to choose to act. On other occasions, such behaviour is seen to be a result of certain features of the society itself, such as its shared cultural beliefs and rules for behaviour, social and economic inequalities and injustices, its class divisions, its poverty levels and so on.

Additionally, it is noted that common-sense and theoretical explanations for why crime happens make ontological assumptions about human nature. Here some view human beings as being egotistical and self-interested concerned with pursuing their own wants and needs. Others stress a communal and altruistic view of human nature. Or that human action is heavily influenced by a range of internal and external forces and drives. These categorising frameworks are used throughout subsequent chapters so you can explore, compare and critically contrast the material presented.

Finally, the chapter reflects on the fact that, as a social science, criminology relies on the rigorous collection of empirical evidence to help shed light on the problem of crime and explore different explanations concerning why it happens. This enhances the persuasive power of the theoretical constructs developed by criminologists and the resulting recommendations for change they make. But this does not mean the criminological endeavour always positively impacts, or influences, crime control and criminal justice policy and practice. There are a number of other experts and professionals whose experiences and opinions influence how society views and responds to crime, including, doctors, probation workers, the police, youth workers, educationalists and clinical psychologists, to name but a few. While discourse and debate surrounding the problem of crime tend also to be shaped and guided not so much by expert knowledge but the beliefs and values of certain interest groups within contemporary society, such as the major political parties in the UK, i.e. the Conservative Party and the Labour Party. Again, these points will be returned to at key points throughout this book as the implications of each theory of crime discussed are explored. The chapter ends by providing a summary of the organisation and subsequent content of this book.

CRIME AND SOCIETY: AN INTRODUCTION

Criminological theory is a subject area every student of crime must familiarise themselves with. Indeed, for many finding out about why people commit crime is why they choose to study criminology in the first place. The purpose of this book is to help the budding theoretical criminologist begin this often difficult, sometimes frustrating, but nevertheless ultimately hugely rewarding exercise in expanding their criminological imagination. It provides an introduction to key material which will help them get started with this task and also points them in the right direction so they can move on with some confidence to explore more advanced material. While those already more advanced in their studies, such as postgraduate students and postdoctoral researchers, will find this book a useful reference point they can refer to periodically to remind themselves of the key theoretical architecture of their chosen discipline.

The subject matter of criminology – human behaviour labelled deviant or criminal by society – seems to be as old as human civilisation. Plato's *The Republic* was written nearly two and a half thousand years ago in around 380 BC and is concerned with the idea of justice and the order and character of the just city-state and the just individual. As such, it bares testimony to the fact that a preoccupation with categorising and labelling human beings and their actions as being good or bad is as old as human civilisation itself. Yet it is debatable if crime has actually been an ever present social phenomenon in all times and all places throughout the ages. We may personally feel that a crime-free society seems very much to be an implausible idea given the evidence of our own lived experience and the testimony of the record of human history. Plato certainly thought so. Hence the need for justice even in his perfect state ruled by philosopher-kings. But being implausible is not the same as being impossible. For all we know several such implausible social worlds may well have existed at one time or another but for some reason their existence has not been recorded in the annals of history.

Additionally, the fact of the matter is that in spite of the obvious advances we have made over the last two and half thousand years we simply do not know at this moment in time if the problem of crime is solvable. Furthermore, even if this were the case, it would be necessary before any solution were implemented to definitively answer the question of whether it would in reality be desirable, or ethical even, for us to act to make sure we live in a world without crime. This may, at first, seem like a counter-intuitive proposition. Particularly if we ourselves or a person close to us has been a victim of crime. While undoubtedly there are some crimes, such as the sexual abuse of children, which are so morally abhorrent that we would find it repugnant to suggest they should not be immediately eradicated forever if it were at all possible to do so. Yet we must remain cautious and not argue that crime is a problem which should be completely eradicated from society in much the same way we might advocate a disease which was a threat to public health and safety should be. Let us turn for a moment to examine why.

A problem we must solve?

What is crime? When asked this question our common-sense may well say that it is something which happens when a person breaks a law that a society has made. Yet as we shall see in later chapters it has been argued by critical criminologists that studying crime must not solely involve looking at the law breakers, that is the individuals who break the law. Indeed, they argue that we should also study the law makers and so those who make and pass society's laws – our governing elites in the modern form of the major political parties – as well as individuals and groups which possess socio-economic, cultural and political influence, such as community and business leaders as well as religious and political organisations and institutions. Not least of all because doing so brings to the fore issues of power and social inequality, along with the role of vested interests and social privilege within society, when it comes to creating laws to govern human behaviour. With a society's social and cultural norms and values often being rhetorically employed by certain groups for their own ends as they seek to engender social consensus about what is good and bad, right and wrong, just and unjust, criminal and law-abiding.

Criminologists tend to agree that it is useful to view deviance and crime as labels attached by society to certain human behaviours deemed to be socially unacceptable, such as for example stealing something which belongs to someone else. These unacceptable behaviours are held to be as deserving of, at the very least, stigmatisation and disapproval, and at most, punishment and retribution. What has and continues to be hotly debated by criminologists, amongst others, is the question of whether the causes of such behaviour come from within the individual themselves, from outside influences acting upon them, or perhaps are somehow a result of the mixture of the two. Clearly, finding an answer to this is very important if we want to know how we can respond to the problem of crime. As we shall see over the course of the chapters in this book, a range of different answers have already been proposed. It is up to you to decide based on the evidence presented which explanations and solutions you prefer, if any.

The presence of healthy ongoing debate between different groups of people advocating particular ways of looking at and solving the problem of crime is perhaps to be expected given its highly complex and seemingly ever changing nature. New types of crime always emerge as societies alter as a result of socio-cultural, economic, political and technological change. For instance, nobody had heard of the now internationally recognised problem that is cybercrime as little as 30 years ago. Yet it has rapidly grown over the last decade and a half in particular to become a multi-billion pound crime industry. One particularly interesting and as yet still emerging area which has spurred much debate recently is the fact that over the last century or so we have begun to develop for the first time the ability to successfully intervene organically, using a mixture of surgery and pharmaceutics, creating the possibility of medicalised solutions to the problem of crime.

Medicalised solutions

Indeed, given the rapid pace of the major advances in medical knowledge, technology and therapeutics in recent years it does not take a great leap of the imagination to consider the possibility that we could soon develop a genetic medical solution to the problem of crime. This could involve directly intervening, possibly without informed consent, to alter the biology of some members of society in some way simply because they have been genetically profiled as being *potentially* at risk of possessing inherited triggers associated with certain behavioural and cognitive tendencies. In much the same way that we would if they possessed an increased genetic tendency for being at risk of heart disease. This profiling and intervention process is justified on the basis that it *might* stop certain biochemical, physiological and neurological triggers from manifesting themselves which can in some circumstances act to increase the tendency for particular emotional states and behavioural and cognitive traits to occur, such as, for example, high levels of aggression, irritability, impulsivity, egotism, emotional apathy and social detachment, which research shows can in some circumstances be associated with criminal behaviour.

Medical research is heavily regulated and scientific developments in genetics and human biology are still in their infancy. But using science and medicine to promote what would for many appear as a eugenic solution to the problem of crime, has been attempted before. Perhaps most notably in Nazi Germany in the early part of the twentieth century. As a result, we may not even wish to contemplate pursuing a solution to the problem of crime that involves somehow using genetic manipulation. But surgical and pharmacological medical solutions are used for dealing with some types of criminal behaviour. For example, pharmaceutically enabled chemical castration along with surgical castration have both been used for dealing with sex offenders in a number of countries, including Sweden, the Netherlands, the US and Germany. Yet as we shall discuss in Chapter 3, the danger here is that once this Pandora's Box of medical solutions to the problem of crime is opened, things can quite quickly escalate.

Such considerations bring to the fore the fact that what is arguably most different about tackling the problem of crime today is that over the last 200 years it has ceased to be solely the concern of certain groups of social elites within society undertaking what can by and large be conceived of as being a moral venture designed (in their eyes at least) to promote the public good, such as the clergy, the social reformer, the wealthy philanthropist, the religiously devout citizen and so on. Modern science, technology and medicine are now key weapons in the war on crime. As we shall explore in the beginning of Chapter 2, within western nation-states a decline occurred in the previously dominant Christian religious worldview from the late eighteenth/early nineteenth century onward, with more secular and scientific points of view gradually coming to the fore and building influence within society. This led to the problem of crime becoming increasingly subject to rational investigation, public administration and governmental experimentation. At the centre of this new governmental project lay an increasingly scientised and medicalised conceptualisation of, firstly, deviant and criminal behaviour; secondly, how society should discipline the body to both punish and correct such behaviour; and thirdly, how society's laws and criminal justice system should be organised to support these punitive and corrective ends. Over the course of this book we will explore how this brought to the fore a number of important questions and ethical dilemmas concerning the place and role of criminology within society, or rather its prevailing social order of the day. Just whose side are we on: that of the law and the criminal justice system, or those who break the law and end up in court and even prison?

Returning to our current question of whether we should act to solve the problem of crime and the issue of medicalised solutions to it, we may well argue, as many do, that society perhaps does possess the right to act to intervene and enforce the use of medical methods such as surgical procedures and pharmaceutical regimes – particularly when, for instance, it comes to taking steps to protect the victims of sex crime from individuals who possess a mental health problem, such as for example a personality disorder psychopathy. Indeed, can it not be said that we have not just the right but also a moral obligation to act, if we can do so, when it comes to protecting the most vulnerable members of society from such harmful behaviour? Here we might point to the fact that the way people think and behave develops as they grow and mature as a result of their everyday contact with family, friends and society at large. We are all socialised from a young age into shared norms and values and ways of doing and thinking about things. A certain amount of intervention and engineering to shape and regulate human behaviour via processes of socialisation and criminalisation may well be said to be a natural and normal part of the human maturation and social conditioning process. Human beings are, after all, social animals and it is the job of any social order to act to ensure a certain minimum degree of behavioural conformity exists amongst group members; as well as to act to punish any infractions as is seen fit so as to enable a society to function and for people to live their lives free from immediate threat of harm from their neighbour. So given that we already do act to shape members of society, what is the problem with acting to remove unwanted behaviour?

Justice in whose interests?

It certainly is generally accepted that limits can and should be placed on human freedom of action, particularly when it comes to behaviours that can either directly or indirectly cause harm to others. So if we can apply a particular surgical procedure, drug therapy or even genetic manipulation with a view to stopping certain behaviours from harming others, shouldn't we feel justified in doing so? Or is there a sliding scale of what type of medical intervention we would feel most comfortable advocating? Here we may consider the fact that medical solutions to the problem of sex crime, such as chemical and surgical castration, were used throughout the twentieth century to tackle homosexual behaviour between consenting adults, which was criminalised in many western countries at that time. Doesn't this point to the fact that we need to be cautious about which human behaviours the state should seek to regulate or change, particularly when it comes to behaviour between two consenting adults occurring in the privacy of their own homes?

Also, what about the fact that justice is imperfect and sometimes people are accused wrongly of something? Isn't it equally the case that just as limits are needed on human freedom to protect the most vulnerable members of society we also, in turn, need to err on the side of caution and place limits on the ability of those in authority to shape human behaviour and create social conformity – particularly when it comes to dealing with behaviour labelled deviant or criminal, regardless of whether we possess the advantages advances of modern medicine provide to help us? After all, we only have to consider examples from history such as the suffragette and civil rights movements, or the more recent Arab Spring protests, to see that human behaviour can sometimes be labelled as deviant and criminal by those in power simply because it serves their interests to do so.

Sometimes being labelled deviant or criminal by the state is a result of the fact that we have exercised our right to use our bodies to signify dissent and our disapproval of the actions and values of other people, our social institutions and the political establishment. Perhaps we might promote and participate in non-violent social protest because we want to change how things are done and promote greater equality and social justice. Many individuals who advocate dissent in this form do so because they cannot accept inequality and injustice, and indeed, strongly feel they have to stand out and make their voices heard. Yet social reformers and Nobel Peace Prize winners such as Martin Luther King, Nelson Mandela and Aung San Suu Kyi were all at first demonised by those in authority and other members of society for doing just this and were accused of deviant and criminal behaviour, often simply because others wished to silence them. As such, the life stories of such individuals do not just act as pertinent reminders of the power each of us possesses to change the world around us for the better. They also serve to remind us of the need to make sure checks and balances are in place on the ability of those in authority to seek to control and regulate human behaviour.

In conclusion, although we may accept that society should act to control the problem of crime and in some instances this may involve constraining our sense of personal freedom, we cannot simply argue that *all* human behaviour labelled by the criminal justice system as criminal must be eradicated from society, even if it were possible to do so. Because definitions of deviance and crime, as well as who gets labelled as such and why, sometimes reflect the entrenched interests and needs of certain powerful sections of society and this can often work to the detriment of other sections of society. Crime is, as a result, always a politically sensitive and morally and ethically loaded topic. Yet the observation that behaviour labelled as deviant or criminal in one society or at one particular point in human history may or may not be labelled as such in other societies or periods in time may not seem at first sight to constitute earth-shattering news. Rather it may just feel like straightforward common-sense. But this should not be taken to mean it isn't important. Sometimes it is only by considering the all too obvious that our understanding of the world around us can be transformed. I would argue that this is a case in point, not least of all because it leads us towards an important starting point from which we can begin to examine the world of criminological theory.

Crime as social label

So far in this chapter I have noted that definitions of what constitutes a crime can vary depending on the nature of the social order present within a society at different points in time. Individuals may recognise and verbally label their own behaviour as having been deviant or criminal. Yet it is the definitions and labels of society which they tend to draw on when doing so. This is because the personal sense of what is right and wrong behaviour which we all possess comes from common, socially shared values which have existed in some form or another long before we were born and will continue to do so long after we pass away. In the sociologist Emile Durkheim's famous dictum, society is *sui generis* to the individual. That is, it exists independently of their person, their life biography and their individual biological or psychological attributes, while at the same time acting to govern their everyday behaviour. Importantly, it establishes shared norms and values from which to define, judge and regulate human behaviour, which, furthermore, individuals themselves internalise and so make their own through processes of socialisation.

In other words, for Durkheim when people get together and create a group, community or society no matter how small or large it is they create shared behavioural rules and a way of organising themselves so they can achieve certain ends. Over time these take on a life of their own and indeed come to shape the very way people think and act without them necessarily being actively and self-consciously aware of it. For the critically minded student of the theory of crime this observation brings to the fore the need to consider not just why people break certain rules of behaviour and how we can stop them from doing so, but perhaps more importantly, who decided what the rules should be in the first place and why. If only so they can better understand for themselves why they tend to act and think as they do.

There are three reasons why it is essential to begin our exploration of criminological theory with this point, as I will now turn to discuss. First, given the size of the field of collective endeavour that is criminology it is impossible to introduce and discuss the entire corpus of criminological theory within a typical one-semester teaching block, let alone to do this in a single-volume book such as the one the reader is currently holding. There simply isn't the space. This means students must be selectively introduced to the study of criminological theory in a gradual fashion, typically using broad brush strokes, in order to outline the key features of the landscape before advancing into more complex terrain at a later date. In part this is why further study questions and key readings can be found in each of the following chapters. Here and now it is simply necessary to note that a certain degree of selection is inevitable in any book which discusses theoretical criminology. Yet the idea that crime is a label attached to human behaviour by society reinforces that underpinning its study is a series of ongoing philosophical debates concerning the nature of what it means to be human and what is the 'right' location of the causes of crime.

One key debate here is whether crime can and should be viewed as being caused by a social phenomenon, such as poverty and lack of social opportunity, or as a characteristic belonging to the individual, including their biological and psychological makeup. This debate is often present in language used by law-abiding citizens, criminologists, politicians, the media and criminal justice practitioners, as they interact and talk about instances of criminal behaviour, as well as disagree with one another, as they often do, about why a crime has happened or indeed how it should now be responded to. Once we recognise this we can use our criminological imagination to explore the different and sometimes competing everyday arguments, forms of empirical evidence and pertinent theoretical constructs which have been used by other people before us to examine the topic. Indeed, once we have familiarised ourselves with this key dichotomy – that is, crime as individual characteristic and crime as social phenomenon – we can use it as an organising construct from which to begin to more critically consider 'crime talk' in all its varied forms. This book is written bearing this fact in mind, with both its choice of content and its general organisation serving as a reminder that when we encounter explanations about why crime happens and what can be done to stop it from happening it is important to also consider what view of human nature is assumed by them.

Crime talk and human nature

This brings us to the second point. This is concerned with the question of what we actually mean when we say that crime can be viewed as a social phenomenon or an individual characteristic. As already mentioned, we are referring here to ideas about where the causes of crime are located. To say that crime is an individual characteristic is to locate its origins within the person labelled as having acted criminally. We do this when we say that the criminal chose themselves out of their own free will to act as they did. Or when we refer to some biological, psychological or developmental feature present in their individual makeup which we say is influencing their action. In contrast, to say that crime is a social phenomenon is to locate its cause within society and its prevailing social order. We do this by referring to one or more elements of it; such as its social mores, cultural values and ways of life, economic realities, cityscapes and geographical spaces, technological achievements, or overarching political ideologies.

Yet as the following chapters will discuss it is important to avoid oversimplification here. For example, Classical criminology by and large generally emphasised the capacity of the individual for free will and rational decision-making when exploring the causes of crime and how it should be responded to by the prevailing social order of the day. But this should not be taken to mean that some if not all Classical criminologists did not also recognise the importance of the influence of social circumstances on human behaviour. Nevertheless, emphasising the focus of Classical criminology on the reasoning criminal helps students approaching the topic for the first time to better understand and familiarise themselves with key theoretical material and the historical development of criminology. It can also help to engage them in comparative study with alternative viewpoints which emphasise the role of social factors in shaping human behaviour, such as Marxist or Critical criminology for example. As such, it can be said to establish the necessary groundwork before they proceed forward towards more fine grained advanced study and critical reflection.

This is particularly the case when disputing parties are at loggerheads about why a crime occurred and what should be done about it. Here it is important to recognise that such disagreements often occur precisely because unspoken assumptions are being made about not just where the causes of crime are located but also about human nature. Sometimes clarifying what these assumptions are can lead to a new insight. The term ontology is used when judgements are made about human nature: it is used by philosophers to refer to the study of what it means to be human. As we shall discuss in subsequent chapters, certain ontological assumptions underpin the social phenomena/individual characteristic dichotomy within criminological theory. One important ontological division is between viewing human nature as being egotistical and self-interested or as communal and altruistic. Another is between determinists, who see human behaviour as the outcome of forces outside an individual's control, and voluntarists who emphasise free will and believe that, while we often find ourselves in unwanted situations, we are always responsible for making the most of any predicament.

As might be expected, the following chapters highlight how the voluntarist viewpoint tends to be (but by no means is always) associated with theories of crime which emphasise the role of individual free will in causing crime, while the determinist viewpoint is often (but by no means always) associated with theories of crime that emphasise the influence of biological, psychological and social phenomena on criminal behaviour. Although the important qualification needs to be made here that these conceptual distinctions are always a matter of degree and in reality the categories involved are not mutually exclusive – ultimately their usefulness lies in their utility as a teaching and learning tool. This is something I will explore in more detail in the next section below. For the moment, we can conclude this discussion by noting that whether we believe human beings are self-interested or altruistic, or that their actions are determined by outside forces or by their own free will, has important implications for how we view, categorise and respond to the behaviour of others. The same can be said, as we shall see, of society and its criminal justice system when it comes to dealing with the problem of crime. As a result, each chapter begins with some ontological reflections on the criminological theory discussed and solution to the problem of crime it proposes. With further readings and study questions being provided to help students further explore the material outlined in light of such considerations.

A biographical note

This brings us to the third point. I have argued it is important we identify the underlying assumptions about human nature and the causes for crime present in each criminological theory discussed in this book. I would suggest it is equally important that we all articulate our own preferences and beliefs about human nature and the cases of crime. As a result I feel it important to briefly highlight my own – if only so the reader is clear in their mind that I do not give preferential treatment to any one point of view found in the following chapters. I have detailed the development of my own criminological imagination elsewhere, so I will not retrace those steps here (see Chamberlain, 2013). In summary, my background is in medical sociology and criminology, with my career to date being largely concerned with the fields of mental health and crime, medical error and malpractice, as well as the profiling and risk appraisal of dangerous offenders (i.e. violent and sex offenders). More lately, I have developed an interest in the role of sports-based interventions in tackling the problem of youth crime and reoffending behaviour.

Throughout my career I have worked with individuals who have been labelled by society as criminals as well as with a range of professionals tasked with looking after them who work in either the criminal justice system or the health and social care system. As a result of this experience, I tend to sympathise with points of view which emphasise the impact of a range of sociological factors in influencing how people come to view and respond to their immediate social environment and the actions of others therein, as well as make the choices they do. For me, these factors particularly include: the spatial design of the cityscape and built environments, social deprivation indicators, race and ethnicity, class, age and gender. This means I am by and large sympathetic to the theoretical positions discussed from Chapter 5 onwards in this book which emphasise the impact in one way or another of social phenomena on criminal behaviour over those discussed in Chapters 2–4, which tend to emphasise the importance of individually bounded characteristics.

This said, my underpinning ontological preference is not for positions which promote deterministic notions of the causes of crime, whether this involves using social factors or referring to matters of human psychology or biology. Rather, I tend to prefer points of view which emphasise a communal and altruistic view of human nature and which also stress human free will and so the potential inside of all individuals to act to change both themselves and their circumstances. This is because my experience of working with offenders has reinforced to me that promoting a sense of community and altruism is vitally important for tackling both individual offending behaviour and the social conditions which help to create the conditions for the problem of crime to emerge. Yet it has also shown me that human beings do indeed possess the personal power to transform themselves and their lives for the better. As a result, although I do actively accept the important role social phenomena play in shaping human behaviour and the choices people make, some would say I wish to have my cake and eat it by also promoting the power of individuals to transcend their circumstances. I do not think I am alone in this. Once we find ourselves outside of the confines of textbook definitions we cannot so readily pigeon hole either ourselves or the world around us into neat and tidy distinct categories. Nor should we do so, no matter how tempting it is to try.

The labels we use to help define a field of study when we approach it for the first time must be regarded as heuristic orientating tools rather than definitive either-or categories. Their usefulness lies in their ability to help each of us to become familiar with how key elements of a disciplinary field first developed and now fit together so we can more critically reflect on the different ways both we ourselves and the society we live in talk about the problem of crime, consider what its causes are, as well as decide what possible solutions to it can and should be undertaken. As members of society crime affects us all in one way or another during our lifetime and it is therefore vitally important we feel able to contribute in a meaningful and informed way to debates about it. To this end, it may well be useful for the reader still familiarising themselves with the field of criminological theory that I acknowledge my own disciplinary inclinations as this might help them in turn to clarify their own starting assumptions. But they must make sure that they do articulate and critically examine their own position in response to what I have said, as well as periodically review their assumptions as they encounter the different theories of crime discussed in this book. For this will help them to come to a more informed decision about the value of each theory of crime they encounter.

Box 1.1   Key summary points

- Deviance and crime are often viewed by criminologists as labels attached to certain human behaviour by society as a result of the need to maintain social order and because certain actions need to be stopped or formally monitored and regulated in order to minimise the risk of harm to others.
- Whether or not certain human behaviours are labelled as deviant or criminal depends on the social norms and cultural values of a society and the point in human history considered. Examples of this can be seen in relation to behaviours such as homosexuality, polygamy, consuming alcohol and committing adultery.
- History proves there is always a danger that people can be falsely labelled as being deviant or a criminal because it serves the interests of others to do so – often social and political elites. As a result of this, the actions of those in authority to ensure social conformity need to possess limits. Criminologists are therefore not just concerned with why some people break certain rules of behaviour and how they can be stopped from doing so. They also examine who decided what the rules should be in the first place and why.
- The causes of crime have been theorised by criminologists in different ways. But generally speaking they see these as being either a result of characteristics which belong to an individual – their biology, their psychology or their ability to use their own free will to choose to act – or due to features of the society to which they belong – its social and economic inequalities, class divisions, poverty levels and so on. Subsequent chapters explore both sides of this individual characteristic/social phenomenon dichotomy.
- Underpinning both common-sense and theoretical explanations for why crime happens are judgements about human nature and so what it means to be human. These are called ontological assumptions. It is important we identify how people are viewed when the causes of crime and how they can be addressed are discussed.
- One important ontological division lies between viewing human nature as being egotistical and self-interested and seeing it as communal and altruistic. Another is between determinists, who see human behaviour as the outcome of forces outside individual control, and those who emphasise free will and believe that, while we often find ourselves in situations not of our own choosing, we are always responsible for making the most of any situation.

RESEARCHING CRIMINAL LIFE: THE PLACE OF THEORIES OF CRIME

Before we begin to explore the world of criminological theory in subsequent chapters it is important to briefly consider its relationship with everyday common-sense reasoning, criminal justice policy and the law, the practice of professionals who work within the criminal justice system, crime data and empirical research. As social scientists, criminologists must be committed to solving the problem of crime by conducting ethical, theory-driven and methodologically rigorous research which is subject to formal peer review. A key methodological rule of criminological research is that it should be as far as possible designed so it actively seeks to disprove what we as criminologists think the answer to the question we are asking is. Part of what makes doing criminological research so exciting is that the possibility always exists that the data we collect will disprove our personal and theoretical preferences and beliefs about what is happening and why. This could be said to stand somewhat in contrast to the actions of various interest groups in society who by and large seek to promote explanations and conclusions to common social problems, including crime, based on their broader beliefs and values – be these the ideological leanings of the major political parties; the moral and ethical views of religious and charitable organisations concerned with promoting social welfare; or the dissenting values of a social movement which is seeking to engender social change.

But no matter how well it explains the facts a theory of crime cannot escape the methodological limitations imposed on it by the manner by which formal expert knowledge is produced within the social sciences. The persuasiveness of rigorously conducted social science research lies in the fact that its conclusions and recommendations are dictated by empirical evidence. Yet all empirical research conducted in the social sciences possesses limitations of design and execution which impact upon the depth and range of findings obtained, while other members of the social science community are more than likely to possess their own empirical data, which may in some ways contradict our own, as well as offer their own alternative explanations and theoretical constructs. As a result, all we can ever say for certain is that the conclusion we think best fits the facts based on the empirical evidence we have collected could actually be one of several possibilities, so we may well be wrong about things, but for the moment, *this* is our best guess.

Formal expert knowledge, of which criminological theory is one example, undoubtedly does play a key role in influencing how society at large conceptualises and responds to social problems such as crime. For example, in one way or another, doctors, lawyers, counsellors, educationalists, probation workers and youth justice workers each possess insights and expertise relevant to the theoretical and practical study of crime and its causes. But all forms of expertise possess their limitations. So it can provide us with alternative points of view, guidelines and recommendations, but never a series of step-by-step instructions for solving things. As a result, common-sense ways of thinking and acting based on practical experience, shared cultural and moral values about what is right and wrong, as well as socio-political ideologies concerning how people should behave and live their lives, all continue to play a role in filling in the gaps left by expert knowledge. Whether or not we feel this to be a good or bad thing is, of course, a matter of personal preference. But this situation undoubtedly serves as a useful reminder that the theories of crime detailed in this book can at best provide us with only part of the answer we seek. Where we choose to look for the rest of it is down to each of us to decide for ourselves.

Box 1.2 Key summary points

- The theories of crime developed and debated by criminologists offer just one way of thinking about and solving the problem of crime. A range of other experts and professionals, including criminal justice practitioners, doctors and educationalists, also influence how we view and respond to the problem of crime. As do common-sense ways of thinking and acting, shared cultural and moral values about what is right and wrong, as well as socio-political ideologies concerning how people should behave and live their lives.

SELF-STUDY TASK

Chapter 1 has introduced the idea that the causes of crime have been theorised by criminologists in different ways and offer different views of human nature. Reflect for a moment on what you think the causes of crime are – can you name at least five? Next to each cause note whether or not you think it is highlighting the role played by a person's free will, their biology, their psychology, or an aspect of the society they live in and their individual circumstances within it. You do not need to go into too much detail here or use specialist language. Simply note down your first impression of where you think the causes of crime are located and why, in your own words. Finally, under your list write down what you think each cause says about human nature and so what it means to be human. Does it reinforce that we are egotistical and self-interested; communal and altruistic; determined by outside forces or free to make our own choices? As you encounter the different theories of crime in each chapter you should return to this list and revise it as needs be. This way you will be able to keep track of your own ideas and assumptions and how they have developed as you learn more about each theory of crime and the particular causes it highlights as important.

2 CLASSICAL CRIMINOLOGY AND CONTEMPORARY RATIONAL CHOICE THEORY

CHAPTER CONTENTS

CHAPTER OVERVIEW

Chapter 2 focuses on the early development of criminology through the emergence of Classical criminology. This emphasised the rational nature of human action and focused on promoting deterrence at the centre of how governments should approach managing the problem of crime. It also discusses the influence of this tradition on contemporary situational crime prevention research in the form of routine activity theory.

The chapter outlines how Classical criminology emerged during the eighteenth century and acted as a humanising force which emphasised the importance of deterrence and proportional punishment when dealing with the problem of crime, how governments across Europe began to deal with criminal behaviour as the nineteenth century progressed and rapid social, political and technological change begun to take place in western nation-states in the wake of the Enlightenment. This was an intellectual movement which argued for the value of focusing on natural instead of religious explanations for events. The chapter introduces two key founding figures for Classical criminology: Cesare Beccaria and Jeremy Bentham. They both subscribed to the political philosophy of utilitarianism, which holds that politics and deeds, particularly those associated with the government, should provide the greatest good for the greatest number of people. Bound up with this is the belief that human beings are rational, calculating, self-interested and hedonistic, and therefore, their goal when they act is always to maximise their own pleasure and minimise their own costs or pain. Criminal behaviour was held by Classical criminologists to be a natural consequence of this state of affairs. Classical criminology stresses the importance of paying close attention to naturalistic explanations for criminality and the role of free will and human agency for understanding the causes of criminal behaviour and dealing with the problem of crime. This position was at odds with the prevailing Christian viewpoint of the time, which by and large held that crime was a result of human beings being born into a state of original sin.

After outlining the influence of Classical criminology on the modern criminal justice system the chapter turns to discuss contemporary rational choice models of crime. Here it discusses the work of Derek Cornish and Ronald Clarke, who both emphasised the situational and opportunistic nature of much of crime, as well as the rationality of the decision of a person who commits a crime. The chapter discusses routine activity theory, which stresses the importance of routine or reoccurring everyday behaviour for understanding crime. Importantly, routine activity theory also holds that they are three essential elements of a crime: (1) a motivated offender, (2) a suitable target and (3) the absence of a capable guardian (Gul, 2009). The basic proposition of the theory is that the probability that a crime will occur at any specific time and place is a function of the convergence of likely offenders and victims in a situation where there is an absence of capable guardians to protect the victim. It is argued that if any of these three elements are lacking then a criminal event will not occur.

The chapter concludes by acknowledging the importance of situational crime prevention theories like routine activity theory for helping to develop targeted crime prevention strategies, i.e. anti-burglary guidelines for home owners. Yet it also notes that a key criticism of the criminological theories discussed in the chapter is that they arguably underplay the importance of a range of sociological factors, including social bonds and shared cultural norms and values, in understanding the causes of crime and why when presented with the same situation some people commit crime and others do not. In doing so, the chapter establishes the groundwork from which we will discuss the development of Biological, Psychological and Sociological criminological perspectives in subsequent chapters.

INTRODUCTION: THE REASONING CRIMINAL AND THE SOCIAL CONTRACT

In this chapter we are going to look at Classical criminology and its impact on the modern criminal justice system as well as how it lives on in today's criminological corpus via the body of work surrounding rational choice theory. A good starting point from which to begin is to consider why as we go about our daily business we don't just do what we like even when we encounter difficult obstacles – why not do things that give you pleasure, even if it involves breaking the law, so long as you won't get in too much trouble for it? This kind of reasoning has intrigued criminologists for centuries and theories of crime have been developed around the idea that people are rational because their behaviour is a result of a personal quest to maximise pleasure and minimise pain. Indeed, the fact that human beings are rational and possess free will and so self-control over their actions arguably in one way or another underpins the entire modern criminological corpus from the eighteenth century onward, and by extension, the entire range of theoretical perspectives covered in this book. Furthermore, this is a fairly popular way of thinking about crime amongst society in general. Certainly, the phrase 'they choose to act that way' is something we often hear during TV debates concerned with why somebody committed a crime, and indeed it is often used by politicians in particular to justify adopting a punitive approach to dealing with individuals who have committed a crime as they deserve their 'just desserts' for acting a certain way when they knew full well what the consequences of their action could be for others.

The logic behind this position is that although environmental conditions can affect a person's views and behaviour, ultimately an individual makes a choice to act, including in ways that are deviant or criminal. Classical criminology emphasises the free will of the individual and therefore, according to this viewpoint, the individual should be the centre of attention when attempting to explain the causes of crime. Modern criminological theory is certainly no stranger to this line of reasoning. For example, we will see that this position underpins Right Realist criminology in Chapter 6. However, as we will discuss later in this chapter, it is important to stress that Classical criminologists did not focus solely on the individual and the choices they make to the exclusion of all background factors which can help to shape their experience of crime, as both victim and offender (i.e. poverty). This said, it is undoubtedly the case that the idea of the freely choosing individual defines the Classical view of crime. While it is often said that the problem of crime may well be as old as society, modern criminology nevertheless begins with Classical criminology and its belief that human beings are rational, calculating, self-interested and hedonistic, and therefore, their goal when they act is always to maximise their own pleasure and minimise their own costs or pain. This is because as a result of their view of human nature deviance and crime are held by Classical criminologists to be fundamentally natural acts – that is acts which result from a person being human – and they therefore occur precisely because breaking a rule is often an easy way to secure things that are wanted. This position, as we will discuss, was at odds with, and eventually replaced as the nineteenth century progressed, the prevailing Christian viewpoint of the time, which by and large held that crime was a result of human beings being born into a state of original sin.

Maintaining social order

Yet it is also important to begin our analysis of Classical criminology by noting the emphasis it places on the need to maintain social order within a society. This is because just as easily as one may commit crime, one may become the victim of crime. In a state of nature, each individual is fearful of being a victim. Indeed, the development of Classical criminology was influenced by the work of Thomas Hobbes, who in his 1651 book *Leviathan* argued that without some restraint over their conduct, human beings are in danger of falling into a war of every person against every person, where there is continual fear and danger of violent death, with the life of many being solitary, poor, nasty, brutish, and short. In a state of nature, therefore, liberty or freedom is rendered practically useless because if I want to have complete freedom to do anything I want, including harm and stealing from you, you also have the same freedom to act in an identical manner towards me. Hobbes argues that to prevent this war of all against all, rational human beings join together and surrender some of their freedom to a government body or state: this is what Hobbes referred to as the Leviathan.

By agreeing not to do some things that might be individually profitable, like robbing and violently injuring others for personal gain, rational beings enjoy the protection that the state offers. Although they may lose some liberty, there is still a net gain in making this social contract because the individual is relatively free from wanton harm in the form of the nasty, brutish and short life. The function of the state, therefore, is to use as little force as possible in order to ensure compliance with the terms of the social contract. This is because the use of force against one's citizens is painful and the purpose of any action, according to Hobbes, is to maximise pleasure while seeking to minimise pain. The ideas of Hobbes influenced a number of liberal thinkers, including Locke, Rousseau and Voltaire, as part of the emergence of modern science, technology and medicine during the period in human history – roughly from the end of the seventeenth century to the middle of the nineteenth century – which came to be known as 'The Enlightenment' (Chamberlain, 2013). Indeed, it is important to remember that this historical social movement, which ultimately led to the birth of modern democracy as we see it today, was grounded in the thinking of individuals who emphasised hedonism, rationality and free will on one hand, as well as the importance of the social contract made between freely choosing individuals and the state on the other hand. Furthermore, at the time, this position was held to be radical, as it stood in stark contrast to traditional religious notions concerning the inherent sinfulness of human beings, as well as the divine right of the monarch to rule and punish in the name of God as they saw fit.

SOCIETY, CRIME AND PUNISHMENT

It is often argued today that what distinguishes human beings from animals is their possession of free will and ability to make decisions and informed choices. Indeed, as already discussed, Classic criminology was built on this idea and as a result argues that individuals are driven by hedonistic pleasure seeking desires, but nevertheless weigh up the costs and benefits and risks of doing a particular action and possible alternative actions, before deciding to choose an action best suited for their goals. Now, of course, this is all well and good, but the problem was that the governing elites in Europe up until the seventeenth century ruled the mass of people by using what we would define today as extreme acts of violence. State-endorsed public torture and execution were commonplace, with forms of punishment such as dismemberment in the public space of the village or town market square, in front of crowds of people, often occurring for relatively minor crimes such as petty theft (Chamberlain, 2013). Furthermore, supernatural and demonological explanations for crime and human behaviour dominated. Indeed, crime was often seen to be in part a product of being possessed by evil spirits, or because human beings were cursed with the burden of original sin.

There can be no doubt that from at least the time of the Middle Ages onwards, church leaders and the aristocracy across Europe together formed a repressive governing regime against the potential amongst the general population (Radzinowicz, 1999), with people tending to explain their lot in terms of superstition and the divine right of traditional kings and queens to rule and punish the population as they saw fit. Justice and punishment were very severe, as Monachesi (1955: 441) states:

> Secret accusations were in vogue and persons were imprisoned on the flimsiest of evidence. Torture, ingenious and horrible, was employed to wrench confessions. … Judges were permitted to exercise unlimited discretion in punishing those convicted of crime. The sentences imposed were arbitrary, inconsistent, and depended upon the status and power of the convicted.

Classical criminology emerged against this background and acted as a humanising force in how governments across Europe began to deal with the problem of crime as the nineteenth century progressed. From the eighteenth century onwards a seismic shift had begun to take place in western nation-states as a result of the rapid and far-reaching technological and scientific progress which emerged in the wake of the Enlightenment. This was an intellectual movement which argued for the value of focusing on natural instead of religious explanations for events. It argued that by applying their innate reason and engaging in active experimentalism human beings could discover laws of nature and even perhaps change things to their liking. Early technological advances, such as the development of the modern steam engine, occurred as a direct result of this approach and led as the eighteenth century progressed to what is now commonly referred to as the industrial revolution. This signalled the early beginnings of the modern era of technological progress as well as mass production and consumption. As the industrial revolution took hold there was a gradual shift in population distribution from rural to urban areas. City-based factory work in particular was attractive to the poor and working classes living in rural areas because it seemed to offer more opportunities for economic prosperity and social ladder climbing than toiling day after day in a field had done for their forebears. The resulting, relatively rapid shift towards city living caused considerable organisational and structural strain on existing urbanised areas at the same time that a growing governmental concern with maintaining social order emerged as democratic and liberal ideas began to challenge existing elitist social hierarchies and monarchical governing structures. Like other human sciences emerging at this time – such as public health, psychiatry, psychology and sociology – criminology was born out of the governmental need to provide workable solutions to a raft of social problems. Most notably criminal justice administration, penology and the planning and policing of growing urban cityscapes.

Criminology as a discipline emerged at a point in history where rapid socio-economic and political change was occurring at the same time that natural explanation for human behaviour began to replace the more traditional religious explanation offered by Christianity. Indeed, what is now called Classical criminology concerned itself with the governmental project of mapping crime patterns and monitoring the criminal justice system to establish a fair, efficient and regulated method of justice to in turn support a better regulated social order which did not necessarily rely on a Christian interpretation of crime, law and society. Classical criminology's emphasis on rational action and free will was inspired by the Enlightenment and the liberal utilitarian political philosophy of Hobbes, amongst others. As already discussed, this holds that people try to maximise pleasure and minimise pain so they rationally calculate the costs and benefits before acting to achieve desired goals. By emphasising free will and the ability of individuals to rationally choose a course of action it highlighted the ability of people to choose their own destiny, rather than be forced into action by spiritual sin or demonic possession, with the relationship between the individual and state being equally built on the idea of ruling through the consent of the people, rather than monarchs and church leaders. As a result, the emergence of Classical criminology is taken to signal the beginning of a shift away from religious explanations for crime and criminality as social elites sought to maintain social order through establishing a more rationalistic system of punishment to deter would-be offenders. It is this focus on deterrence that the chapter will now turn to consider.

CLASSICAL CRIMINOLOGY AND CRIME DETERRENCE

Cesare Beccaria and Jeremy Bentham are two key founding figures for Classical criminology. They both subscribed to the political philosophy of utilitarianism, which holds that politics and deeds, particularly those associated with the government, should provide the greatest good for the greatest number of people (Young, 2011). Bound up with this viewpoint was the belief that the governing apparatus of the state should seek to minimise its influence over the freely choosing individual. In his 1764 book, *On crime and punishments*, Beccaria wrote that 'every act of authority of one man [*sic*] over another, for which there is not an absolute necessity, is tyrannical. It is upon this then that the sovereign's right to punish crimes is founded' (Beccaria, 1764: 58). Beccaria and Bentham argued that the end of criminal law is to promote happiness. They argued that the general objective all legislative laws and legal systems should have in common is to augment the total happiness of the community. As a result, they were both opposed to the torture of prisoners and capital punishment.

The reasoning of Beccaria and Bentham is compatible with contemporary notions of the presumption of innocence, judicial neutrality and proportionality in sentencing. It is certainly the case that as Classical criminology developed and began to influence those in governmental authority we see a gradual humanising shift in western criminal justice systems away from more traditional punitive approaches. Classical criminologists emphasised that punishment was a necessary evil and only justifiable if based on reasonable, humane and rational processes. For example, in his 1789 book, *The principles of morals and legislation*, Bentham argued that punishment should not be given when it is:

- Groundless (the act is not really deviant or criminal)
- Inefficacious (ineffective as a deterrent)
- Too expensive (where the trouble it causes exceeds the benefits)
- Needless (where the crime may be prevented or dissolved in some other way)

According to this position, punishment should be proportional to the harm caused to society, not tailored to the individual victim's preferences or the particular qualities of the individual offender, i.e. if they were poor or rich or male or female. This approach is encapsulated in the commonly used phrase, 'let the punishment fit the crime'. In this way Classical theory's main focus is on the crime not the offender. Furthermore, all individuals are assumed to be operating under the same kind of rationality. Indeed, criminal behaviour, like all behaviour, is held to be a result of the rational calculation of the costs and benefits associated with the act by an individual. A central prediction stemming from this idea is that people would be more likely to commit a crime if the pleasure – the perceived benefits – from the behaviour outweigh the pain – the perceived cons. It is important to note that the Classical school did not possess a negative or judgemental view of human beings – that an individual typically pursues their self-interest and so tends to use their reason to act in their own interests, even if this involves breaking the law, is taken to be a natural consequence of human nature rather than a result of some moral defect. While in regard to criminal behaviour, Classical school thinkers thought that the most likely cost in the cost–benefit equation would be detection, apprehension and punishment.

Beccaria's 12 principles of justice

This focus on deterrence and the use of punishment to deter criminal behaviour advocates that threatened punishment for criminal behaviour works best as a deterrent if it is, firstly, certain, secondly, proportionate to the harm caused by the crime, and thirdly, swiftly imposed. Indeed, Beccaria (1764) argued that punishment worked best as a deterrent when it was inescapable, arguing that the certainty of a punishment, even if it was a moderate form of punishment, will always make a strong impression on human behaviour. Hence, if the criminal justice system met the deterrent conditions of Classical criminology, it was held that the individual would be less likely to commit a crime for they would know that they would be caught and punished, that the punishment would happen soon after the offence, as well as that the punishment mirrored the seriousness of the crime. For Bentham and Beccaria the severity of a punishment is the least important element of deterrence, what is most important is the certainty of capture.

To establish this principle of deterrence at the centre of the criminal justice system, Beccaria advocated 12 principles:

- Enact laws that are clear, simple and unbiased, and that reflect the consensus of the population.
- The law should place as few restrictions as possible on individual freedom.
- Educate the public.
- Eliminate corruption from the administration of justice.
- Reward virtue.
- The justification of punishment is retribution not revenge, and to protect individual rights.
- Punishment must be proportionate and strictly limited. It should not exceed the harm done. The evil inflicted on an offender should exceed an advantage gained from the crime. Beyond this it is superfluous and tyrannical.
- Penalties should correspond with the nature of the offence and its extent in society.
- Punishment should be certain and speedy. Deterrence was more effective if it was certain, fast and mild.
- Exemplary punishment, such as public execution, should be prohibited. Nor should punishment be imposed to reform beyond pain that which is proportionate to the harm done. Nor should it be varied to suit the personality or circumstances of the crime.

- The potential offender is a reasoning, independent individual who calculates and thus all are equally responsible and all deserve the same punishment for the same crime.
- It is better to prevent crimes than to punish them, this is the chief aim of every good system of legislation.

Source: Beccaria, C (1764) *On crime and punishments* New York: Bobbs-Merril.

Beccaria's principles went on to influence modern models of criminal justice and still possess resonance today. It is conventional to distinguish between two classes of potential offenders who may refrain from crime because they fear punishment. First are people who have directly experienced punishment for something they did in the past. If these people refrain from future criminal activity because they fear being punished again, then this is called specific deterrence. Second are people who have not experienced punishment themselves but are deterred from crime by the fear that they might get the same punishment experienced by others. This is general deterrence. This distinction is important because the deterrent effect of experienced punishments may be quite different from that of threatened punishments. When a judge hands down a sentence and tells the offender 'this ought to make you think twice next time', the judge is thinking of the penalty as a specific deterrent. But if the judge says 'I intend to make an example of you', the penalty's general deterrent value is being emphasised. This is because Classical criminology is concerned not so much with the question of why some individuals commit certain crimes and others do not. Classical theorists viewed this issue as irrelevant as criminal motivation is a given as part of the cost–benefit equation. This is why they adopted a non-judgemental view of the individual. Rather, their concern is with social control, and furthermore, with ensuring that the criminal justice system is more robust, humane and, of course, rational.

NEOCLASSICAL CRIMINOLOGY

Although we can say that Classical criminology continues to this day to influence thinking around crime, one immediate problem encountered when people began to apply its principles from the early nineteenth century onwards related to what is called Bentham's 'felicity calculus'. Bentham had tried to measure the cost–benefit calculation using a pseudo-mathematical model which was really just based on the arbitrary criteria of his personal estimation of the consequences of an act (Maguire et al., 2012). So it should come as no surprise to learn that when the French criminal justice system began to apply Classical criminology's principles from around 1791 onwards it became immediately clear that it was impossible in practice to ignore the determinants of human action and to proceed in practice as if punishment and incarceration could be easily measured on some kind of universal calculus without regard for individual situation. The central assumption of Classical criminology that people and their actions were driven purely by free will alone, without any influence from environmental conditions such as social deprivation and poverty, proved in practice to be problematic. This led to early criminologists such as Rossi, Garaud and Joly to develop what came to be called the Neoclassical school of criminology. Neoclassicism proposed three modifications of the classical position. What is more, they are still with us today and indeed are key foundational principles within criminal justice systems throughout Europe.

First, Neoclassicism holds that free will is important but also that sometimes it can be constrained by physical and environmental factors. Hence factors such as that a person stole some food from a shop because they lived in abject poverty or had a mental health problem need to be taken into account by the legal system. Leading on from this was the second modification. Namely that a court needs to take into account an offender's past biographical and criminal history when making a decision about their sentence. And thirdly, was the recognition that certain individuals – such as children, the mentally ill and in some cases the elderly – are generally less capable of exercising their reason, and hence, should be given special treatment. Together, these changes did lead to a greater focus within the criminal justice system on rehabilitation, rather than punitive punishments, such as hard labour. Not least of all because there is a tentative recognition that criminal behaviour can occur for reasons other than the exercise of the cost–benefit calculation associated with free will by Classical criminologists. Undoubtedly, people can sometimes be driven to commit crime because of their social circumstance or mental capacity. But it is important to stress that as with Classical criminology, Neoclassical criminology heavily emphasises free will and human rationality; it simply sought to refine these ideas slightly so they worked in practice in the real world of the day-to-day operation of the criminal justice system.

CRITIQUING CLASSICAL/NEOCLASSICAL CRIMINOLOGY: DOES DETERRENCE WORK?

Having outlined the development and historical influence of Classical and Neoclassical criminology, with their focus on the day-to-day operation of the criminal justice system, it is important to ask if it is right to focus on the question of whether deterrence actually works. After all, as the chapter has discussed, although quite revolutionary when it first emerged two and a half centuries ago, saying that people choose to engage in crime and that punishment deters if it is certain, swift and reasonably severe, is these days very much part of conventional criminological wisdom and common-sense thinking. Yet it is still important to critically consider if these assumptions actually work in practice. Because when we do so it comes to light that we really haven't been able to confirm or deny whether or not deterrence works. This is quite naturally something many people find difficult to understand. Most of us can think of anecdotal illustrations of deterrence from our own personal experience perhaps, or from hearing about people who have refrained from a crime because they were fearful of the consequences. But criminological researchers find that the complexities of the subject present formidable obstacles to developing conclusive answers. This is not to say that there has been absolutely no support in the literature for deterrence theory. Limited support of deterrence has been found in the areas of car crime, drunk driving, luggage theft, as well as petty crime trends in general (Maguire et al., 2012). However, we haven't been able to get conclusive proof for the deterrent effect of, for example, capital punishment. Indeed, there is no good methodologically sound research which supports the oft-heard claim that there would be fewer murders if more killers were executed rather than kept in prison. Neither is there much evidence that deterrence works for hardened repeat offenders (Radzinowicz, 1999; Chamberlain, 2013).

Indeed, on balance, the research seems to show that the threat of formal punishments is much less worrisome to potential offenders than the threat of informal punishments imposed by relatives, friends, co-workers or other close acquaintance. In short, it seems to be the case that the average law-abiding citizen seems to be too concerned about losing their job, being ostracised by friends and family to engage in crime even when the benefits outweigh the costs. Indeed Pogarsky (2002: 432) argues that 'some people are acute conformists so that moral inhibition or worries over social isolation may so effectively inhibit conduct that consideration of the cost and benefit are not even brought into play'. Conversely, we should note that some criminals engage in criminal behaviour as an act of defiance when they think an unfair punishment is in place. In short, they act out of defiance to society, and perhaps not surprisingly, Pogarsky (2002) discusses how research has shown that some youth and first-time offenders engage in crimes such as petty theft or street graffiti as acts of social defiance. As sometimes do murderers in prison who commit further crimes inside against fellow inmates because, for example, they feel they should have had a lighter sentence. In summary, deterrence does not necessarily work. Yet the lack of strong robust evidence overall does not mean that deterrence theory is disproved. We can reasonably assume on a general level that the thought of swift, certain and relatively severe punishment will undoubtedly deter some individuals from committing some crimes in some circumstances. But it is the case that the emphasis placed by Classical and Neoclassical criminology on free will and rationality does not help to explain why not all individuals can be deterred from crime by the thought of punishment, regardless of the type of crime, or perhaps more importantly, their practical situation. In the following chapters we will focus on some theories of crime, such as Right Realism for example, which to varying degrees acknowledge, like Classical and Neoclassical criminology, the importance of the free will and rationality of the individual, and so emphasise their personal responsibility for the choices they have made, while also stressing the role of a range of factors, such as psychological abnormality and social deprivation and poverty, in influencing human behaviour.

Box 2.1   Key summary points

- Classical criminology emerged through the writings of Cesare Beccaria and Jeremy Bentham, as part of the broader intellectual movement known as the Enlightenment which developed across Europe from the late seventeenth and early eighteenth century onwards, and emphasised naturalistic explanations for events and scientific forms of enquiry.
- Classical criminology emphasises the free will and rationality of the individual. Arguing against religious interpretations of individual behaviour it holds that the causes of crime are not a result of the inherent sinfulness of the individual. Rather they are a natural outcome of the rational application by the individual of a cost–benefit analysis of their situation so they can maximise pleasure and minimise pain. As a result, Classical criminologists are crime-specific; rather than focusing on the offender themselves, they advocate focusing on deterring crime.
- Classical criminology heavily influenced the development of criminal justice systems across Europe from the early nineteenth century onwards through advocating a focus on ensuring the legal organisation and delivery of justice served the idea that the threat of punishment could deter crime if it was firstly, certain, secondly, proportionate to the harm caused by the crime, and thirdly, swiftly imposed.
- Neoclassical criminology emerged during the nineteenth century as a result of the recognition that the actions of individuals could be influenced by factors other than their reason, such as their social circumstances for example. Nevertheless, Neoclassical criminology continued to heavily emphasise the rationality and the free will of the individual.
- Classical and Neoclassical criminology emphasise human agency over social structure and as such have been criticised by sociological forms of criminology, including Critical criminology in particular, for ignoring the importance of key categories such as class, gender and race and ethnicity, in understanding the causes of crime.

Further reading

Beccaria, C (1764) *On crime and punishments.* New York: Bobbs-Merril.

Bentham, J (1789) *The principles of morals and legislation.* Oxford: Clarendon Press.

Maguire, M, Morgan, R and Reiner, R (2012, 5th edn) *The Oxford handbook of criminology.* Oxford: Clarendon Press.

Monachesi, E (1955) Pioneers in criminology: Cesare Beccaria. *Journal of Criminal Law, Criminology and Police Science* 46: 440–5.

Pogarsky, G (2002) Identifying deferrable offenders: implications for research on deterrence. *Justice Quarterly* 19 (3): 431–532.

Radzinowicz, L (1999) *Adventures in criminology.* London: Routledge.

Young, J (2011) *The criminological imagination.* Cambridge: Polity Press.

CONTEMPORARY RATIONAL CHOICE THEORY

In addition to its influence on contemporary models of criminal justice, the legacy of Classical criminology continues to this day in theories of crime which emphasise the rationality of criminal decision-making processes. One of the best known contemporary applications of rational choice theory in criminology is that of Derek Cornish and Ronald Clarke (1986). From the 1970s onwards Cornish and Clarke developed a modern form of rational choice theory which they applied to crimes such as burglary. They accepted the Classical position that human beings are rational beings who exercise free will in deciding upon a course of action. In their 1986 book *The reasoning criminal*, Cornish and Clarke argued that their conceptual starting point was the classical assumption that offenders seek to benefit by their criminal behaviour, that this involves the making of decisions and choices, however rudimentary on occasion these processes might be, and that these processes therefore exhibit a measure of cost–benefit reasoning behaviour. They held that even crimes which may well seem to be impulsive and unpredictable, such as drunken brawls, have rational components.

These assumptions led Cornish and Clarke, like their Classical criminology forebears, to focus on crimes rather than criminals. Their approach is crime specific. That is, they argue that different crimes may meet different needs for different offenders. In addition, situational factors and available information also may vary amongst different types of crime. Consequently, relatively fine distinctions should be made amongst types of crime if we are to fully understand them and develop effective strategies for dealing with them. For example, it is not enough to talk about the differences between burglary committed in homes and burglary committed in large corporate organisations. We also need to distinguish between burglaries committed in middle-class areas, student heavy areas, in welfare housing and wealthy residential areas, to name but a few of the options. Because, and empirical studies do seem to suggest this, the individuals involved have different motivations, see different benefits from committing the offence, and also can vary considerably in their methods (Maguire et al., 2012).

The emphasis placed on the crime rather than the individual does not mean offenders are ignored completely. It is argued that each offender has individual skills, experiences and needs which interact with their choices. In other words, an offender's characteristics – their age, life experience and so on – combine with offence characteristics in shaping criminal decisions. This process is referred to by Cornish and Clarke (1985) as 'choice structuring' and since the 1980s a number of different models have been developed. One insightful and informative example of this modelling of the decision-making process is what Cornish calls 'crime scripts' (Cornish, 1994). This scripting helps us to look at the decision sequences in an event in order to understand why they happen so that crime prevention strategies can be developed. They are five somewhat overlapping scripting stages: preparation, target selection, commission of the act, escape and the aftermath. For example, during the preparation stage, the offender plans the activity to ensure they have the knowledge (i.e. how to force open a closed window), resources (i.e. a bag to carry stolen items) and skills (i.e. breaking and entering skills) necessary to handle the job at hand (i.e. a burglary); during the target selection stage, they find a suitable location or person (i.e. a residential home containing items worth stealing); during the commission of the act they commit the crime (i.e. force the window lock, enter the house and steal items); during the escape, they leave the scene of the crime (i.e. leave the house via the way they entered or perhaps by another exit point); and finally, during the aftermath, they may do a range of things depending on the nature of the crime (i.e. identify and visit a 'fence' to sell the stolen items to). It is by breaking down this scripting process for a range of crimes – for instance, burglary, pocket picking, embezzlement and insurance fraud – that crime prevention strategies, such as guidance to home owners on how to prevent domestic burglary, has been developed by criminal justice practitioners over the last two decades, for the benefit of law-abiding citizens (Maguire et al., 2012).

SITUATIONAL CRIME PREVENTION, OPPORTUNITY THEORY AND ROUTINE ACTIVITY

One particularly important development in contemporary rational choice theories of crime, which has emerged as a result of the work of Cornish and Clarke (1985) and Cornish (1994), is situational crime prevention, which is sometimes called opportunity theory, with one popular approach being routine activity theory. Opportunity theory stresses that the choice to commit a crime is in no small part shaped by the opportunities which are present in real everyday situations. This approach starts with crime as an event which happens somewhere within a social situation which fortuitously brings together a series of factors which facilitate it. The 10 main principles for situational crime prevention are:

- Opportunities play a role in causing all crime.
- Crime opportunities are highly specific.
- Crime opportunities are concentrated in time and space.
- Crime opportunities depend on everyday movements of activity.
- One crime produces opportunities for another.
- Some products offer more tempting crime opportunities.
- Social and technological changes produce new crime opportunities.

- Crime can be prevented by reducing opportunities.
- Reducing opportunities does not usually displace crime.
- Focused opportunity can produce wider declines in crime.

Source: Felson, M and Clarke, RV (1998) *Police research series, paper 98: Opportunity makes the thief.* London: Home Office.

From this perspective, the common element found in all events, criminal or otherwise, is opportunity. An opportunity makes an event possible. Therefore, a criminal opportunity makes a crime possible. One cannot rob a bank without the opportunity to do so. There has to be a bank in the first place and it has to be organised in a certain way, open at certain times, closed at others, employ certain security devices and so on. One version of situational crime prevention or opportunity theory is routine activity theory. Routine activities are activities which reoccur and at a day-to-day level our everyday lives are full of them: eating, sleeping, working, keeping fit, going to the cinema, having sex, are all routine activities. So is crime. For example, we would expect that handgun crime would occur depending on the routine activities of offenders and victims and the relationship between the two. Research has shown that it certainly appears to be the case that, due to their routine activities at the day-to-day level of lived human experience, handgun crime involving relatives is likely to occur in the home and those involving strangers in the street.

Importantly, routine activity theory also holds that there are three essential elements of a crime: (1) a motivated offender, (2) a suitable target and (3) the absence of a capable guardian (Gul, 2009). The basic proposition of the theory is that the probability that a crime will occur at any specific time and place is a function of the convergence of likely offenders and victims in a situation where there is an absence of capable guardians to protect the victim (Cohen and Felson, 1979). It is argued that if any of these three elements are lacking then a criminal event will not occur. This brings to the fore that the central contribution of contemporary rational choice-based models of criminality to understanding the causes of crime is twofold. Firstly, that criminal behaviour occurs in everyday situations and as such it must be examined and explained in and through those situations and the opportunities for criminal and non-criminal behaviour which exist within them. In short, the focus is on the crime itself and the reasons for it within the situation it arose in. Secondly, that criminals decide to commit a crime and this decision is fundamentally a rational one (Felson and Clarke, 1998).

Routine activity is about situations, not people, and within that context the lifestyle routines which people follow, as these are held to significantly affect their chances of being assaulted, robbed and so on. But this is not about victim blaming. Rather, it is about looking at how situations and opportunities therein cause crime to happen, in order to develop preventative strategies to help stop them from happening. Hence the emphasis is on what is sometimes referred to as the crime triangle of victim, location and offender (Eck, 1994). However, in spite of the apparent value of this approach, situational crime prevention approaches such as routine activity theory are open to the criticism that due to their focus on situational opportunity they tell us very little about who the offender is, and most importantly, the role played by sociological factors, such as cultural and ideological norms and values and shared social bonds, in influencing the decision-making process and why some individuals refrain from criminal activity and others do not – particularly when the same situational opportunity presents itself to different people (Gul, 2009).

Box 2.2   Key summary points

- Classical rational choice theory has influenced contemporary situational crime theories where the presence of everyday opportunity and the rationality of the criminal reasoning process are held to be key to understanding and controlling the problem of crime.
- One important version of situational crime prevention or opportunity theory is routine activity theory. This holds that there are three essential elements of a crime: (1) a motivated offender, (2) a suitable target, (3) the absence of a capable guardian.
- Routine activity theory highlights that social environments and living spaces impact on crime and in doing so it brings to the foreground the possibility that crime prevention strategies can be developed to tackle the problem of crime.
- Situational crime prevention approaches such as routine activity theory are open to the criticism that they tell us very little about who the offender is, and most importantly, the role played by factors such as shared social bonds in influencing the decision-making process and why some individuals refrain from criminal activity and others do not.

Further reading

Cohen, LE and Felson, M (1979) Social change and crime rate trends: a routine activity approach. *American Sociological Review* 44 (4): 588–608.

Cornish, DB (1994) The procedural analysis of offending and its relevance for situational prevention. In Clarke, RV (ed.), *Crime prevention studies, volume two.* St Louis, MO: Willow Tree Press.

Cornish, DB and Clarke, RV (1985) Modelling offenders' decisions: a framework for research and policy. *Crime and Justice* 6: 147–85.

Cornish, DB and Clarke, RV (1986) *The reasoning criminal.* New York: Springer.

Felson, M and Clarke, RV (1998) *Police research series, paper ninety-eight: Opportunity makes the thief.* London: Home Office.

Gul, S (2009) An evaluation of rational choice theory in criminology. *Sociology and Applied Science* 4 (8): 36–44.

Write a maximum of 750 words outlining the historical background to the emergence of Classical criminology alongside its key features, strengths and weaknesses, and its influence on contemporary criminological theory. As part of this process critically reflect on the idea that a person rationally weighs up the costs and benefits *before* committing a crime. Can you think of some situations where this might hold true and some where it seems not to? What other factors do you think play a role in a person's decision to commit crime?

3 BIOLOGICAL CRIMINOLOGY

CHAPTER CONTENTS

CHAPTER OVERVIEW

Chapter 3 examines Biological criminology. The chapter highlights how, like Classical criminology and Psychological criminology, Biological criminology locates the causes of crime inside the individual. Although rather than emphasising free will, it is argued that our actions are to some extent determined by our biological makeup and its interaction with the natural and social environment.

The chapter begins by outlining the early origins of Biological criminology in physiognomy, which emerged in ancient Greece and Rome and introduced the central idea that physical structure, or more precisely human biology, determines a person's personality and behaviour. It then discusses the emergence in the eighteenth century of phrenology which established the focus of Biological criminology on naturalistic as opposed to religious causes for human behaviour through experimenting with the developing medical sciences of the time; including, most importantly, the emerging disciplines of anatomy and physiology.

It then turns to discussing the work of Cesare Lombroso (1876, 1895) who is regarded as the founding father of modern Biological criminology and was influenced by the evolutionary theory of Charles Darwin and the ideas of natural selection. Lombroso's central theory was that the criminal was a biological throwback to an earlier stage in human evolution, more ape-like than human. He called this degeneracy atavism. Atavism manifested itself, according to Lombroso, in certain physical characteristics that he called stigmata. The stigmata did not cause criminality, atavism did. But the stigmata were useful for identifying atavists, or born criminals, as Lombroso called them.

The chapter then turns to explore the influence of Lombroso's research and ideas, tracing its intellectual development into the first half of the twentieth century, and how this both built on and critiqued the atavistic theory of Lombroso. It discusses how Charles Goring (1913) and Earnest Hooton (1939a, 1939b) found no difference in the physical measurements of stigmata between criminals and law-abiding citizens. It also discusses how Ernst Kretschmer (1921) and William Sheldon (1940) examined the relationship between body type and personality type, finding little evidence as they did so to support the viewpoint that there is a link between physical appearance and criminal behaviour. The chapter highlights how some Biological criminologists during the first half of the century were criticised for advocating social eugenics and state sterilisation of individuals they nevertheless deemed to be biologically inferior, including the mentally ill and habitually criminalistic.

The final part of the chapter examines developments in Biological criminology since the 1960s, and how these have focused on the role played by genetics, brain structure, development and injury, as well as biochemistry, hormones and diet, in influencing human behaviour, including antisocial and criminal behaviour. The chapter discusses how no serious biologist would argue that there is a single 'criminal gene'. Furthermore, contemporary research has highlighted the importance of environmental factors in shaping the impact of genetic inheritance on actual human behaviour: including parenting style, levels of family income and educational achievement, social support and stressful life events. As a result, contemporary Biological criminologists stress the importance of both genetic and environmental factors when examining human behaviour.

INTRODUCTION: CLASSICISM, POSITIVISM AND THE DEVELOPMENT OF BIOLOGICAL FORMS OF CRIMINOLOGY

Although its origins stretch back much further, the historical development of modern forms of Biological criminology from the beginning of the nineteenth century onwards overlaps with the emergence of Classical criminology from the eighteenth century, as well as Psychological criminology at the turn of the twentieth century (Beirne, 1987). Classical criminology emphasised rational action and free will, a viewpoint that Chapter 2 noted was inspired by utilitarian political philosophy. Certainly, the emergence of modern criminology as an academic discipline was bound up with broader socio-political, economic and intellectual changes during the seventeenth and eighteenth centuries. This was a point in human history where rapid socio-economic and political change was occurring at the same time that natural explanation for human behaviour began to replace more traditional religious explanation. Classical criminology held that people try to maximise pleasure and minimise pain, so they rationally calculate the costs and benefits before acting to achieve desired goals. In doing so it signalled the beginning of a shift away from religious explanations for crime and criminality as social elites sought to maintain social order through establishing a more rationalistic system of punishment to deter would-be offenders (Radzinowicz, 1999). Consequently, to begin with, following the tenets of Classicism, criminologists concerned themselves with the governmental crime control project of mapping crime patterns and monitoring the criminal justice system to establish a fair, efficient and regulated method of justice to in turn support a better regulated social order. Yet Classicism did not thoroughly engage in observation and experiment, preferring instead to 'armchair theorise'. In contrast to this, the development of modern forms of scientific expertise, including advances in human anatomy and medical science, led to the emergence during the nineteenth century of what is referred to today as Biological criminology (Chamberlain, 2013).

As this chapter discusses, spurred on by achievements of natural and social scientists during the nineteenth century, including Charles Darwin and Auguste Comte, Biological criminology emerged in the form of 'the Lombrosian project', which built on the modern scientific principle of careful observation and experiment (Garland, 2001). Drawing on Darwinian evolutionary theory Lombrosian criminology popularised the idea that it was possible to 'spot the criminal type'. It argued that criminals were a distinctive type of biologically determined human being who are physically and psychologically different from law-abiding citizens. This signalled the beginning of widespread penal expansionism and experimentalism across Europe. Prisons became vast experimental laboratories where a raft of newly emerging professionals (notably psychiatrists, penal reformers and criminologists) sought to identify and contain criminality under the guise of developing scientifically informed efficient punishment systems and effective rehabilitative regimes. The central idea of Lombrosian criminology that criminals represented a different type of human being was subsequently widely discredited, but it is nevertheless recognised today as marking the early beginnings of the 'scientific study of the criminal and the conditions under which he commits crime' (Wolfgang, 1973: 286).

For Garland (2001), amongst others, for better or worse the historical heritage of criminology as an empirically grounded scientific enterprise lies within Lombrosian criminology, and it is this which makes it an academic discipline with a strong policy orientation. Yet before examining the historical emergence of Biological criminology it is important to note the influence of positivism. This is discussed in the context of Psychological criminology in Chapter 4 and again in Chapter 8 in relation to the examination of contemporary critical forms of criminology. Positivism advocates the adoption of a scientific approach to the study of human behaviour. Emphasis is placed on identifying and systematically collecting 'the facts' through careful observation and experiment. Positivism assumes there is an objective reality that exists independently of human beings and emphasises the need for a researcher to engage in systematic observation and experiment in a value-neutral and dispassionate manner in order to discover underlying causal laws of behaviour. Positivist criminologists, be they focusing on the biological or psychological factors which contribute to the problem of crime, focus on criminals, not on crimes, as Classical criminologists did. This because the goal of Biological and Psychological forms of criminology is to discover the underlying causes of criminal behaviour within the makeup of the human being. Consequently, these forms of positivism reject Classical criminology and its focus on explaining human behaviour in general, and criminal behaviour in particular, as being the end product of individuals' rational exercise of their free will. Instead, human behaviour is seen as being more or less determined, or at least heavily influenced by factors either within the individual or their natural environment. This tension between criminological views based on human free will (for example, Classical criminology) and those which stress more deterministic structures which shape human behaviour (for example, Biological criminology and Marxist criminology) is a theme which runs through the chapters of this book but is examined more closely in Chapter 9. Beginning in the next section of this chapter we will look at three overlapping perspectives which belong in the more deterministic biological camp; namely, traditional evolutionary theories as influenced by the early thinking of Darwin, later genetic theories which focus on inherited traits, defects or deficiencies, as well as more recent biochemical theories that focus on hormonal or chemical imbalances. The next section begins this discussion by looking at the origins of Biological criminology in the Grecian and Romanic tradition of physiognomy.

PHYSIOGNOMY AND PHRENOLOGY

There are a number of commonly known injunctions against judging a person by the way they look; such as, for example, 'appearances are deceiving' and 'you can't judge a book by its cover'. Yet it is also a fact of everyday life that we often do judge other people, at least initially, by how they look. We may try to strike up a conversation with someone because we find him or her attractive. Or we may deliberately avoid another person because he or she is physically unappealing to us. We may hear someone described as 'shifty looking' by a friend or when the photograph of a suspected criminal is flashed on our TV screens for a news report we may say he or she must have done it because they 'look bad'. Indeed, in today's image saturated multi-media world of 24-hour news, we often cannot help but make inferences about another person's character based on their appearance. But this state of affairs is not new. In fact, the notion that an individual's character can be read from their physical appearance dates back to the ancient Greeks and Romans. First mentioned in the fifth century BC in the writings of the Athenian artist and playwright Zopyrus, physiognomy (which means nature's judge) studied faces, skulls and other physical features such as hands and feet, which it was commonly believed revealed a person's character and natural disposition (Rowe, 2002). For example, ancient physiognomists warned against trusting beardless men and bearded women as they were held to be inherently deceitful. While individuals with particularly dark complexions were also to be avoided as they were judged to be naturally more violent and envious of others. The socio-political, cultural and intellectual heritage of the Roman Empire ensured physiognomy's continued influence across Europe well into the sixteenth and seventeenth centuries. For example, in Medieval England there was even a law which stated that if two people were accused of a crime, the uglier of the two was more likely the guilty party (Beirne, 1987).

By the beginning of the seventeenth century, and certainly by the middle of the eighteenth, physiognomy began to fall into disrepute, so much so that a British statute made all persons pretending to have skill in it liable to being whipped as rogues and vagabonds (Rowe, 2002). In no small part this was because there had always been a tension between the beliefs and practices of physiognomy and the Christian faith, which had come to dominance across Europe from the third century onwards. But perhaps most importantly, physiognomy's decline predominately happened because it was being replaced by the increasing emphasis being made across Europe from the eighteenth century onwards on developing a more rigorous and scientifically informed understanding of human behaviour using the methodological tools of reason and experiment. Indeed, it was this change which led to the development of the practice of phrenology. However, as we shall see, by today's standards phrenology was not as intellectually rigorous as would normally be required by the scientific community.

Physiognomy is important as it introduced the idea that physical structure determines personality and behaviour. Yet it is with phrenology that we see a beginning point for the scientific study of crime. Thomas Foster first coined the term in the nineteenth century (Simpson, 2005). Although defined as a science of the mind, it is more accurate to say that it was concerned with the development and shape of the brain and how this affects personality and human behaviour, including social interaction. Although its proponents by and large (but not always) emphasised naturalistic as opposed to religious causes for human behaviour, a key difference with Classical criminology was that phrenology experimented with the developing medical sciences of the time, including most importantly the emerging disciplines of anatomy and physiology (Parssinen, 1974). Francis Gall (1835) is considered to be the founding father of phrenology and he is credited with the discovery that various brain functions are localised within certain structures of the brain. In other words, specific areas of the brain control particular types of behaviour and personality traits (Simpson, 2005). Gall theorised that the more important the brain area, the greater its size. Phrenologists argued, similar to the anatomists and physiologists of the time, that one could study the brain through surgery and dissection, but short of that one could always examine and measure the cranium and skull. This is because, according to Gall (1835: 45), 'the skull precisely and accurately covered the cranial cortex, so that organs of disproportionate importance produced concomitant protuberances (i.e. bumps) on the skull'. Gall identified some 26 distinct bumps, with later phrenologists expanding these to 35 (Parssinen, 1974). These bumps were felt to reflect major regions or compartments of the brain which Gall set about defining as being related to key aspects of human personality: including higher intellectual reasoning, moral faculties and what he viewed as more animalistic needs such as that for sex. Perhaps not surprisingly, it was particular parts of our animalistic natures, such as anger and destructiveness for instance, which phrenologists localised to an area just above the ear and argued was overdeveloped in criminals and responsible, for example, for instances of violent criminal behaviour.

Although Gall saw crime as having biological causes, he was generally optimistic about the possibility of preventing or inhibiting criminal behaviour (Rowe, 2002). For Gall, an individual's higher moral and intellectual faculties could be developed and strengthened through careful training and exposure to a good social environment to help them control or suppress their 'lower' criminal faculties. Consequently, like Classical criminologists, Gall and his fellow phrenologists supported punishments designed to rehabilitate criminals and generally opposed the death penalty and the practice of exiling prisoners to the colonies, both of which they felt served no useful purpose (Simpson, 2005). Phrenology enjoyed particular popularity in Europe, England and the US in the first part of the nineteenth century. Yet perhaps not unsurprisingly it came under pressure from religious leaders who thought dissecting brains was prying into God's creation as well as that it was morally dangerous to assert as phrenologists did that it was the brain, rather than the heart, or more precisely the human spirit or soul, which was the centre of human reason (Parssinen, 1974). In addition, a number of what today would be regarded as charlatans started to practise 'reading' the heads of people for money, in much the same way as fortune tellers and palmists. This led to a growing effort by religious leaders and socio-political elites to curtail phrenology by making such practices petty crimes. But most importantly, a key determining factor in the demise of phrenology was its displacement by the work of Lombroso and his theory of atavism.

LOMBROSO AND ATAVISM

Lombroso was an Italian doctor who was interested in phrenology and the anatomy of the brain. Like Gall he emphasised the importance of studying human behaviour using scientific means in the pursuit of naturalistic as opposed to religious explanations for human behaviour (Rowe, 2002). Indeed, Lombroso is usually recognised as the father of positivism within criminology and the founder of what is referred to as the Italian School, which emphasised the scientific study of criminal behaviour. Influenced by Darwin and the ideas of natural selection, Lombroso's central theory was that the criminal was a biological throwback to an earlier stage in human evolution, more ape-like than human. He called this degeneracy atavism. Atavism manifested itself, according to Lombroso, in certain physical characteristics that he called stigmata. The stigmata did not cause criminality, atavism did. But the stigmata were useful for identifying atavists, or born criminals, as Lombroso called them. Stigmata, according to Lombroso, included: ears of unusual size; fleshy, swollen and protruding lips; receding or protruding chin; premature and abundant wrinkling of the skin; an inability to blush; anomalies of hair colour; extra or overly large fingers, toes or nipples; greater strength in left limbs; insensitivity to pain; and finally, excessive tattooing (Wolfgang, 1973).

In his 1876 book, *Criminal man*, Lombroso discusses his research examining 383 Italian male convicts (Lombroso, 1876). Lombroso reports that 21 percent had just one of his stigmatic traits, but 43 percent had five or more. And from this he concluded that the presence of five or more stigmata indicated atavism (Knepper and Ystehede, 2012). By today's methodological and experimental standards Lombroso's work cannot be regarded as robust and conclusive. But for the time in history in which he was working his focus on actually going out and examining criminals and attempting to build theory from empirical data revolutionised criminology and directly challenged Classical criminology. As a result, Lombroso has rightly earned a place as a founding father of modern criminology. At the time, his theory of atavism was much debated in legal and penal circles, as well as society at large, during the latter part of the nineteenth century. It was criticised on moral grounds from religious groups for advocating anatomical experimentation. Meanwhile Lombroso himself, after he collected more data during the 1880s, realised that he needed to revise how many atavists he thought were in the criminal population down from 70 percent to around 30 percent. The rest of the criminal population, he argued, were either people who had committed crimes involuntarily – such as harming or killing somebody in self-defence – or who seemed to be habitual criminals, primarily because of weak parenting, mental health issues or poor education (Knepper and Ystehede, 2012). It is important to note that, alongside the emergence of Classical criminology, the work of Lombroso had a significant impact on Italian and French criminal justice systems in the nineteenth century. However, by modern-day standards, Lombroso's legacy is perhaps not congruent with concepts of human rights and core humanistic notions of due process and innocent until proven guilty. It is impossible to know how many people were convicted of crimes simply because they failed to blush, were heavily tattooed, or had sticky out ears or unusually large jaws or arms (Chamberlain, 2013).

Additionally, Lombroso's analysis of women and crime can in no uncertain terms be criticised for being misogynist, albeit with the proviso that it broadly reflects the sexist and patriarchal social and cultural assumptions and stereotypes which dominated the historical period, which will be discussed further in Chapter 6 when Feminist criminology is examined (Walklate, 2004). Lombroso observed that in official records women had a far lower crime rate than men. He examined this matter closely in his book *The female offender*, which was published in 1895. He argued that, as a group, women were less evolved than men. This, he felt, was evidenced in various primitive traits they possessed, such as being naturally jealous, vengeful and prone to emotional outbursts, including bouts of hysteria and crying. Ordinarily, he held, these defects were neutralised by other feminine traits, such as passivity, physical weakness, low intelligence and the maternal instinct. In short then, the normal everyday woman is for Lombroso an atavist, and he held that criminal women displayed more masculine traits, such as increased strength and intense erotic passions. Female offenders were more sexually active than normal women, as Lombroso sees them, who in accordance with the common standards of the time were meant to be loving but chaste. Hence female offenders are the atavistic women transformed, as Lombroso put it, into deviants and monsters; they had become monstrous women. As a result of his analysis Lombroso argued against giving women the same education and occupations and social opportunities as men, as this only gave them the means and opportunity to commit crimes. As Chapter 6 discusses, Lombroso's ideas have been criticised by Feminist criminologists and Critical criminologists more generally for scientising somewhat commonly held patriarchal assumptions about women, However, this hasn't stopped some criminologists seeing the value of his work in looking for the causes of crime in human biology, or rather physical types of humans.

Box 3.1   Key summary points

- The idea that an individual's character can be read from their physical appearance dates back to the ancient Greeks and Romans and can be found in the writings of Zopyrus, an artist and playwright who lived in Athens during the fifth century BC. Known as physiognomy, which means nature's judge, practitioners studied faces, skulls and other physical features, such as hands and feet, which they believed revealed a person's natural disposition.
- Physiognomy introduced the central idea of Biological criminology that physical structure, or more precisely human biology, determines a person's personality and behaviour. Yet it is the emergence in the eighteenth century of phrenology which established the focus of Biological criminology on naturalistic as opposed to religious causes for human behaviour through experimenting with the developing medical sciences of the time; including, most importantly, the emerging disciplines of anatomy and physiology. Phrenologists such as Francis Gall argued that various brain functions are localised within certain structures of the brain. That is, specific areas of the brain control particular types of behaviour and personality traits. Gall identified some 26 distinct bumps, with later phrenologists expanding this to 35 bumps, which where felt to reflect major regions or compartments of the brain and related to key aspects of human personality, including higher intellectual reasoning, moral faculties and what were viewed as more animalistic needs such as that for sex. Although influential during its time, phrenology was gradually discredited and replaced by the work of Lombroso.
- Cesare Lombroso was an Italian doctor who was influenced by the evolutionary theory of Charles Darwin and the ideas of natural selection. Lombroso's central theory was that the criminal was a biological throwback to an earlier stage in human evolution, more ape-like than human. He called this degeneracy atavism. Atavism manifested itself, according to Lombroso, in certain physical characteristics that he called stigmata. The stigmata did not cause criminality, atavism did. But the stigmata were useful for identifying atavists, or born criminals, as Lombroso called them.
- In his 1876 book, *Criminal man*, Lombroso discusses his research examining 383 Italian male convicts. Here is argued that the typical forms of stigmata include: ears of unusual size; fleshy, swollen and protruding lips; receding or protruding chin; premature and abundant wrinkling of the skin; an inability to blush; anomalies of hair colour; extra or overly large fingers, toes or nipples; greater strength in left limbs; insensitivity to pain; and excessive tattooing.
- In his 1895 book, *The female offender*, Lombroso argued that women are naturally atavistic, but this is kept in check by their feminine nature, and that criminal women displayed more masculine traits, such as increased strength, a capacity for aggression and violence and intense erotic passions. Hence the female offender is the atavistic woman transformed, as Lombroso put it, into deviant and monster; they had become monstrous women.

(Continued)

(Continued)

- Although heavily influential in his time, Lombroso's research and ideas have subsequently been criticised for being sexist and misogynist, for their lack of methodological and conceptual robustness, as well as supporting prejudicial processes within the criminal justice system which are at odds with contemporary notions of human rights and presumptions of innocent until proven guilty.

Further reading

Beirne, P (1987) Adolphe Quetelet and the origins of positivist criminology. *American Journal of Sociology* 92 (5): 1140–69.

Gall, FJ (1835) *On the functions of the brain and of each of its parts: with observations on the possibility of determining the instincts, propensities, and talents, or the moral and intellectual dispositions of men and animals, by the configuration of the brain and head.* Boston: Marsh, Capen and Lyon.

Knepper, P and Ystehede, PJ (2012) *The Cesare Lombroso handbook.* London: Routledge.

Lombroso, C (1876, 2006 edn) *Criminal man.* Durham, NC: Duke University Press.

Lombroso, C (1895, 2006 edn) *The female offender.* Durham, NC: Duke University Press.

Parssinen, TM (1974) Popular science and society: the phrenology movement in early Victorian Britain. *Journal of Social History* 8 (1): 1–20.

Simpson, D (2005) Phrenology and the neurosciences: contributions of F. J. Gall and J. G. Spurzheim. *Australian and New Zealand Journal of Surgery* 75 (6): 475–80.

Walklate, S (2004, 2nd edn) *Gender, crime and criminal justice.* Cullompton: Willan Publishing.

Wolfgang, ME (1973, 2nd edn) Cesare Lombroso. In Mannheim, H (ed.), *Pioneers in criminology.* Montclair, NJ: Patterson Smith.

LOMBROSO'S HERITAGE: IN SEARCH OF THE CRIMINAL TYPE

For all its limitations, Lombroso's Biological criminology is regarded as the first truly positivist form of modern criminology, emphasising scientific methodology, with theory being developed and tested using observation, measurement and experimentation. It is with the Lombrosian project that the criminal first gets placed firmly under the scientific microscope (Garland, 2001). For example, Quetelet and Guerry complied criminal statistics and used them to make predictions and comparisons about what crimes would happen in certain city areas at certain times in the year (Rowe, 2002). This growing positivist orientation within criminology sees the emergence of crime being thought as a 'social fact'. The concept of crime as social fact is discussed in Chapter 5 when

Durkheim's sociological positivism is examined. Viewing crime as social fact means seeing it not as being a result of original sin or deviation from religious doctrine, but rather as something which exists in society and has its own natural regularities, and so is quantifiable, measurable, and in principle, open to manipulation and change. In other words, at the heart of positivist criminology is the idea that by knowing what causes crime it can be stopped. Indeed, post-Lombrosian Biological criminology arguably influenced the introduction of rehabilitative ideals within criminal justice systems across Europe from the late nineteenth century onwards, in much the same way as Classical criminology did (Chamberlain, 2013).

The subsequent development of Biological criminology both built on and critiqued the work of Lombroso. For example, in 1913 the English Biological criminologist Charles Goring published *The English convict: a statistical study* (Goring, 1913). This was a hugely comprehensive study involving the analysis of over 3000 convicts and non-convicts. He found no difference in the physical measurements or physical abnormalities between the two groups and concluded that 'the physical and mental constitution of both criminal and law-abiding persons, of the same age, stature, class, and intelligence, are identical. There is no such thing as an anthropological criminal type' (Goring, 1913: 370). Goring's research essentially ended the influence of Lombroso within criminology. However, his central idea – namely that structure determines function, that is, a person's physicality determines their criminality – was not extinguished completely. Indeed, Goring himself concluded that it is an 'indisputable fact that there is a physical, mental, and moral type of normal person who tends to be convicted of crime: that is to say, our evidence conclusively shows that, on average, the criminal of English prisons is markedly differentiated by defective physique – as measured by stature and body weight, by defective mental capacity' (Goring, 1913: 370). Goring even went so far as to say that it might be advisable to seek to 'regulate the reproduction of those degrees of constitutional qualities – feeble-minded, inebriety, epilepsy, social instinct, etc' (Goring, 1913: 370). Such statements run close to advocating a programme of social eugenics, a point this chapter will discuss more shortly.

One criminologist who was particularly influenced by Goring was the American criminologist Earnest Hooton, who as a result of his anthropological fieldwork with offenders published two books in 1939, *Crime and man* and *The American criminal* (Hooton, 1939a, 1939b). He argued that his research into links between crime and race showed that 'within every race it is the biologically inferior, the organically unadaptable, the mentally and physically stunted and warped, and the sociologically debased – who are responsible for the majority of crimes committed' (Hooton, 1939a: 123). While Hooton advocated eugenic sterilisations of those deemed insane, diseased and criminalistic, he emphasised there was no justification to correlate such degeneracies, as he saw them, with race. The idea of racial difference, in particular that ethnic minorities were more likely to engage in crime than people from majority white backgrounds, was socially and culturally prevalent during this time and influenced the research conducted by Biological criminologists during the period (Garland, 2001). Indeed, although he did not link crime and race directly as many did at the time, Hooton has nevertheless been subsequently criticised for propagating racial stereotypes about black athleticism and moral inferiority in his research (Radzinowicz, 1999). Yet the response to Hooton's work from the scientific community was nevertheless mostly negative, with many criticising him on the grounds that his qualitative fieldwork was highly impressionistic and lacked a necessary statistical and experimental robustness. However, one area of research into physicality and crime which was given slightly more credence centred around body build and crime. For example, in 1921 Ernst Kretschmer published *Physique and character*, which divided people into three body types: people with long and thin limbs and narrow shoulders and underdeveloped muscles who had a tendency to prematurely age; people who were the opposite and so more athletically built with a strong skeleton; and finally, people who were small and round with a pronounced tendency for a distribution of fat around the trunk of the body, who he said were likely to be friendly and sociable (Kretschmer, 1921). Kretschmer began his research because he was interested in seeing if any of these body types correlated with crime. However, he did not find any relationship, although perhaps unsurprisingly he discovered that athletically built people who are criminals are able to do crime for longer as they are more generally robust that other physical types.

Another example of research into physical type and criminality was that of William Sheldon (1940). Like Kretschmer, Sheldon held that people could be classified into three body shapes, which for him also corresponded with three different personality types: firstly, endomorphic (fat and soft) who tend to be sociable and relaxed; secondly, ectomorphic (thin and fragile) who are introverted and restrained; and finally, mesomorphic (muscular and hard) who tend to be aggressive and adventurous. Sheldon found that many convicts were mesomorphic, and they were least likely to be ectomorphic. However, a key problem arising from his research was that he used his data to argue for adopting a eugenic programme based on selective breeding. Indeed, he argued that governments needed to begin adopting stringent birth control programmes to prevent what he referred to as 'bad stock' from reproducing, including the mentally ill, habitually criminal and socially abnormal. Morally and politically, his ideas were unpalatable to the majority of people, and were subject to heavy criticism from the broader scientific community (Rowe, 2002). While methodologically, although at first it seemed he had been rigorous in his study, on closer inspection it turned out that the majority of young offenders he studied had committed relatively minor offences, such as vandalism (Rowe, 2002). Indeed, increasingly throughout the first part of the twentieth century criminological research showed that there was 'no specific combination of physique, character and temperament to be found which would determine whether an individual becomes a delinquent' (Laub and Sampson, 1991: 1435). In conclusion, by the 1950s the scientific community had put to bed the idea that there is a relationship between physical appearance and criminal behaviour. However, criminologists continue to be interested in the fact that people still judge each other on the basis of their physical appearance (Wolfgang, 1973). This point will be returned to in Chapter 5 when Sociological criminology in general and labelling theory in particular are discussed. The remainder of this chapter will focus on more recent developments in Biological criminology in the last few decades. These are much more sophisticated than simply seeking to look at physical appearance. Indeed, one particularly fruitful area of research has involved the examination of the role of genetic factors in influencing human behaviour.

Box 3.2 Key summary points

- The development of Biological criminology into the first half of the twentieth century both built on and critiqued the atavistic theory of Lombroso. For example, Charles Goring (1913) found no difference in the physical measurements of stigmata between criminals and law-abiding citizens. While Earnest Hooton (1939a, 1939b) examined a proposed link between race and crime, noting as he did so that within every race there is 'the biologically inferior, the organically unadaptable, the mentally and physically stunted and warped, and the sociologically debased – who are responsible for the majority of crimes committed' (Hooton, 1939a: 123). Finally, Ernst Kretschmer (1921) and William Sheldon (1940) examined the relationship between body type and personality type, finding little evidence as they did so to support the viewpoint that there is a link between physical appearance and criminal behaviour. As a result, by the middle part of the twentieth century criminologists by and large rejected the idea that criminals were biologically distinct from the law-abiding population.
- Some early Biological criminologists were criticised for advocating morally dubious positions as a result of their research. For example, although Hooton (1939a, 1939b) found no relationship between racial type and crime, he nevertheless advocated social eugenics and state sterilisation of individuals he deemed to be biologically inferior, including the mentally ill and habitually criminalistic.

Further reading

Goring, C (1913) *The English convict: a statistical study.* London: HMSO.
Hooton, EA (1939a) *The American criminal.* New York: Greenwood Press.
Hooton, EA (1939b) *Crime and man.* New York: Greenwood Press.
Kretschmer, E (1921) *Physique and character.* New York: The Humanities Press.
Laub, JH and Sampson, RJ (1991) The Sutherland–Glueck debate: on the sociology of criminological knowledge. *American Journal of Sociology* 96 (6): 1402–40.
Sheldon, WH (1940) *The varieties of human physique.* London: Harper and Brothers.

GENES AND CRIME

The study of genes is linked to evolutionary theory (Rowe, 2002). Genes operationalise the Darwinian notion that we humans, like all animals, have a biological inheritance, which has been passed down over the generations. Since the late 1960s Biological criminologists have looked at the role of genetics in making criminal behaviour more probable through influencing human behaviours, such as impulsivity or a willingness to take risks, as well as looking at their role in influencing the production of certain enzymes which may act to trigger aggressive behaviour. An important and fruitful research area in this regard has been the study of twins. Clearly, identical twins share the same genes and non-identical twins and brothers and sisters share half their genes. So it is possible, in principle, to look at twins and their criminal records and perhaps draw conclusions about the role of genes in influencing certain types of behaviour associated with crime, such as aggression and antisocial behaviour. There are two types of twins: monozygotic (MZ) twins share the same egg and so 100 percent of their DNA; and dizygotic (DZ) twins are separate eggs and so have 50 percent of their DNA in common. What Biological criminological researchers have done since the late 1960s and early 1970s is study the role of genetics in criminal behaviour by determining the degree of concordance – that is similarity – in the behaviour of MZ twins and comparing them with the concordance – or similarity – for DZ twins. Here the concordance runs from zero – where there is none – to 100 percent – where it is exactly the same, meaning if one twin is a criminal then the other is too. Furthermore, we can divide the studies into two parts. In MZ together studies the twins are brought up together and in MZ apart studies they live separately and have no contact with each other. Twins are rare and twins growing up apart is even rarer. As a result, the samples in some cases are small. But this research has been going on for several decades now, and there are some key larger-scale studies, so it is possible to draw together some important conclusions.

For MZ and DZ together studies, Christiansen (1977) studied 3586 twin pairs born between 1870 and 1920 and found 799 twin pairs where at least one had been involved in crime, with the statistics showing 31 percent for MZ and 13 percent for DZ. Cloninger and Gottesman (1987) managed to add even more data to the Christiansen database, updating it and expanding its sample and statistical power, and the figures increased to 74 percent for MZ and 47 percent for DZ. Additionally Bartol (1999) brought together a number of 'MZ apart' studies – that is where identical twins have been brought up apart – and here the average concordance rate is 55 percent for MZ twins and 17 percent for DZ twins. Finally, an extensive review by Button et al. (2005) highlights the importance of genetic influence on aggressive behaviours and traits often associated with engagement in criminality. These studies show the powerful role genes can play in influencing behaviour. Not least of all because the twins all shared the same immediate social environment growing up. The data certainly at first glance appear to indicate that the more DNA you share in common the more likely you are to engage in criminality, regardless of environmental factors.

However, there are some methodological problems with the twin studies. Perhaps most importantly, the different studies define criminality in different ways. For example, traffic violations and drunk and disorderly offences are not defined in the same manner across the studies belonging to different countries. Also sampling problems exist in relation to key social categories such as class and race and ethnicity, with some ethnic minority groups in particular being under-represented (Rowe, 2002). Other research shows that MZ twins tend to be dressed and treated the same by others and also tend to spend considerably more time together than DZ twins. So the greater similarity in behaviour between the MZ twins may actually be down to environmental factors, particularly upbringing and social interaction with family and immediate peer group members. Indeed, studies have provided considerable evidence for the influence of non-genetic environmental factors on behaviour, including parenting style, levels of family income and educational achievement, social support and stressful life events (Kendler and Baker, 2007). For example, delinquent behaviour has been shown to increase amongst adolescents, both twins and otherwise, living in families with high rates of dysfunction, including alcohol and substance misuse as well as domestic violence (Button et al., 2005). Furthermore, a large number of adoption studies have shown that genetic markers for antisocial and aggressive behaviour are more likely to be associated with the development of aggressive and criminal behaviour in adulthood when there are adverse adoptive environmental conditions, particularly when these do not promote and reward emphatic behaviour or are physically or mentally abusive (Rowe, 2002). This lends weight to the argument that both genes and social environment are equally important in influencing behaviour. Indeed, repeated studies into children with genetic markers for impulsivity and aggression has noted the importance of the environmental caregiver role in particular when it comes to predicting the likelihood of higher levels of aggression and impulsive traits in infants and pre-schoolers (Bakermans-Kranenburg and van Ijzendoorn, 2006). In conclusion, no serious biologist would argue that there is a single 'criminal gene' (Rowe, 2002). Indeed, most contemporary Biological criminologists argue for the need to take into consideration both biological and environmental factors when it comes to analysing the effect of genetics on human behaviour, as the available evidence indicates that neither nature (genes) nor nurture (upbringing and social environment) are sufficient in themselves to cause antisocial and criminal behaviour.

Box 3.3   Key summary points

- From the 1960s onwards Biological criminology has focused on the role played by genetic markers in predicting human behaviour.
- An important and fruitful research area in this regard has been the study of twins. The data certainly at first glance appear to indicate that the more DNA you share

(Continued)

(Continued)

in common the more likely you are to engage in criminality, regardless of environmental factors. However, no serious biologist would argue that there is a single 'criminal gene' and these twin studies possess several key methodological and sampling flaws. Furthermore, contemporary research has highlighted the importance of environmental factors in shaping the impact of genetic inheritance on human behaviour, such as parenting style, levels of family income and educational achievement, social support and stressful life events. As a result, contemporary Biological criminologists stress the importance of both genetic and environmental factors when examining human behaviour.

Further reading

Bartol, CR (1999) *Criminal behaviour: a psychosocial approach.* Englewood Cliffs, NJ: Prentice-Hall.

Bakermans-Kranenburg, MJ and van Ijzendoorn, MH (2006) Gene–environment interaction of the dopamine d4 receptor (drd4) and observed maternal insensitivity predicting externalizing behaviour in pre-schoolers. *Developmental Psychobiology* 48 (5): 406–9.

Button, TM, Scourfield, J, Martin, N, Purcell, S and McGuffin, P (2005) Family dysfunction interacts with genes in the causation of antisocial symptoms. *Behavioural Genetics* 35 (2): 115–20.

Christiansen, KO (1977) Seriousness of criminality and concordance amongst Danish twins. In Hood, R (ed.), *Crime and public policy.* New York: The Free Press.

Cloninger, CR and Gottesman, I (1987) Genetic and environmental factors in antisocial behaviour disorder. In Mednick, SA, Moffitt, ET and Stack, SA (eds), *The causes of crime: new biological approaches.* Cambridge: Cambridge University Press.

Kendler, KS and Baker, JH (2007) Genetic influences on measures of the environment: a systematic review. *Psychological Medicine* 37 (5): 615–26.

Rowe, D (2002) *Biology and crime.* Los Angeles: Roxbury.

BRAIN DEVELOPMENT, INJURIES AND MAPPING

The research into genetics and crime has reinforced that we cannot rely solely on biological or environmental factors to understand criminal behaviour. In all genetic research there is the problem that people with a similar genetic inheritance who are exposed to similar environmental stimuli can and do often behave differently when placed in situations. In short, human beings are neither born as blank slates, with their characteristics and actions determined somehow by their environment, nor are they biologically destined to behave in a certain way. All that it is possible to conclude from the available research is that a person's biological makeup may produce certain individual characteristics that might influence for better or worse their susceptibility to environmental influences and social interactions which may in turn trigger criminal behaviour (Rowe, 2002).

That said, one particularly important contemporary area for biological research has been in the area of brain development and injury. This has advanced considerably over the last four decades as a result of the emergence of magnetic resonance imaging (MRI), which has allowed researchers for the first time to map brain activity. This field of research had led to the development of neurocriminology – the examination of brain structure on behaviour – which has its intellectual origins in phrenology with its advocacy of the influence of biological structure on behaviour (Raine, 2013). Mapping technology has confirmed that certain structures in the brain – the hindbrain, the midbrain and limbic region – are responsible for core cognitive processes and motor skills, including human movement and coordination, blood pressure, heart rate, respiration and involuntary responses such as vomiting, our sense of smell, as well as the fight or flight response. The pituitary gland and hypothalamus, which are located in the limbic region and play a key role in controlling the release of growth and sex hormones and so the regulation of aggression, have been linked to excessive violent behaviour in children and young adults, particularly when they are damaged as a result of childhood physical or sexual abuse (Raine, 2002). Temporal lobe dysfunction, either through impact injury or developmental abnormality, has been associated with sex offenders who commit incest or paedophilia (Raine, 2013).

Similarly, damage to the prefrontal lobe – which is responsible for processing emotional responses to situations and forming moral judgements about how to act – has been associated with an increased propensity for aggression and violent crime, including homicide (Davidson, 2004). Indeed, the position of the prefrontal lobe at the front of the head makes it more likely to experience damage and research has shown that damage to the left side of it in particular often leads to an individual feeling more negative about life and other people, with the result that they are more likely to engage in behaviour regarded by others as antisocial, deviant or even criminal (Rowe, 2002). Yet it is important to treat such research with caution. The structure of the brain is highly complex and there are a range of different processes occurring within it at any one time – a fact which is further complicated and affected by the presence of hormones, biochemistry and diet in influencing brain functioning, as the next section of the chapter discusses. Nevertheless, it is important to recognise that advances in brain imaging and research have shown that it is important in some cases to consider the effect of the structure of the brain – either as a result of biological development or impact trauma and injury – on human behaviour, including that labelled as deviant and criminal. It is a conclusion which raises the interesting moral and ethical question of whether we should always adopt the position that individuals are solely responsible for their actions.

BIOCHEMISTRY, HORMONES, DIET AND CRIME

An important but very much still developing area of research over the last two decades within Biological criminology which has reinforced the importance of environmental factors acting on human biology, as well as raised interesting ethical questions surrounding just how much conscious control we have over our actions, has been the examination of the interaction of biochemistry, hormones and diet on human behaviour (Golomb et al., 2000; Gesch, 2002). It is commonly held by nutritionists that brain chemistry can be influenced by diet, additives in food, pollution or hypoglycaemia (low blood sugar levels associated with forms of diabetes). This is because the structure of the brain is made up of cells called neurons, which communicate with one another by way of chemical messages called neurotransmitters. Neurotransmitters are chemical compounds found between nerve cells which send signals from one neuron to another, thus having a direct impact on behaviour, emotion, moods and learning. There are a number of transmitters produced by the body. Three in particular have interested criminologists: serotonin, dopamine and norepinephrine. This is because these particular neurotransmitters are thought to help regulate such behaviours and traits as aggression, irritability and excitability – all of which can be readily associated with criminal behaviour. Most of the research, however, has been conducted with animals, not humans, although that is fast changing (Rowe, 2002).

The evidence suggests that increased dopamine and norepinephrine may trigger inter-male and territorial aggression in animals, but at the same time inhibit predatory aggression. Serotonin appears to play a role in inhibiting all types of aggression. There is some research on habitually violent and dangerous offenders, as well as impulsive offenders such as arsonists, which does seem to show that they have lowered serotonin levels (DeFeudis and Schauss, 1987). Importantly, the production and efficient utilisation of neurotransmitters by the body is to a large extent dependent on diet. For instance, serotonin is produced from tryptophan, which is an amino acid found in high-protein foods such as eggs, fish, dairy products and some types of meat. The production of both dopamine and norepinephrine depends on the amino acid tyrosine, which is also found in most protein foods. Consequently, it has been suggested that certain behaviour patterns, such as aggression, are due to low serotonin levels, and may be correctible through a high-protein diet (Stevens et al., 1995). There are also several possible other ways diet can be linked to criminal behaviour. Attention in particular has been focused on the role of refined sugars and carbohydrates, such as white rice, sugar, as well as high-sugar foods, including junk food, as our bodies break these down slowly, converting them to glucose as it does so, which it injects into the bloodstream, causing the pancreas to secrete insulin. Usually this happens at a pace our bodies can handle. But with refined foods it causes glucose spikes which can lead to the behavioural systems associated with hypoglycaemia, including irritability, nervousness, depression and destructive outbursts. It should not be a surprise, therefore, that criminologists have become increasingly interested in this research area. For example, Gesch (2002) found in a study of convicted violent offenders that they tended to suffer from reactive hypoglycaemia. This is an abnormal tolerance to glucose caused by an excessive consumption of sugar, carbohydrates and stimulants such as caffeine.

Zalberg (2010) found young adult prisoners who had exhibited aggressive and rule-breaking behaviour tended to prefer a high-sugar processed food diet and suffered from poor nutritional levels associated with a lack of key vitamins and minerals. However, it has been highlighted that this is very much a growing area of research within Biological criminology and the evidence base is far from conclusive. Indeed, it is difficult, if not impossible, to confidentially assert a direct link between nutrition and diet and human behaviour, particularly outside laboratory-based conditions. As the already discussed research into the role of genes illustrates, a range of environmental factors influence how human beings behave in social situations, and so mediate the relationship between human biology and a person's behaviour in social situations. The same can be said when it comes to considering the impact of biochemical and diet and nutritional factors on behaviour (Rowe, 2002). Psychological and Sociological criminologists, as the following chapters discuss, certainly reinforce the importance of paying close attention to cognitive and socio-cultural factors when it comes to analysing the causes of human behaviour, including that defined as deviant or criminal.

Box 3.4   Key summary points

- The research into genetics and crime has reinforced that we cannot rely solely on biological or environmental factors to understand criminal behaviour.
- Another important but very much still developing area of research over the last two decades within Biological criminology, which has reinforced the importance of environmental factors acting on human biology, has been the examination of the interaction of biochemistry, hormones and diet on human behaviour. There certainly is evidence to suggest that nutrition and diet in particular can impact on human behaviour, particularly excessive consumption of sugar, carbohydrates and stimulants such as caffeine. However it is difficult to conclusively link diet to aggressive and rule-breaking behaviour, particularly as a range of psychological and socio-cultural factors influence how human beings behave within social situations.

Further reading

DeFeudis, FV and Schauss, AG (1987) The role of brain monoamine metabolite concentrations in arsonists and habitually violent offenders: abnormalities of criminals or social isolation effects? *International Journal of Biosocial Research* 9 (1): 27–30.

(Continued)

(Continued)

Gesch, B (2002) Influence of supplementary vitamins, minerals, and essential fatty acids on the antisocial behaviour of young adult prisoners. *The British Journal of Psychiatry* 181: 22–8.

Golomb, BA, Stattin, H and Mednick, S (2000) Low cholesterol and violent crime. *Journal of Psychiatric Research* 34 (4–5): 301–9.

Raine, A (2002) Biosocial studies of antisocial and violent behaviour in children and adults: a review. *Journal of Abnormal Child Psychology* 30 (4): 311–26.

Raine, A (2013) *The anatomy of violence: the biological roots of crime.* New York: Pantheon.

Rowe, D (2002) *Biology and crime.* Los Angeles: Roxbury.

Stevens, LJ, Zentall, SS and Deck, JL (1995) Essential fatty-acid metabolism in boys with attention-deficit hyperactivity disorder. *American Journal of Clinical Nutrition* 62 (4): 761–8.

Zalberg, Z (2010) Effects of nutritional supplements on aggression, rule-breaking, and psychopathology among young adult prisoners. *Aggressive Behaviour* 36 (2): 117–26.

SELF-STUDY TASKS

1. Produce a 20-minute PowerPoint presentation which outlines the empirical evidence for the work of Lombroso and his theory of atavism and the presence of stigmata in Italian criminals. Provide visual examples from the contemporary context to show why it is dangerous to try and 'spot the criminal type' as if offenders are physically different from law-abiding citizens.

2. Write a maximum of 750 words outlining the historical background to the emergence of Biological criminology alongside its key features, strengths and weaknesses. How is it similar to and different from Classical criminology with its emphasis on free will, rational choice and deterrence? What potential threats to personal freedom and social equality do you think contemporary Biological criminology potentially possesses due to its tendency to emphasise genetic inheritance and biological normality, even when the importance of environmental factors is acknowledged?

4 PSYCHOLOGICAL CRIMINOLOGY

CHAPTER CONTENTS

INTRODUCTION: THE CLASSICAL SCHOOL AND PSYCHOLOGICAL AND BIOLOGICAL THEORIES OF CRIME

This chapter introduces psychological explanations of crime by focusing on personality and cognitive development as well as psychosocial learning theories in the form of social learning and differential association theory. It also considers the contribution of research into violent and sex offenders to understanding the causes of crime. Chapter 2 highlighted how the emergence of Classical criminology was bound up with a shift from the seventeenth and eighteenth centuries on towards naturalistic as opposed to religious explanations for the world and human behaviour. However, as was noted in Chapter 3, a key problem with Classical criminology relates to the fact that its advocates felt they had solved the problem of crime. It was argued by Beccaria and Bentham that as the causes of crime lie in the rational choices of the individual, criminal behaviour could as a result be managed by using different forms of deterrence to make deviance and crime appear unattractive to the reasoning individual. Whatever the merits of this emphasis on deterrence the starting position of the Classical school that the rationality of human beings was a self-evident truth meant that by and large they did not advocate the rigorous collection of empirical data to investigate criminal behaviour (Chamberlain, 2013). After all, why would the learned gentleman criminologists of the eighteenth century need to get their hands dirty collecting data from criminals when they already knew why they committed crime, i.e. because they perceived the benefit of doing so as outweighing the perceived costs? In contrast, although they share the emphasis of Classical criminology in locating the cases of crime within the individual, the development of Biological and Psychological forms of criminology emphasised systematically collecting empirical facts and figures through the use of careful observation and experiment. As a result, Psychological and Biological forms of criminology are regarded as positivistic forms of criminology, as they by and large advocate the adoption of a scientific approach to the study of crime (Young, 2011).

As was discussed in Chapter 3, positivists argue for the adoption of the methodology of the natural sciences within the social sciences and claim that objective and value-neutral knowledge about the causes of human behaviour, including criminal behaviour, is possible. Positivism is discussed again in Chapter 8 in relation to contemporary postmodern constructivist approaches in criminology. For the moment, it is important to note that Biological and Psychological approaches to the study of crime, as discussed in this and the previous chapter, emphasise this positivistic approach to studying the causes of crime, and this fundamentally separates them from what can be broadly defined as the Classical school of criminology as well as religious and popularist 'common-sense' positions concerning the problem of crime. Yet, like Classical criminology, Biological and Psychological forms of criminology locate the causes of crime inside the individual. It's just that rather than holding that these lie in human free will and our ability to exercise reason and choice, they hold our actions are to some extent determined by our biological or psychological makeup. This contrasts with the Sociological theories of crime discussed from Chapter 5 onwards. Here it is important to note that Classical, Biological and Psychological theories of criminality each to varying degrees do recognise the importance of 'the social'. However, some authors working in these traditions emphasise 'the social' more than others, and all are limited by their focus on viewing the social causes of crime in terms of childhood developmental and family and interpersonal relationships. In contrast, Sociological approaches to the study of crime focus on social-structural and ordering factors such as culture, economics, class, gender, urban geography and the design of cityscapes. Indeed, it is important to remember that 'the social' can and has been expressed in different ways by different authors and different theoretical traditions. The various Biological and Psychological perspectives covered in Chapters 3 and 4 reinforce this viewpoint. In this chapter, we begin to look at Psychological theories of crime by looking at the work of Freud on personality development.

FREUD AND PERSONALITY DEVELOPMENT

The main focus of the work of Freud was on personality structure and its influence on human behaviour (Freud, 2012). His key idea is that people have natural drives and urges, some of which are buried in the subconscious and unconscious. Freud conceived of the human personality as having three inter-related parts – the id, the ego and the superego. The id is present at birth. It is entirely unconscious and is composed of powerful forces, called drives and instincts. The two most important drives and instincts are sex (Eros) and destruction or aggression (Thanatos). The id operates on the pleasure principle: it wants immediate gratification so as to relieve the psychic tension produced by its powerful drives. That is, it seeks to maximise pleasure and minimise displeasure. Freud, like the Enlightenment scholars before him and Classical criminologists, viewed human nature humanistically, arguing that human beings are not inherently evil or born sinful, but rather as a species we evolved within a natural environment, and so our drives and urges are normal and tied up with the maturation and developmental processes which naturally occur within it. At the core of this lies the normal and natural goal of minimising pain and injury while maximising a sense of personal wellbeing and good health. Following the innate pain–pleasure drive means we are more likely to continue to survive and reproduce collectively as a species.

For Freud and his followers, who are called psychoanalysts, the id is not evil but simply amoral. In contrast to this, the ego operates on what is called 'the reality principle', in that it tries to satisfy the needs of the id in socially acceptable ways. The ego first begins to develop when we are between six and eight months old from our experiences in our environment as we come to understand that we are separate or distinct from other people and things around us. The ego is best described as the aspect of the personality that is rational, oriented towards solving problems, and able to delay gratification. As the ego grows, so does the individual's ability to deal with reality through engaging in self-discipline. Finally, there is the superego. This is typically defined as the conscience. It develops when we are three to five years old. The superego is the internalisation of the values and norms of our society which we are taught initially by our parents or other caregivers, and later by other authority figures we may encounter, such as teachers and famous role models for example. It is the superego that produces feelings of guilt. Freud held that given the various demands and functions of these different aspects of the personality the possibility for psychic conflict is great. Usually, though, the three components of the personality work together in relative harmony, under the leadership of the ego, to achieve pleasurable yet safe discharges of tension. The ego of a healthy individual successfully represses id impulses or channels them to some acceptable outlet – what is often called sublimation – while also keeping the superego in check, making sure it does not become too rigid or perfectionistic. But what if something goes wrong? For example, if the ego is weak, or the superego overdeveloped? For Freud and his followers, criminal behaviour is one possible consequence. It is argued that the most important conflicts occur in childhood, and these can have immediate and long-term knock-on effects on our personality as we grow. Key events, such as physical and sexual abuse, neglect, or overindulgence by parents, can lead to personality problems which may manifest themselves in adulthood. Hence from a Freudian perspective a major cause of criminal and delinquent behaviour is a malfunctioning ego or superego, as these are the mechanisms which keep the id and its untamed desires and wants in check.

Following Freud, Alexander and Healy (1935) suggested that children need to progress from the pleasure principle (being id dominated and therefore needing instant gratification) to the reality principle (where the ego is dominant). They argued that a child needs a stable home environment in order to successfully make this transition and that criminals are those children who do not make this transition. There was some early research to support the view that most criminals come from unstable homes. For example, in 1944 Bowlby conducted research with 44 juvenile delinquents and compared them with non-criminal disturbed juveniles (Bowlby, 1969). Thirty-nine percent of the delinquents had experienced complete separation from their mothers for six months or more during the first five years of their lives compared with 5 percent of the control group. However, later research has shown that it isn't separation from a mother which is the problem (Webber, 2009). What seems to be critical is a lack of opportunities for positive bonding with any caregiver, be this a family member or not. Furthermore, it was increasingly recognised from the 1950s onwards by Criminal psychologists that it is a gross oversimplification of the complex social environment a child grows up in to focus solely on early childhood experiences and family relationships alone when looking for possible influences on criminal behaviour. This said, Freud and later research conducted by his fellow psychoanalysts has contributed to the criminological corpus by reinforcing the importance of childhood experience when examining criminality. Indeed, as we will discuss later in the chapter, when profiling violent and sex offenders we often do see that they have had deeply negative childhood experiences. Nevertheless, a key problem with this approach is that because psychoanalysis relies on looking at the unconscious it is not in reality empirically testable. It is impossible to prove or disprove that internal conflicts and unconscious desires and emotions are driving behaviour. It was for this reason why from the 1950s onwards psychologists focused on observable behaviour. Hence the name given to this development was behaviourism.

Behaviourism and classical and operant conditioning

Classical conditioning is key to understanding behaviourism in particular and contemporary psychological models of criminality more generally. Here the focus is on how behaviour is learned. That is to say, a defining feature of humankind is taken to be their ability to model their actions on others. Poor classical conditioning has been proposed as one of the fundamental problems amongst antisocial groups by Eysenck (1952). Classical conditioning is an association learning process whereby a neutral stimulus – called the conditioned stimulus or CS – takes on the properties of an unconditional stimulus – called a UCS – and comes to elicit a conditioned response – a CR – following repeated pairings of the neutral stimulus, or CS, with the unconditional stimulus, the UCS. The process of classical conditioning was discovered by the Russian physiologist Ivan Pavlov, who found that his laboratory dogs could learn to salivate to the sound of a bell. The presentation of food – UCS – normally elicits salivation in dogs – an unconditioned response or UCR. When the sound of a bell – the CS – was repeatedly paired with the presentation of food – the UCS – the sound of the bell alone – the CS – eventually became enough in itself to elicit salivation – the CR – in the dogs even when food wasn't presented. Similarly punishment – UCS – naturally causes feelings of distress, which is an unconditioned response – or UCR – for most children. Each time a child is caught stealing, he or she is presumably punished, thereby leading to feelings of distress. According to classical conditioning theory, the repeated pairing of stealing with punishment will eventually cause the child to feel distress when thinking about stealing something. It is the association between stealing and the feeling of distress caused by punishment that will deter most children from stealing, according to this approach. And it is this pairing of a stimulus – stealing – with a response – punishment – which has led behaviourism and classical conditioning to be called stimulus–response theory. Studies seem to show that antisocial individuals may well have poor classical conditioning (Webber, 2009).

Burrhus Frederic Skinner, more commonly known as BF Skinner, agreed that it is more productive to study observable behaviour rather than internal mental events. Building on the work of early behavioural psychologists, notably Edward Thorndike, Skinner introduced a new term, the Law of Effect, into the psychological lexicon. This holds that reinforced behaviour tends to be repeated (i.e. strengthened) while behaviour which is not reinforced tends to die out (i.e. weakened). Skinner identified three types of responses or operant that can follow behaviour:

Neutral operants: responses from the environment that neither increase nor decrease the probability of a behaviour being repeated.

Reinforcers: responses from the environment that increase the probability of a behaviour being repeated. Reinforcers can be either positive or negative.

Punishers: responses from the environment that decrease the likelihood of a behaviour being repeated. Punishment weakens behaviour.

Hence to understand why somebody commits a crime it is necessary to understand their individual learning history and what has reinforced this behaviour. However, while this approach may well work under laboratory conditions, in the real world several factors interact with situations to produce affects. It is certainly difficult to apply behaviourism to criminal life histories and identify clear stimulus–response situations, as well as measure the impact of various operants on complex human behaviours; including that labelled deviant or criminal. As the next section discusses, this state of affairs led later social psychologists such as Eysenck to draw together personality traits and environmental considerations to look at why certain people commit crime.

Box 4.1 Key summary points

- Freud (2012) conceived of the human personality as having three interrelated parts – the id, the ego and the superego – and that given the various demands and functions of these different aspects of the personality the possibility for psychic conflict is great, with deviant and criminal behaviour being one result of this state of affairs.
- Freud contributed to the development of Psychological forms of criminology from the early nineteenth century onwards by reinforcing the importance of childhood experience when examining the causes of crime.
- Critics highlighted that the focus of Freud and his followers on the unconscious lacked empirical and experimental depth, which led to a focus from the 1950s onwards on observable human behaviour.
- Behaviourism developed as a result of the research of Pavlov into classical conditioning and of Skinner into operant conditioning – where a certain stimulus elicits a certain response and an environment can be tailored to condition an emotional response. However, while behaviourism may well work under laboratory conditions, in the real world several factors interact with situations to produce affects. It is certainly difficult to apply behaviourism to real world criminal life histories and identify clear stimulus–response situations. With the result that from the 1960s onwards Criminal psychologists increasingly focused on drawing together personality traits, social factors and environmental considerations, to look at why certain people commit crime.

Further reading

Alexander, F and Healy, W (1936) *Roots of crime: psychoanalytic studies.* Montclair, NJ: Patterson Smith.
Bowlby, J (1969) *Attachment and loss: volume 1. Loss.* New York: Basic Books.
Eysenck, HJ (1952) The effects of psychotherapy: an evaluation. *Journal of Consulting Psychology* 16: 319–24.
Freud, S (2012 edn) *A general introduction to psychoanalysis* (Wordsworth classics of world literature). London: Wordsworth Editions Ltd.
Webber, C (2009) *Psychology and crime.* London: Sage.

EYSENCK, DIMENSIONS OF PERSONALITY AND CRIMINAL BEHAVIOUR

Working under the influence of the work of Freud's psychotherapy and Pavlov and Skinner's behaviourism, Hans Eysenck argued that it is impossible to ignore the social causes of offending while also advocating the need to look at underlying biological and psychological causes for crime (Eysenck and Eysenck, 1976). Eysenck did not consider social conditions such as class and poverty, rather he concentrated on the biological foundations to the human personality and how these interacted with social environments in the form of social bonds and relationships. The essence of his theory is that some people are born with cortical and autonomic nervous systems which affect their ability to be conditioned by environmental stimuli. Behaviour, influenced by both biological and social factors, is taken by Eysenck to define an individual's personality (Eysenck, 1997). However, he did not think people were predestined to commit crime in the same way as Lombroso and the Biological positivists discussed in Chapter 3 suggest. Rather, his point is that the autonomic or central nervous system of the criminal is different from non-criminals in some significant ways. In essence, Eysenck holds that some people have nervous systems that are more reactive or sensitive to stimuli than others, and this makes them more excitable and less able to exercise self-control.

Eysenck's theory explains the criminal personality as resulting from the interaction between three psychological traits: neuroticism (N), extroversion (E) and psychoticism (P) (Eysenck, 1997). To begin with, a neurotic can be loosely defined as a person suffering from anxiety and appears nervous and moody. However, the manner in which neurotics are defined by Eysenck's theory is not the strict clinical disorder. The second and perhaps most integral part of this explanation of criminal personality is the dimension known as introvert to extrovert. Generally introverted people are described as quiet, withdrawn people, and conversely, extroverts as outgoing and impulsive. Explanations for this vary, but from within Eysenck's theory cortical or brain stimulation is important. Extroverts have low cortical arousal and seek excitement to maintain levels of stimulation. Introverts, however, are overstimulated and avoid stirring situations to avoid becoming over-aroused. Finally, psychoticism – which is similar to the modern-day term of psychopath or sociopath – describes people whose personality is characterised by poor emotion, sensation-seeking behaviour and a general lack of empathy for others. The relationship between these three personality dimensions is for Eysenck the essence of the criminal personality (or lack thereof) (Webber, 2009). Specially, the interplay between these three variables is assumed to limit severely the ability of an individual to be conditioned or socialised into a non-criminal way of thinking and behaving. Conversely, people who were introverted and scored low on neuroticism and psychoticism were seen as ideal candidates for social conditioning and less likely therefore to be involved in criminal activity. Interestingly, Eysenck reports little in his research in the way of gender differences and that young offenders were more likely to be highly extroverted than adult offenders.

Eysenck's theory led to a growth in the psychological profiling of offenders, with academics and criminal psychologists using it as a model from which to increasingly categorise different types of offenders in terms of criminal personalities. Yet his work was heavily criticised, mainly on the instrumental grounds of how the questionnaire he developed captured the different personalities, but also because it was argued the real world is too complex to pigeonhole people into personality categories. Sociological criminologists, in particular, felt Eysenck adopted a very simplistic view of socialisation and the influence of a range of social factors, including education, class, race, geographical location, on individual personality and decision-making processes. This said, the idea of linking extrovert personality types to crime has led to some interesting research findings. For example, Kirkcaldy and Brown (1999) looked at data from 37 countries and found that extrovert personality types did correlate with crime rates. One study from Brazil, for example, shows that extroverts were more likely to use dramatic weapons like guns when committing crime (Webber, 2009). However, a key issue is that Eysenck's theory links biology with crime via its emphasis on the influence of the nervous system on personality type. Although many criminal psychologists and social scientists recognise the usefulness of looking at personality in this way, just as they recognise the value of stimulus and response conditioning, they nevertheless for moral and ethical reasons tend to prefer to de-emphasise deterministic biological approaches to human behaviour as these can lead to, on the one hand, criminals seeking to excuse their behaviour on the grounds that they couldn't choose to act differently, and, on the other hand, be used by political parties and governing elites to justify punitive interventions and preventive measures towards certain groups of individuals on the basis that they might act a certain way in the future, as was discussed in more detail in Chapter 3. The work of Eysenck and subsequent critiques of it brought to the fore an emphasis within social psychology and criminal psychology from the 1980s onwards on how people learn certain behaviours, not through a process of stimulus and response, but rather through modelling their behaviour on others. The resulting research, broadly classified as social learning theory, has been influential in criminology. Although as the next section outlines, one key criminology social learning theory, differential association theory, was first developed in the 1930s.

Box 4.2 Key summary points

- Working under the influence of Freud's psychotherapy and Pavlov's behaviourism, Hans Eysenck argued that it is impossible to ignore the social causes of offending while also advocating the need to look at underlying biological and psychological causes for crime.
- Eysenck holds that some people have nervous systems that are more reactive or sensitive to stimuli than others, and this makes them more excitable and less able to exercise self-control.
- Eysenck's theory led to a growth in the psychological profiling of offenders, with academics and criminal psychologists using it as a model from which to

(Continued)

increasingly categorise different types of offenders in turns of criminal personalities. However, his work has been criticised on instrumental grounds, with concerns being raised over whether his questionnaire could capture personality types.

- Eysenck's theory has also been criticised on moral and ethical grounds for potentially providing a deterministic model of criminal behaviour whereby it is justified on the basis that a person couldn't choose to act differently given their nervous system physiology.

Further reading

Eysenck, HJ (1997) *Dimensions of personality.* London: Transaction Publishers.
Eysenck, HJ and Eysenck, SBG (1976) *Psychoticism as a dimension of personality*. London: Hodder and Stoughton.
Kirkcaldy, BD and Brown, JM (1999) Personality, socioeconomics and crime: an international comparison. *Psychology, Crime and Law* 6 (2): 113–25.
Webber, C (2009) *Psychology and crime.* London: Sage.

SUTHERLAND, DIFFERENTIAL ASSOCIATION THEORY AND SOCIAL LEARNING

The idea that people who break the law are psychologically different or atypical is highly problematic. Some offenders undoubtedly do have mental health problems. It might be comforting to think that criminals have a different psychological makeup to the rest of us which can be identified through testing and profiling them. However, in reality, this is more than a little problematic as it is based on the false dichotomy that an individual is always either a criminal or not a criminal. Indeed, most run of the mill day-to-day criminals, in fact, aren't psychologically abnormal. Rather, it is better to think of a continuum. After all, few, if any, people are criminal all the time, and few, if any, people are always law-abiding or conformist all the time. Given this situation, it is possibly better to be able to know some other things about individuals who commit crime. Here differential association theory states that we gain most by looking at which people these individuals associate with. This theory was first put forward by the sociologist Edwin Sutherland (Sutherland, 1939). He believed that an individual's behaviour is directed by the primary groups they belonged to and has nine propositions:

1. Criminal behaviour is learned.
2. Criminal behaviour is learned in interaction with other persons in a process of communication.
3. The principal part of the learning of criminal behaviour occurs within intimate personal groups.

4. When criminal behaviour is learned, the learning includes (a) techniques of committing the crime, which sometimes are very complicated, sometimes very simple, and (b) the specific direction of motives, drives, rationalisations and attitudes.
5. The specific direction of motives and drives is learned from definitions of the legal codes as favourable or unfavourable.
6. A person becomes delinquent because of an excess of definitions favourable to the violation of law over definitions unfavourable to the violation of law.
7. Differential associations may vary in frequency, duration, priority and intensity.
8. The process of learning criminal behaviour by association with criminal and anti-criminal patterns involves all of the mechanisms that are involved in any other learning.
9. While criminal behaviour is an expression of general needs and values, it is not explained by those general needs and values because non-criminal behaviour is an expression of the same needs and values.

Some of these statements may seem pretty simplistic. But at the time Sutherland was putting forward his theory – in the 1930s – each proposition contained key points which subsequently significantly influenced the development of criminology as an academic discipline. The first proposition – criminal behaviour is learned – is an explicit rejection of the dominant causal theories of the late nineteenth and early twentieth centuries – especially the work of Lombroso and Biological criminology discussed in Chapter 3 – as these were still being taken seriously at this point in time and Sutherland was concerned with distancing mainstream criminology from this perspective, not least because he was worried about associating criminology as a discipline with eugenics and right-wing political concerns with racial purity, which were dominating political discourse in Germany in particular during this period. The second proposition augments the first, but reinforces that all learning is a social process. Persons come to crime not through purely personal or private experience, but rather through contacts with others. This bedrock tenet of Sutherland's theory placed it squarely within the mainstream of social-psychological thought, where it remains today. The third proposition narrows the field of 'others' to intimate associates. This qualification illustrates the strong emphasis placed on primary socialising groups; including family, friends, neighbours and co-workers, and face-to-face social interaction on a day-to-day basis. The fourth proposition asserts that the process of learning crime not only involves the acquisition of motives to commit crime but also knowledge about the methods of how to commit crime.

The fifth proposition is inherited from symbolic interactionism, which is a theory of collective human behaviour discussed in Chapter 5, and which states that human behaviour is affected by the meanings or definitions that individuals place on objects, events, or acts, and which is acquired in and through social interaction. The sixth proposition is the heart of Sutherland's theory. It sets forth the mechanism by which a person becomes delinquent; namely, an excess of definitions favourable to violation of the law. In other words, a person commits a crime or does not commit crime, due to the external influence of other people saying and acting like it is OK to do so, or not OK to do so as the case may be. The seventh proposition highlights the dynamic nature of the relationships involved in this process. While the eighth proposition reinforces that the process of learning criminal behaviour by association with criminal and non-criminal patterns involves all the mechanism that are involved in other types of learning. What this means then is that learning to be a criminal is not simply about imitating other people who are criminals: people can be seduced into committing crime, or even deliberately educated by others into thinking what they are doing is right. But it also means that we must view criminal behaviour as behaviour, that is, not as something abnormal and different. Here Sutherland is again arguing against Biological criminology as he holds that criminal behaviour differs from lawful behaviour because of the standards by which it is judged, not because the causes of criminality lie inherently inside of somebody. The ninth, and final proposition further reinforces that criminologists up until Sutherland's time had tried to explain criminal behaviour in terms of the pleasure principle of rational choice theory, or by using biological explanations for criminal behaviour, and what he wanted to argue was that it was the social context an individual lives which was key to understanding why criminal behaviour happens.

Underpinning Sutherland's theory is the argument that crime is a social and political label placed on certain behaviours, and what is crime in one society or local culture may well not be a crime in another. This is a social-psychological theory of crime which links the personal to the social which will be discussed later in this book from Chapter 5 onwards. Indeed, no theory of crime has received more attention from researchers in the US and UK over the last 70 years than differential association theory (Deflem, 2006). The literature on the topic is daunting and diverse. But the single strongest piece of evidence in its favour can be stated succinctly: no characteristic of individuals known to criminologists is a better predictor of criminal behaviour than the number of delinquent friends an individual has (Chamberlain, 2013). A range of data has been used to show this, both qualitative and quantitative. Few correlative regularities in criminology have proven as consistent as that between delinquency and delinquent friends. Nevertheless, some people have pointed out that people do not become delinquent because they acquire delinquent friends. Often they acquire delinquent friends after they have themselves become delinquent. The evidence to date is not yet sufficient to settle the issue one way or another, and it remains one of the key unresolved questions in criminology today (Webber, 2009). But this doesn't take away from the fact that young offenders in particular engage in delinquency and crime in groups, as well as that the group nature of teenage delinquency episodes is one of the few established facts of criminology.

Notwithstanding the evidence in favour of differential association, one aspect of Sutherland's theory has consistently failed to receive support from research. Sutherland argued that individuals become delinquent because they acquire definitions or attitudes favourable to the violation of law through differential association. Here he is arguing that delinquency is the result of attitude transference, whereby the attitudes of one individual are adopted or absorbed by others. However, a number of studies over the last three decades have consistently indicated that attitude transference is not the process by which differential association operates (Webber, 2009). For example, Deflem (2006) discusses how research reinforces that the effects of friends' attitudes on teenagers is small in comparison to that of friends' actual behaviour, which does not necessarily operate through changing attitudes, rather it is largely an embodied and physically direct experience, most of which cannot be fully verbalised. Indeed, human beings, like most animals, communicate more through non-verbal means than verbal. This fact led Burgess and Akers (1966) to develop a broader social learning theory, which emphasises conditioned behaviour and imitation, and how socially learned behaviour – criminal and otherwise – is direct and vicarious and behavioural. For example, a teenager may imitate the smoking, theft or drug use behaviour of friends because they observe the adult status this confers on them in the eyes of their peers, rather than because they are directly talked into doing them, although of course this more than likely will also play a role.

In conclusion, Sutherland's differential association theory contrasted to the reigning theories of the day and he brought to the fore that criminal behaviour is extrinsic to the individual rather than intrinsic. That is, he foresaw later Sociological approaches to crime by highlighting that the causes of crime do not necessarily lie within the individual themselves, as is claimed by Classical and Biological criminologists, amongst others. Sutherland asserted that criminal behaviour can be learned by anybody. Indeed, Vold and Bernard (1986: 225) conclude that 'Sutherland's theory, more than any other, was responsible for … the rise of the view that crime is the result of environmental influences acting on biological and psychologically normal individuals'. As such, perhaps his lasting contribution to criminology as a discipline is that his work reinforces that the analysis of criminal behaviour cannot be divorced from the social and political context in which it occurs, which is an axiom that has lain at the centre of academic criminology for the last several decades.

Box 4.3   Key summary points

- Sutherland proposed that the idea that people who break the law are psychologically different or atypical is highly problematic. In contrast, he proposed the theory of differential association, which states that we gain most insight into the causes of crime by looking at which people individuals associate with, as like any other type of behaviour criminal behaviour is socially learned in and through interaction with other people.
- Differential association theory has been tested repeatedly over the last 80 years and it does seem to be the case that it is a key predictor of delinquent and criminal behaviour.

(Continued)

(Continued)

- However, it does not help us to understand non-verbal cues for human behaviour and it is not known if people become delinquent because they acquire delinquent friends or acquire delinquent friends after they have themselves become delinquent.

Further reading

Burgess, R and Akers, RA (1966) Differential association-reinforcement theory of criminal behavior. *Social Problems* 14 (2): 128–47.

Chamberlain, JM (2013) *Understanding criminological research: a guide to data analysis*. London: Sage.

Deflem, M (2006) *Sociological theory and criminological research: views from Europe and the United States*. London: Elsevier.

Sutherland, D (1939, 3rd edn) *Principles of criminology*. Chicago: University of Chicago Press.

Vold, GB and Bernard TJ (1986, 3rd edn) *Theoretical criminology*. New York: Oxford University Press.

Webber, C (2009) *Psychology and crime*. London: Sage.

PSYCHOLOGICAL CRIMINOLOGY AND MENTALLY DISORDERED OFFENDERS

Whatever its limitations, Psychological criminology has played an important role in examining and managing the problem of mental illness and crime, particularly in relation to how mentally disordered offenders are cared for within the criminal justice system. More than 70 percent of the prison population in the UK has two or more mental health disorders, including depression, addiction, anxiety and compulsive behaviour, with similar statistics being reported worldwide (Webber, 2009). Male prisoners are 14 times more likely to have two or more disorders than men in general, and female prisoners are 35 times more likely than women in general. Furthermore, the suicide rate in prisons is almost 15 times higher than in the general population (Howitt, 2006). A key contribution Psychological criminology has played in this regard pertains to the diagnosis and treatment of violent and sex offenders, including serial killers. Research shows that several psychological traits are often found in individuals who commit violent and sex crimes, including a lack of self-control, a lack of victim empathy, high levels of social hostility and aggression, deviant sexual fantasy, as well as cognitive distortions and rationalisations for undertaking violent sexual behaviour. As a result, various questionnaire-based tools have been developed to help identify violent and sex offenders, i.e. Hare's Psychopathy Checklist, the VRAG, the HCR-20, the SORAG, the R-RASOR and the Static 99. These tools are variously used by psychologists and psychiatrists to clinically diagnose and risk-manage the care and treatment of mentally dis-ordered offenders (Webber, 2009).

Profiling homicide and the serial killer: Biological, Psychological and Sociological theories

Another important area which Psychological criminology has explored is serial murder. This is typically defined as involving the murder of three or more people over time. We frequently think serial murder is a highly preva-lent feature of modern life due to TV crime dramas and the fact that it seems not a month goes by without another case cropping up in the news. Criminologists are perhaps also guilty of reinforcing the view that serial kill-ers are everywhere around us. It has been argued that there are between 3500 and 4000 serial murder victims per year in the US (Gresswell and Hollin, 1994). This estimate is based on the view that serial murderers are responsible for two-thirds of the 5000 or so unsolved US homicides each year. The prob-lem with this viewpoint is that it is based upon the flawed assumption that serial killers are responsible for unsolved or apparently motiveless killings (Haggerty, 2009). In reality, serial murder is far less common than is pre-sumed. For example, the Homicide Index in the UK shows that between 1995 and 2012, 4.1 percent of homicide victims were killed in episodes that could be defined as multiple homicides (Chamberlain, 2013). In terms of gaining a profile of the serial killer, they tend to be white males in their thirties who shoot, burn, stab or strangle their victims, while the majority murder their friends and family (Webber, 2009). Indeed, what is known about serial killers shows that not only do we need to question the common perception that the number of serial killers are on the increase, we also need to seriously question how they are portrayed by the media in terms of the common profile of the 'mad loner'. Rather, they generally appear to be men who for some reason kill their family or friends, often in response to the need to exercise power and control.

It is commonly argued that serial killers are born not made; often by either making the case for genetic difference or organic brain structure malfunction (Webber, 2009). However, in reality no distinctive, purely biological basis for the drive to commit serial murder and sex crime has been conclusively found. Rather, the majority of Psychological criminologists stress the importance of life events creating psychological disturbances and trigger points which can subsequently lead to criminal acts (Holmes and DeBurger, 1985). Research shows that while three-quarters of homicide perpetrators do not have a history of mental illness, serial sexual homicide perpetrators commonly have a dual diagnosis of sexual sadism and antisocial personality disorder (Stone, 2001). Often they have violent sexual fantasies and it has been argued that these act as an internal drive mechanism for repetitive acts of sexual violence. However, the key question here is what specific factors enable a sadist fantasist to move to act out their fantasy in real life? Stone (2001) highlights a range of possible destabilising factors which come from the environment in which the offender lives: these include an unstable home life as a child, death of a parent, divorce and physical and/or sexual abuse, as well as, importantly, an inability to cope psychologically with such events. Additionally, Hickley (2010) describes what he calls a 'Trauma Control' model of serial killing, suggesting that drug abuse, pornography and, in particular, violent sexual fantasy act as facilitators for serial sexual offending, with this enactment being an attempt on behalf of the offender to contain negative feelings associated with early childhood trauma, which is frequently based around childhood experiences of sexual abuse. As Hickley (2010: 34) notes, 'childhood trauma for serial murderers may serve as a triggering mechanism resulting in an individual's inability to cope with the stress of certain events'. Underpinning the Trauma Control theory is the view that the serial sex offender increasingly psychologically identifies with the individual who abused them as a child and subsequently as an adult re-enacts their own abuse on other individuals to release underlying unresolved psychological tensions and trauma.

Holmes and DeBurger (1985) categorise serial murderers into four main types: the Visionary Motive Type (who is commanded to kill by voices or visions); the Mission Oriented Motive Type (who kills to achieve a goal or mission); the Hedonistic Type (who kills for pleasure and the emotional thrill of committing murder); and the Power/Control Oriented Type (who kills to achieve total control over another human being). In contrast to this form of psychologically based categorisation of the serial killer, other criminologists have focused on exploring sociological factors in explaining serial violent and sex offenders. Leyton (1986), for example, argues for a 'Homicidal Protest' model whereby homicides and serial murder and sex crime are viewed as products of their time and reflect society's critical tensions. Moreover, Leyton argues that the social characteristics and origins of the killer change over time and identifies what he calls three broad periods of 'Homicidal Protest': the pre-industrial age, industrial age and modern age. He argues serial homicide occurs in response to changing social-economic conditions within each time period. These are fundamentally about the exercise of power and control and maintenance of social position by a group member in the face of competing social groups and the threat they are seen to pose to that status as a result of social change. So in the pre-industrial age, the serial homicide perpetrator is the wealthy aristocrat testing the limits of their power. While during the industrial age it is the wealthy bourgeois checking the threat to their hard-won status from the growing mass of the proletariat working class. Finally, during the modern age it is the excluded individual taking vengeance on society. What Leyton is touching upon here is the development in modern times of the idea that the serial killer kills not to enact and contain early childhood trauma, as Psychological criminologists hold, but rather to seek revenge on society and make a name for themselves. In a nutshell, Leyton is capturing the very modern idea of killing for fame. He comments:

Both killer and victim have altered their form because the nature of homicidal protest has changed most radically: it is no longer the threatened aristocrat testing the limits of his power, no longer the morbidly insecure bourgeois checking the threat to his hard won status; now it is an excluded individual wreaking vengeance on the symbol and source of his excommunication. (Leyton, 1986: 287–8)

In conclusion, it is often argued that serial killers aren't the same as the rest of the population, that they are somehow 'born different'. Psychological criminologists may well sympathise with viewpoints which stress the importance of biological factors, such as genetics and brain structure, in influencing mental states. Yet they nevertheless tend to stress the importance of life events in creating psychological disturbances and trigger points which can subsequently lead to violent physical and sexual acts. While other criminologists note that no definitive scientific statement can yet be made concerning the exact role of biology and psychology in determining the serial killer personality (Stone, 2001), noting as they do so the role of society's institutions, its cultural expectations and the social pressures of work, family and friends, and how these together often act on individuals and so create stress and strain and feelings of internal conflict and aggression. Furthermore, the powerful role of the media in feeding the public fascination with crime, fame and serial killers does seem to have created the modern idea of 'killing for fame'. This arguably serves to further reinforce the importance of combining Psychological and Sociological approaches when examining the causes of criminal behaviour.

Box 4.4 Key summary points

- Psychological criminology has played an important role in examining and managing the problem of mental illness and crime.
- Research shows that several psychological traits are often found in individuals who commit violent and sex crimes, including a lack of self-control, a lack of victim empathy, high levels of social hostility and aggression, deviant sexual fantasy, as well as cognitive distortions and rationalisations for undertaking violent sexual behaviour.
- Various questionnaire-based diagnostic tools have been developed to help identify violent and sex offenders, i.e. Hare's Psychopathy Checklist, the VRAG, the HCR-20, the SORAG, the R-RASOR and the Static 99. These tools are variously used by psychologists and psychiatrists to diagnose care and treat mentally disordered offenders.
- While some criminologists focus on psychological trauma and trigger points in causing an offender's behaviour, others note the role of society's institutions, its cultural expectations and the social pressures of work, family and friends, and how these can together act on individuals and so create stress and strain and feelings of internal conflict and aggression, which can in turn lead to the enactment of violent physical and sexual behaviour. The important role of the modern media and the emergence of the idea of 'killing for fame' have also been noted.

(Continued)

(Continued)

Further reading

Chamberlain, JM (2013) *Understanding criminological research: a guide to data analysis.* London: Sage.

Gresswell, DM and Hollin, CR (1994) Multiple murder. *British Journal of Criminology* 341: 1–44.

Haggerty, KD (2009) *Crime, media, culture: modern serial killer.* London: Sage.

Hickley, EW (2010) *Serial murderers and their victims.* Belmont, CA: Wadsworth, Cengage Learning.

Holmes, WM and DeBurger, J (1985) Profiles in terror: the serial murder. *Federal Probation* 44 (3): 29–34.

Howitt, D (2006) *Introduction to forensic and criminal psychology.* Harlow: Pearson.

Leyton, A (1986) *Compulsive killers.* New York: New York University Press.

Stone MD (2001) Serial sexual homicide: biological, psychological and sociological aspects. *Journal of Personality Disorders* 15 (1): 1–18.

Webber, C (2009) *Psychology and crime.* London: Sage.

SELF-STUDY TASKS

1. Write a maximum of 750 words outlining the contribution of psychology theories to understanding criminality. How does Psychological criminology enable criminologists to gain a deeper understanding of possible determinate causes underpinning apparently 'rational' and freely chosen offender decision-making? What about the broader social context? Can you think of three key consequences for contemporary criminal justice policy and practice if we accept that some human actions might be influenced by psychological disturbances?

2. Outline in no more than 500 words the main features of Leyton's (1986) concept of 'Homicidal Protest' and critically evaluate the contribution of this to understanding serial murder and sex crime. How do you think the idea of 'Homicidal Protest' could be used to supplement Hickley's (2010) 'Trauma Control' model of serial murder?

5 STRAIN THEORY, SOCIAL DISORGANISATION THEORY AND LABELLING THEORY

CHAPTER CONTENTS

Chapter 5 focuses on the early development of sociological approaches to the study of deviance and crime through outlining the emergence from the beginning of the twentieth century onwards of the American 'Chicago School', with its concern for developing a 'sociology of deviance'. The chapter focuses on three key early theories of crime: Strain Theory, Social Disorganisation Theory and Labelling Theory. These highlight the role of social change and anomie, the organisation of city spaces and urban environments and the stereotyping and labelling of human behaviour by socio-cultural elites and interest groups within society, in both shaping and defining certain acts as antisocial and deviant or criminal.

The chapter outlines how, inspired by the work of Emile Durkheim and George Herbert Mead, sociologists of deviance and criminality such as Robert Merton, Stuart Agnew, Clifford Shaw, Henry McKay, Charles Lemert, Howard Becker, Kai Erikson and John Braithwaite have together established the importance of paying close attention to the role of 'the social' in understanding the causes of criminal behaviour and dealing with the problem of crime. Furthermore, it notes that a tension exists within these sociological theories of crime between acknowledging the determining role of social factors while also stressing the ability of individuals to change their circumstances. In doing so, the chapter establishes the groundwork from which we will discuss the development of Marxist, Feminist, Critical and Cultural criminological perspectives in Chapters 6 and 7.

INTRODUCING THE SOCIOLOGICAL STUDY OF CRIMINAL LIFE

In previous chapters we have looked at Classical, Biological and Psychological approaches to the study of crime. In doing so we noted that whereas Classical criminology emphasised free will and so our personal responsibility for how we act, Biological and Psychological approaches in contrast tend to be associated with a more deterministic position which emphasises the impact of factors outside of our direct control on our individual human agency and so the choices we make. In this chapter we move towards looking at sociological explanations for crime. These, as we shall see, hold that crime and deviance must be explored and understood in terms of social structures and forces which are external to the individual but in many ways are also internalised within them in the form of shared cultural understandings, norms and values. These structures and forces have been conceptualised by different sociologists in different ways, such as for example in terms of a society's social and economic inequalities, its class divisions, its poverty levels, its cityscapes and urban geographies, as well as its cultural norms and values and common-sense ways of doing and thinking about things.

Clearly we are talking here about a wide range of possible factors that can be said to influence human thought and behaviour and the following chapters explore the main different ways these have been conceptualised and explored by criminologists. In doing so, we explore how some theoretical positions emphasise the importance of external and/or internalised sociological factors, in determining human thought and action, while others emphasise human freedom and agency and in some instances the ability of individuals to overcome their social circumstances and change the world around them to their liking. We start this exploration in this chapter through the lens of what has been called 'the Chicago School' (Chamberlain, 2013). Established in 1892, the University of Chicago was home to the first academic department of sociology in the United States. In this chapter we focus on the development of three key sociological theories of crime to emerge from the Chicago School: anomie and Strain Theory, Social Disorganisation Theory and Labelling Theory.

The chapter outlines how the early Durkheim-influenced Chicago School, with its focus on anomie, strain as well as urban space, held a somewhat deterministic view of crime and deviance. This contrasts with the later Median-influenced Chicago School, with its focus on societal reaction and the negative labelling of deviant behaviour, which emphasises human agency while also acknowledging the importance of deterministic social-structural factors (i.e. economic disadvantage in the form of poverty). We will begin by outlining the influence of Durkheim on the Chicago School.

DURKHEIM: SOCIAL FACTS, SOCIAL SOLIDARITY AND ANOMIE

Established in 1892, as noted above the University of Chicago founded the first academic department of sociology in the US. It was heavily influenced by Durkheim and his concern with the impact of social change on society in general and crime in particular. Durkheim is one of the most important social theorists of all time and his influence in the social sciences is far-reaching. It is difficult to isolate as most important any single contribution of such a prominent writer and thinker, but certainly amongst his greatest achievements was the role he played in getting sociology recognised as a legitimate science in the academic world and his specification of the unique concerns of social sciences that set them apart from the other sciences.

Durkheim emphasised that much human behaviour, including criminal behaviour, is caused by social rather than biological or psychological factors and argued that it therefore must be understood in sociological terms. He outlines his approach to the analysis of society and crime in his 1885 book *Rules of sociological method* (Durkheim, 1964). For Durkheim, when people get together and create a group, community or society, no matter how small or large it is, they create shared behavioural rules and ways of organising themselves so they can achieve certain ends. Over time these take on a life of their own, become embodied in the form of a society's political, socio-economic, educational and cultural institutions, and in doing so, come to shape the way people think and act without them necessarily being actively and self-consciously aware of it. In other words, they become what Durkheim referred to as 'social facts'. He argued that when we perform our duties as a brother, a husband or a citizen and carry out the social commitments associated with these, we fulfil obligations that are defined in law and custom and so are external to us and our individual actions, thoughts and feelings. They act as a frame of reference from which to shape our own behaviour and also view the behaviour of others around us.

Durkheim also held a particular view of human nature. According to Durkheim humans have innate needs and desires that must be satisfied if they are to be content. However, unlike other animals, most human needs and desires are not physical; they are social – we crave knowledge, status, power, recognition, money and so on. Furthermore, according to Durkheim the more one has the more one wants. Because of this human behaviour must be regulated by the collective order – that is society. How this happens depends on the type of society one lives in. Durkheim distinguished between two types of society – those characterised by mechanical solidarity and those characterised by organic solidarity. A society of mechanical solidarity is one in which the members are very much alike and there are few individual differences between them. The members of such a society do the same types of work, fulfil the same social roles, have the same worldview – what Durkheim called a collective or common consciousness – and have the same understandings of right and wrong. It is this collective conscience that binds people together and promotes conformity in the society of mechanical solidarity.

But this society is not crime free. Durkheim believed that crime is inevitable. Indeed, he argued that the problem of crime can never ever be resolved. This is because he held that in all societies there will be individuals who violate social norms. Owing to the high degree of uniformity in mechanical societies norm violators meet with a strong social reaction. Durkheim characterised law in such societies as repressive: its goal is punishment and revenge. But despite the negative light in which crime is held, Durkheim also recognised that crime serves some positive social functions. For one thing, it highlights and reinforces the moral boundaries of the society. In addition, it enhances social solidarity among conforming members by inducing feelings of moral superiority and righteousness. This is a point we will return to later when we discuss the work of the later Chicago School on societal reaction and labelling.

Mechanical societies are, by necessity, small and relatively undeveloped technologically. As a society undergoes population growth and technological advancement social diversity increases and the collective conscience is weakened. Still, social order is preserved because the proliferation of diverse jobs, roles and ideas actually creates interdependence amongst the society's members. This leads to an interdependent division of labour which replaces the collective conscience as the binding force in society. The boundaries of acceptable behaviour are widened, and punishment becomes less harsh. Law becomes more civil-administrative, with the primary goal of preserving contracts amongst the society's members – a kind of law Durkheim called restitutive. This society is characterised by organic solidarity, and this humanisation of the criminal justice system is certainly broadly what can be seen to be happening in Europe from the nineteenth century onwards.

Crime in organic societies may still serve positive functions, but Durkheim was particularly concerned about such societies because he saw them as being susceptible to conditions that could cause crime and for other social problems to become rampant. Durkheim argued that key forces for social change in such societies – namely population growth, industrialisation, urbanisation and technological and communication change – could occur so quickly that the society would not have adequate time to develop appropriate regulations to govern social interaction. Durkheim called this condition of inadequate or inappropriate social control anomie. He most fully developed the concept of anomie in his classic work *Suicide*, which was first published in 1897 (Durkheim, 1979). In analysing suicide rates, he noticed that suicides not only go up during periods of economic depression, but also during periods of sharp economic growth. While to most people this seems paradoxical, Durkheim pointed out that under the latter circumstances confusion about social norms frequently prevails. Though some have interpreted anomie to mean normlessness, in which norms no longer seem applicable and the individual consequently feels cast adrift in a sea of uncertainty, it is probably more accurate to describe it as a condition in which traditional norms no longer seem applicable but new ones have not yet fully developed. It consequently arises when disruption of the collective order allows people's aspirations to rise beyond all possibility of their fulfilment. Here a person aspires to goals which either they cannot attain or find difficult to reach. For example, the unemployed teenager who wants to wear only designer gear and live the life of a celebrity footballer suffers from anomie. For Durkheim, in such social circumstances a rise in the suicide rate is one result, a rise in the crime rate is another.

It is perhaps no surprise to learn then that Durkheim's ideas were taken up by early criminologists interested in the idea that crime is normal and serves a social function, how modern organic societies provide more room of deviance and crime, as well as by extension, how if we view crime as being a social fact it can in the broadest sense of the term be learnt by anybody. This latter idea is particularly important as it offers an alternative to the excesses of viewpoints which see the causes of crime as lying within the individual, either as a result of their rational choices alone, or as a result of their psychology or biological difference from the mass of people. Indeed, three important early developments in criminological theory that we are going to discuss in this chapter, namely Strain Theory, Social Disorganisation Theory and Labelling Theory, reinforce how Durkheim's ideas heavily influenced early criminological thinking.

MERTON AND AGNEW: ANOMIE AND STRAIN THEORY

Both Robert Merton (1938, 1949) and Stuart Agnew (2006) were heavily influenced by Durkheim and further developed his concept of anomie into a more general theory of anomie referred to as Strain Theory. As Agnew built his conceptualisation on that of Merton, we shall begin our discussion with him. Working in the shadow of social upheavals caused by the communist revolution in Russia, the great depression in America, as well as two world wars, it is perhaps unsurprising that Merton felt that Durkheim was on to something with his concept of anomie. Yet whereas Durkheim conceived of anomie as a problematic social condition resulting from sudden and rapid social change, Merton saw it as an endemic feature of the everyday operation of certain types of societies.

To understand this better, let's consider how Merton views society in general. Merton divides society into two parts, the cultural structure and the social structure. The cultural structure consists of the society's goals; in other words, it is what the members of the society value and strive for. The social structure is the institutionalised means by which the goals are supposed to be achieved. In a well-balanced society these two structures will be integrated. That is, all members know and accept the goals and have at their disposal the means to achieve them. Not everyone will be uniformly successful in achieving the goals. But in the ideal society people derive satisfaction from being in competition with others working towards the same ends. Merton used academic community and pursuit of scientific truth as an example of this.

In some societies, however, an undue emphasis is placed on one of the societal structures. Here Merton turns his attention specifically to the United States where, he says, the most important goal is material success. In other words, money and the social status symbols associated with it. For Merton the culture of US society seems to value money and the accumulation of material wealth above all else. Whatever our personal views on this state of affairs, Merton notes that the important point is that in principle this goal is not in itself problematic. Rather what is a problem is the fact that in the US the institutionalised means to achieve material success are not equally available to everyone. Indeed, we could expand this line of thinking to all modern-day liberal-democratic states in the West as although mainstream political discourse employs the rhetoric of equality as a key part of what it means to be a democratic society, in fact we aren't all born equal as we don't all start from the same running blocks: wealth, and perhaps more importantly, the availability of avenues to pursue it are unequally distributed. As a result, for Merton, social problems such as crime arise because of the fact that in spite of the modern-day democratic ideology of egalitarianism – which embodies the notion that everyone who is honest and hardworking will be successful – some groups in society, including women and ethnic minorities, find the institutionalised means to success blocked or closed to them. Indeed, it is the egalitarian ideology that exacerbates the problem of the disjunction between goals and means. This disjunction itself is what Merton calls anomie.

Anomie produces strain in those who experience it. Merton delineates several different ways that people may respond to this strain. These responses are referred to collectively as the typology of adaptations. Three of the adaptations – innovation, retreatism and rebellion – are considered deviant, the other two – conformity and ritualism – are not. Conformity, according to Merton, is the most common adaptation as it makes social order possible. Conformists accept cultural goals and play by the rules to achieve them, no matter how difficult that may be because of a lack of legitimate opportunities. This helps to explain why even in high crime areas there are always residents who are not criminals. Ritualism also involves adhering to the rules, that is the institutionalised means of achieving goals, such as making sure you do well at school, but it also involves a personalised scaling down of the goals so that satisfaction may be obtained through a much lower level of success. Interestingly, Merton believes this adaption is most common among the middle classes, because of the strict patterns of socialisation in this class which expect them to achieve certain goals – such as getting a degree – but nevertheless also recognises that there are ultimately a limited number of opportunities for advancement on offer for those with degrees.

Among the deviant adaptations, innovations are considered most important by criminologists. Innovators have brought in the cultural goals but, having found the institutionalised means blocked or closed, they utilise more expedient, though illegitimate means, to achieve these ends. This often leads them to commit crime. Significantly, Merton argues that the tremendous emphasis on material success in the US and other western countries causes some members of the wealthy and upper middle classes to engage in innovation and commit white-collar and corporate crimes, i.e. fraud and tax evasion. He argues that for individuals who sit on the top economic levels, the pressure towards innovation not infrequently erases the distinction between right and wrong in the world of business. Yet although Merton recognises that innovation occurs amongst elites, his primary focus is on those at the lower end of the social hierarchy. And in his view we shouldn't be too surprised that crime rates are highest amongst these groups, as this response is a somewhat natural outcome within nations where the cultural emphasis on material success has been absorbed by those individuals at the bottom of the social ladder, but where there is little access to conventional and legitimate means for becoming successful. Merton considers retreatism to be the least common adaption. Retreatists are individuals who have been socialised to accept the cultural goals as well as the institutionalised means to achieve them. However, upon failing to succeed through institutionalised means, retreatists do not innovate, instead, they essentially drop out of society. For Merton, retreatists include drug addicts, alcoholics and homeless people. Finally, rebellion is the adaptation of those who reject the current cultural and social structures, but seek to replace them with new ones. Merton left this area a little unexplored, but clearly we can place social movements and pressure groups in this category.

Merton's Strain Theory was highly influential in subsequent sociology and criminology, not least because it recognises that people are constrained by their position in the social structure of society. However it has been criticised for being too rigid in its assessment of which adaption is most probable amongst which social group. Certainly, many subsequent criminologists felt that innovation as the result of blocked opportunities was spread across all social groups not just those at the lower end of the social hierarchy, as Merton claimed. Also many commentators pointed out that conformists are few and far between even within social groups, such as the upper classes, who according to this theory shouldn't experience that much strain. Indeed, it was argued that Merton failed to account for how some people can escape being labelled deviant and criminal while others can't – he doesn't really get to grips with power and control and who defines people as criminal or not criminal. Finally, he was criticised for treating the culture of the United States of America as if it were a single entity, when in fact most societies are highly diverse, and indeed, the idea that all members of society hold uniformly common values was felt to be wide of the mark of what happens in reality. Although here we should perhaps say that Merton was possibly right in stressing that modern liberal democracies do seem to stress consumerism, consumption and material success.

Box 5.2   Key summary points

- Merton develops Durkheim's ideas to look at the cultural and structural makeup of the US. He highlights how anomie arises as a result of conflict between a shared belief in equality and democracy and the presence of inequality and blocked opportunity for certain social groups, i.e. ethnic minorities, the poor and socially disadvantaged, as well as women. This state of affairs, he argues, results in a feeling of strain amongst certain sections of society and leads to common social problems such as crime.
- Merton's Strain Theory is a sociological theory of crime because it recognises that a person's freedom of action is constrained by their position in the social structure of society, which can lead them to experience anomie that in turn can lead to personal feelings of strain, with the result that they might respond to this sense of strain by engaging in deviant and criminal behaviour. Therefore, for Merton, the causes of crime are not wholly located within an individual and their biology, their psychology, or their free will to act as they wish. Rather, according to Strain Theory, they are in no small part a result of contradictions present within the organisational and ideological fabric of the everyday social worlds we inhabit as we live out our lives.

Further reading

Merton, RK (1938) Social structure and anomie. *American Sociological Review* 3 (5): 672–82.
Merton, RK (1949) *Social theory and social structure*. New York: The Free Press.

Merton's Strain Theory is sometimes called institutional anomie theory for the obvious reason that it focuses on the macro level of social structure, meaning that it is a large-scale theory which focuses on social conditions and patterns which transcend particular social situations. In contrast, Robert Agnew (2006; Agnew and White, 1992) in what is often referred to as General Strain Theory seeks to take Merton's ideas and use them to help him look at the micro level of everyday social interactions. He starts with the assumption that negative relationships with others cause strain or stress in people's lives. Negative relationships are those in which others are not treating the individual as he or she would like to be treated. Agnew argues that Mertonian Strain Theory relies too heavily on the relationships that prevent the individual from reaching positive valued goals. Agnew agrees that this is important, but he also considers three other sources of strain that may lead to crime and delinquency: anticipated, vicarious and experienced strains.

Anticipated strains are just that, strains which an individual anticipates will happen in the future. Vicarious strains are strains experienced as a result of events which happen to close others, including family, friends and reference groups. Experienced strains are just that, they happen as we go about our everyday lives. For Agnew, these three types of strain share in common two key characteristics: they either remove, or threaten to remove, positively valued stimuli which a person possesses, or present or threaten to present a person with negatively valued stimuli. The first of these, the failure to achieve positively valued goals, suggests that people have in some way not met their goals, expectations, or have received unfair or inequitable outcomes in social relationships. Examples include not meetings one's expectations to earn good grades in school, financial reward and security from working and so on. The second characteristic stems from situations in which others remove or threaten to remove things that a person positively values. Think for a moment about the kinds of stressful life events we all probably encounter, such as the loss of partners and friends; these events place stress on people.

Agnew argues strain can trigger involvement in crime if the social situation is right. He also argues that when others threaten us we experience strain and this likewise can lead to us lashing out and can even lead us to commit criminal acts. In other words, he is saying that we all experience strain and all have the potential to react in deviant or criminal ways because of it. Here Agnew is following the Durkheimian maxim that the criminal type is no different from the mass of people. Agnew argues that some people aren't able to develop appropriate coping strategies to deal with strain. Generally people can use coping strategies to moderate the effects of strain, to blow off steam, without it affecting anybody else negatively, or downplay it and seek to put it into perspective. Agnew argues that personality traits, temperament and social learning and bonding with other people all help to determine whether a person adapting to strain is criminal or not.

Research does seem to show the value of taking this approach (Agnew and White, 1992). It is suggested that men in particular who lose family members when young and have negative relationships with adults do tend to manifest their loss and anger externally, projecting it onto others, and can engage in violent and disruptive behaviour as a result (Agnew, 2006). Other research with young girls seems to show that they internalise these emotions and suffer from anxiety, depression, self-harm and other disorders such as anorexia and bulimia (Agnew, 2006).

However, the utility and applicability of Agnew's Strain Theory seems to be limited to the type of crime we are dealing with. The strong points for the theory are certainly fairly easy to see when looking at inner-city crime. Much of the proceeds of this crime are not centred on providing basic needs, but for the collection of cash, jewellery, expensive cars, social status, 'bling' and expensive clothing. Children growing up in this environment see that illegal activity, such as drug sales or theft, is easier and more profitable than going to school, getting a job, buying a home and working their way up the social ladder. In such circumstances, it is easy to see how Agnew's Strain Theory will predict the development of coping strategies which involve engaging in criminal behaviour. However, Strain Theory doesn't explain how different people living in the same environment choose different paths, both legal and otherwise. It doesn't help either to explain white-collar or corporate crime, or crime committed by the wealthy and powerful. These individuals already have all the benefits of society that Strain Theory implies should prevent crime, so why are they committing crime? Yet in spite of these limitations, Strain Theory remains to this day an important theory of crime which highlights the key role played by social circumstances in creating crime and deviance.

Box 5.3   Key summary points

- Agnew's Strain Theory is sometimes called General Strain Theory. He takes Merton's ideas and uses them to help look at the micro level of everyday social interactions between people.
- Agnew focuses on the coping strategies people develop to deal with strains they directly experience (experienced strain), see happening to others who are close to them or who they feel an affinity with (vicarious strain), or are worried may happen to them or others close to them in the future (anticipated strain). He argues that the positive or negative stimuli people feel as a result of these strains can result in them adopting coping strategies which lead them to undertake deviant or criminal behaviour.
- At its core Strain Theory says that people choose to commit crime because of the disparity between the social goals that encourage monetary and material success, and the opportunities to achieve this through socially approved means. It is therefore a Sociological theory of crime as it holds that deviant and criminal behaviour are coping strategies adopted by individuals as they seek to adapt to the circumstances they find themselves in. However, a key criticism of Strain Theory is that it can't explain why people adopt the coping strategies they do.

Further reading

Agnew, R (2006) *Pressured into crime: an overview of General Strain Theory.* London: Sage.
Agnew, R and White, H (1992) An empirical test of General Strain Theory. *Criminology* 30 (4): 475–99.

PARK AND BURGESS: SOCIAL DISORGANISATION THEORY AND THE BROKEN WINDOWS HYPOTHESIS

In addition to the work of Merton, the presence of Durkheim can also be seen in the early Chicago School through the development of Social Disorganisation Theory. Sometimes the early Chicago School is called the ecological school as it tended to see the social world as an interconnected ecosystem. In part, this is because following Durkheim, the Chicago School saw crime as a social rather than individual phenomenon. But whereas Durkheim stressed how rapid social change brought about anomie, the ecological school focused on urban geographic areas and argued that social change caused social disorganisation within them, with crime being one result of this state of affairs. What we are seeing here then is an early concern with place and crime. This is a concern which is very much with us today over 100 years later in modern criminology.

From the early 1900s onwards, under the guidance of Robert Park and Ernest Burgess (1969 [1921]; Park et al., 1967 [1925]), the Chicago School focused on social deviance. This, following Durkheim, was broadly defined as a violation of society's norms and values for appropriate behaviour. The term social deviance came to be used synonymously with the term social problems. The goal for these sociologists was to study and explain deviance or social problems so as to devise practical means for eliminating them. Park and Burgess identified several distinct zones that expanded out in a pattern of concentric circles from the centre of the city – the outlying zones, which they called the commuters' zone and residential zones. These were populated predominately by white, middle- and upper-class homeowners who had lived in their communities for many years and who were well integrated in the dominant culture. In the area between the centre of the city and the outlying zones was the working-class zone, where second and third generation immigrants live. In contrast, the heart of the city – zones I and II – which were constantly encroached on by business, has high concentrations of transient populations, the homeless, African American migrants and newly arrived immigrants, all of whom occupied street corners and run down housing.

The Chicago sociologists observed that not all the urban zones were plagued equally by alcoholism, drug abuse, high rates of mental illness, delinquency and crime. Indeed, the further one moved away from the centre of the city the lower the incidence of social problems. According to the Chicago School this was the result of the social disorganisation that characterised the inner-city areas. Social disorganisation, they argued, was caused by rapid social change that disrupts the normally smooth operation of a social system. In a socially disorganised area, dominant values and norms compete with other, sometimes illegitimate, values and norms. Various cultures conflict and members of younger generations clash with one another as well as members of older groups. Social cohesion breaks down, and social deviance is one common result. Of particular interest for the Chicago School was youth offending and general delinquency and the work of Clifford Shaw and Henry McKay (1942) specifically focused on this area.

Shaw and McKay believed that the foundation for an adult criminal career was laid early in life, so the best way to control crime was to prevent juvenile delinquency. To study this they used two methods – one quantitative and one qualitative. The quantitative one was the cornerstone of what they termed their neighbourhood studies. Using police and court records they plotted on a series of maps: (1) the houses where juvenile delinquents lived (what they called spot maps); (2) the percentage of the total juvenile population in specific census tracts who were involved with the criminal justice system (what they called rate maps); and (3) the distribution of delinquency throughout the various parts of the city (what they called zone maps). They then supplemented their data with qualitative life history interviews with a number of young offenders, including a detailed account of the social and familial relationships, their school experiences, and so on.

They published the results of their research over a 20-year period from the early 1920s to the early 1940s. They concluded that in terms of such characteristics as personality, intelligence and physical condition, young offenders were for the most part not too much different from young people who didn't get involved in crime. Again then we see the Durkheim-inspired Sociological criminological concern with highlighting the normality of the offender; that is, at least in terms of biological and psychological characteristics. Of equal significance was their finding that crime and delinquency were not consistently dominated by any particular racial or ethnic group. This could be seen in the fact that although the composition of certain neighbourhoods changed over the years the levels of crime did not. Rather the rates remained fairly constant. In other words, crime appeared not to be about the individuals themselves but rather the social space – the ecological urban zone – that they occupied. More specifically, Shaw and McKay reported that the neighbourhoods with the worst delinquency problems also had the highest rates of other serious problems, including deteriorated housing, infant mortality, lower life expectancy and various other social and health-related problems. The residents of these neighbourhoods were the most economically disadvantaged in the city. These neighbourhoods were in or right next to zones I and II.

A key feature of these zones was that they were in transition; they were undergoing a process they conceptualised as being of invasion, dominance and succession. On one hand the neighbourhoods were being invaded on a periodic basis by newly arriving immigrants and migrant groups, which resulted in the flight of most of the current residents. These new groups did not have the resources to live in better areas of the city and they also had to face the difficulty of adjusting to life in a different society. At the same time, business and industry continued to encroach upon these areas allowing conditions to deteriorate further. It was, then, the instability of the neighbourhoods which caused traditional social controls to break down and immoral values to creep in. From this perspective then, the solution to the crime problem lies not with the treatment of individual offenders, but with programmes to shore up traditional social controls in disorganised neighbourhoods until they become stable.

This was precisely Shaw's goal in 1932 when he set up the Chicago Area Project, or CAP, in three high-delinquency neighbourhoods. The CAP was composed of neighbourhood councils whose members were committed to bettering their communities from within. From the outset then the sights of the CAP were turned inward. CAP activities were designed primarily as social programmes, including sports and recreation areas, as well as the traditional American pastime of summer camps for kids focused around various activities ranging from sports and camping to science and education and even of course religious retreats. The CAP project lasted for over 25 years until Shaw died in 1957, although the state of Illinois eventually took over and kept the project funded until the mid-1970s.

Although the CAP project has a number of positive outcomes, including providing inner-city young people with recreational, educational and even occupational opportunities, it didn't have a significant affect in lowering the delinquency and crime rates of neighbourhoods (Kubrin and Weitzer, 2003). It has been argued that this is because such projects can't really address broader underlying socio-economic and political realities relating to society at large and the social norms and values present within a society aren't isolated to particular cities let alone zones within them (Chamberlain, 2013). In other words, there is more going on in these neighbourhoods than meets the eye and what we are dealing with here may well be localised social problems occurring within inner-city areas but they nevertheless are caused by inherent power inequalities which underpin western nation-states as a whole, not just these isolated cityscapes. This is a point we will return to when we look at Radical criminology in the next chapter.

It has also been pointed out that like Strain Theory, Social Disorganisation Theory does perhaps follow Durkheim a little too much in thinking that there is only one set of dominant norms and values available to transgress, when clearly several compete against each other, particularly within multicultural societies. However, Social Disorganisation Theory has had a long-lasting effect on criminology and its development as an academic discipline. Not least of all because it brought to the fore the need to look at place and crime together: it established urban and cityscape geographies as central units of analysis for examining and dealing with the problem of inner-city crime. One particularly influential area has been the development of what has been called the 'Broken Windows' hypothesis (Wilson and Kelling, 1982). This idea was developed out of the key idea which emerged from the work of the Chicago School: namely, that visual cues of physical and social disorder within an urban living space could over time if not dealt with lead to further disorder and crime.

Working in the ecological tradition of the early Chicago School, Wilson and Kelling argued that physical signs of disorder – litter, graffiti, property damage – along with social signs of disorder – prostitution, drug dealing, begging – indicate a breakdown of order and suggest that crime and deviance are permitted; therefore by tackling seemingly minor infringements and disorder we can tackle more serious crime. This hypothesis was most famously tested in New York City in the 1990s by Police Chief William Bratton (George and Kelling, 1998). Here an approach called 'zero tolerance policing' operated where all signs of disorder are quickly and punitively addressed by proactive community policing. Zero tolerance policing involves the police more strictly enforcing the law against drinking in public, subway and bus fare evasion, for example, and did indeed lead to a year-on-year reduction in crime rates. Although criticised for being costly and highly punitive, similar results have been found elsewhere; for example, Keizer et al. (2008: 1683) from the University of Groningen in the Netherlands found from their research that 'one example of disorder, like graffiti or littering, can indeed encourage another, like stealing'.

It is undoubtedly the case that Social Disorganisation Theory and the Broken Windows hypothesis have had a significant effect on contemporary situational crime prevention studies, crime mapping technology and the like. We will return to Broken Windows and zero tolerance policing in Chapter 6, when we look at Radical criminology and Left and Right Realism. However, for the moment we should note that a key criticism of Broken Windows is that it conflates causation with correlation. Just because certain high crime rate urbanised areas tend to possess evidence of social disorganisation (that is, they tend to correlate with each other) does not in itself mean that the one causes the other. Not least of all because to say they do ignores the important role played by overarching socio-economic and political inequalities which exist at the large nation-state level and permeate through local urban geographies.

Box 5.4 Key summary points

- The early Chicago School is sometimes called the ecological school as it tended to see social world as an interconnected ecosystem. Influenced by Durkheim and his arguments for the value of exploring sociological explanations for deviance and crime, the ecological school led by Park and Burgess focused on urban geographic areas and argued that social change caused social disorganisation within them, with crime being one result of this state of affairs. Social disorganisation theory and later developments, such as the Broken Windows hypothesis, are sociological theories of crime as they seek to connect the structure of urban environments with participation in criminal activity.
- Park and Burgess identified several distinct zones in Chicago that expanded out in a pattern of concentric circles from the centre of the city. They noted that the heart of the city – zones I and II – were constantly encroached on by business, have high concentrations of transient populations, the homeless and newly arrived immigrants, all of whom occupied street corners and run down housing. They noted that these 'zones of transition' tended to be areas with a high level of social unrest and crime.
- Following on from this Shaw and McKay looked at juvenile delinquency. They believed that the foundation for an adult criminal career was laid early in life, so the best way to control crime was to prevent it within local urban areas and their research reinforced the need to promote positive community-led provision to steer young people away from criminal activity rather than to pursue punitive criminalising measures, while at the same time recognising the importance of creating a safe urban space.
- One particularly influential outcome of this work has been the development of what has been called the Broken Windows hypothesis. This emerged out of the key idea that visual cues of physical and social disorder within an urban living space could over time, if not dealt with, lead to further disorder and crime.

(Continued)

(Continued)

- This hypothesis was most famously tested in New York City in the 1990s by Police Chief William Bratton. He used an approach called 'zero tolerance policing' where all signs of disorder are quickly and punitively addressed by proactive community policing. Zero tolerance policing involves the police more strictly enforcing the law against drinking in public, subway and bus fare evasion and did indeed lead to a year-on-year reduction in crime rates. However, zero tolerance policing has been criticised for being overly punitive and costly.

Further reading

Agnew, R and White, H (1992) An empirical test of general strain theory. *Criminology* 30 (4): 475–99.

George, L and Kelling, GL (1998) *Fixing broken windows: restoring order and reducing crime in our communities*. New York: Simon and Schuster Touchstone.

Keizer, K, Lindenberg, S and Steg, L (2008) The spreading of disorder. *Science* 322 (5908): 1681–5.

Park, RE and Burgess, EW (1969 [1921]) *Introduction to the science of sociology*. Chicago: University of Chicago Press.

Park, RE, Burgess, EW and McKenzie, RD (1967 [1925]) *The city: suggestions for the investigation of human behaviour in the urban environment*. Chicago: University of Chicago Press.

Wilson, JQ and Kelling, GL (1982) Broken windows. *The Atlantic Monthly* 249 (3): 29–38.

MEAD AND BLUMER: SYMBOLIC INTERACTIONISM AND LABELLING THEORY

A second key influence on the Chicago School was the distinctively American pragmatic philosophical tradition known as symbolic interactionism, which as we shall see led to the development of what would become a key sociological theory of crime and deviance: Labelling Theory. From this perspective, crime is not an objective condition, nor is the law, the criminal, or the criminal justice system. Criminologists operating from this paradigm might build theories to explore questions such as 'who defines crime and for what purpose?', 'how and why are labels attached to certain people and to certain acts at particular moments in time?' and 'what are the consequences of the application of labels to people and groups over time?'

Typically, criminologists arguing from a Labelling Theory position are critical of more deterministic approaches, be they sociological, biological or psychological. This is because they believe human beings are creative social actors, who make the world around them in and through language and social interaction, and the meanings and understandings they attach to both. Although the degree to which human agency is held to dominate over deterministic social structure varies between different advocates of the Labelling Theory position, they nevertheless tend to emphasise human agency and free will over constraining social structure. What we are dealing with here then is a point of view which acknowledges that people are constrained by the social environments in which they live. Labelling theorists certainly do accept that factors such as where we are born, who our parents are, what gender we are, what our immediate social circumstances are, where we went to school, and suchlike, all help to shape our life chances and lifestyle choices. Nevertheless, they argue that a defining feature of humanity is that we are able to change the world around us to our liking, and perhaps most importantly, we can also change ourselves and how we see ourselves, the world around us and our place in it. This is because of its grounding in symbolic interactionism.

Symbolic interactionism is a school of thought based on the ideas of George Herbert Mead, John Dewey, WI Thomas and Charles Horton Cooley, amongst others. Herbert Blumer (1969) coined the term 'symbolic interactionism' to refer to the writings of these scholars, which emphasise the way that meaning arises in social interaction – through communication using language and symbols. Blumer summarised the key assumptions of symbolic interaction as:

1. Human beings act towards things on the basis of the meanings that the things have for them.
2. These meanings are the product of social interaction in human society.
3. These meanings are modified and handled through an interpretative process that is used by each individual in dealing with the signs each encounters.

These three assumptions correspond roughly with the three sections of Mead's (1934) *Mind, self and society*. Mead's starting point is the discussion of the crucial feature that separates human beings from other animals. Like many other thinkers, he settles on language and he is concerned to elaborate the implications of this. Animals engage in conversations of gestures, but it would be wrong to say that they communicate like human beings. When a dog snarls at another and the other backs away, one dog is feeling aggressive and the other is feeling scared, but there is no mutual understanding. When I want to get out of a conversation with somebody because I am pressured for time, I don't bare my teeth and snarl at the person, I give him or her a reason why I can't talk which I believe they will understand. In other words, there is mutual understanding. And the difference between humans and animals is that the significant symbols we use, unlike the animal gesture, bring out the same reaction in myself as they do the other person – each of us in the exchange, that is our social interaction, puts us in the position of the other.

It is this ability to use symbols to communicate and to put ourselves in the position of others and see their point of view which makes the difference and is uniquely human. Social interaction produces meaning and meaning makes up our world. We create our world by giving meaning to it and as our meaning changes and develops, so does the world. Another key aspect of our ability to use significant symbols is that it means we have the ability to stand back and pause our reaction to a situation, using our imagination to rehearse what we are going to say in social interaction. In other words, our symbols enable us to both name objects in the world that we can see and can't see – such as an apple tree and gravity – and do thought experiments, that is consider alternative choices and what might happen if we follow one particular line of action instead of another.

This brings us to Blumer's third assumption. So far we have covered the first two assumptions by noting that we use shared symbolic meanings to negotiate social reality, including the objects, people and situations within it. That is, we have looked at how symbolic meanings operate in the external world around us. Blumer's third assumption concerns our internal world. Now Mead said that to negotiate the world around us we also obviously need to have internal conversations within ourselves – and he argued that there were two parts or phases to this –the Me and the I. Now remember the significant symbol is socially shared and brings out the same reaction in me as it does in others. In essence, what it does then is allow me to look at myself as others see me. The Me phase of the internal conversation is precisely that – it is myself as others see me. The I phase is the part that looks at the Me: remember here the phrase 'I am thinking about myself'. Mead argues that the I is a source of creativity and originality and spontaneity as it is constantly moving backwards and forwards between the different possible Me's and exploring new possibilities. Mead held that the internal conversation between the Me and I – most of which happens without us giving much thought to it – provides a channel through which all our external conversations and patterns of interaction with others must pass.

This conception of the self then involves a description of the process of socialisation – society and other people in a very real way are part of who we are, and even though we may feel alone in our heads, strictly speaking, we always have other people talking to us. Mead uses a child to illustrate his point. In the life of an infant initially random gestures are narrowed down as the child grows to recognise those that have meaning for others – first words like mummy, daddy, cup, food and so on, are learnt because of this process – and then through play she learns to take the role of individual others – so she dresses up and gets a pretend medical kit and plays at being a doctor – and then as she grows older she learns through games like hockey or football to coordinate her activities with others, and to see herself as others see her. Indeed, through family and friends she comes to see herself in an increasingly wider context until she takes on what Mead calls 'the role of the generalised other'. Here she views herself as how society as a whole views her. Another way of putting it is that as she grows she increasingly takes on a sort of social conscience.

What we have here then is a social-psychological view of human beings as creative social actors who are moulded by their environment but at the same time possess the potential to change the world around them due in no small part to their innate 'role taking' ability. Like Durkheim, Mead and Blumer argue that individual identity formation is highly influenced by important or significant others, who tend to be members of our primary groups, such as families and friends. These are sometimes referred to as reference groups because they provide the individual with a perspective, a point of reference, and a comparison, for their own behaviour and thinking. Mead, then, argued that we are able to rehearse various lines of action in our heads in the same way actors rehearse scenes before going on stage. Moreover, because role taking involves considering lines of action from the standpoint of reference groups, it follows that behaviour is in part controlled by social groups. For symbolic interactionism the exercise of self-control by the individual is simultaneously the exercise of social control by the social group to which they belong. Hence the appraising or labelling of individuals by social groups affects the individual's sense of self as well as their sense of social identity: their idea of their place in the world and of themselves as an individual are tightly linked together. So much so that it is impossible to think of being an individual self without having other people. It is this tension between its acknowledgement of the in no small part determined and fundamentally social nature of human beings and its simultaneous emphasis on the creative and transformative potential within every human being which makes symbolic interaction and by extension Labelling Theory, an important development of the sociological study of deviance.

Box 5.5   Key summary points

- Symbolic interactionism is a school of thought based on the ideas of George Herbert Mead and along with Durkheim was heavily influential on the development of the Chicago School and the sociological study of deviance.
- Herbert Blumer (1969) coined the term 'symbolic interactionism' from Mead and summarised the key assumptions of symbolic interaction as:

  o Human beings act towards things on the basis of the meanings that the things have for them.
  o These meanings are the product of social interaction in human society.
  o These meanings are modified and handled through an interpretative process that is used by each individual in dealing with the signs each encounters.

- Symbolic interaction emphasises the role of language and symbols in constituting the role around us and our perceptions of ourselves in it.
- Like Durkheim, Mead and Blumer argue that individual identity formation is highly influenced by important or significant others, who tend to be members of our primary groups, such as families and friends. These are sometimes referred to as reference groups because they provide the individual with a perspective, a point of reference, and a comparison, for their own behaviour and thinking.

(Continued)

(Continued)

- For symbolic interactionists and by extension labelling theorists, the exercise of self-control by the individual is simultaneously the exercise of social control by the social group to which they belong.
- Underpinning this sociological analysis of human beings and their behaviour lies a tension between its acknowledgement of the in no small part determined and fundamentally social nature of human beings and its emphasis on the creative and transformative potential within every human being to change the world and themselves.

Further reading

Blumer, H (1969) *Symbolic interactionism: perspective and method*. Englewood Cliffs, NJ: Prentice-Hall.

Mead, GH (1934) *Mind, self and society.* Chicago: University of Chicago Press.

LEMERT, BECKER AND ERIKSON: TOWARDS THE SOCIOLOGY OF DEVIANCE

Lemert and primary and secondary deviation

Edwin Lemert was influenced by the ideas of Mead and Blumer and in 1951 published *Social psychology* (Lemert, 1951), exploring what he called primary and secondary deviance. Primary deviance refers to the initial acts of deviance which only have minor consequences for a person's status, social relationships, or subsequent behaviour. Primary deviance tends to be situational, transient and idiosyncratic. Indeed, Lemert noted that most people violate many laws during their lifetime and that the average law-abiding citizen commits many acts that technically are crimes, but they are not serious enough to be viewed as crimes either by the perpetrator or the rest of society. Secondary deviance, in contrast, is explicitly the societal reactions to deviance and has major consequences for a person's status, relationships and future behaviour. Secondary deviance occurs when society's response to initial deviance – which Lemert argues revolves around stigmatisation, punishment and segregation – causes fundamental changes in the person's social roles, self-identity and personality, resulting in additional deviant acts.

Whereas the primary deviant's life and identity are organised around conventional activities, the secondary deviant's life and identity are organised around the facts of deviance. In other words, when you get arrested by the police for causing public disorder, for example after drinking too much alcohol, you are involved in the secondary deviance stage, as how others see you, particularly agencies of social control, becomes increasingly focused on your deviant act to the exclusion of everything else about you. Lemert argues that societal reactions to deviance can be warranted – where society is responding to behaviours that are objectively deviant – or unwarranted – where society is falsely responding to behaviours that are not objectively deviant. If society labels as a murderer someone who has committed a murder then the label is warranted. If society labels as mentally ill a person who was merely eccentric then the label is unwarranted. Lemert uses the term punitive deviation to refer to 'that portion of the society reaction which has no foundation in objective behaviour' (Lemert, 1951: 56).

But what does the 'societal reaction' consist of? Society's responses to crime and deviance are highly variable, ranging from the expression of moral indignation to formal prosecution, stigmatisation and punishment. The most important societal reaction is the response of social institutions of control, such as the criminal justice system and mental health institutions. Not least of all because these can lock people away against their will. Processing in the criminal justice system stigmatises the individual at every stage – from arrest, detention and court appearance to sentencing and punishment. Lemert noted that often the labelled criminal faces more scrutiny and is subject to more rules than other members of society. Often the process leading to secondary deviance is not immediate, but unfolds over time, as primary deviants are reacted to by agents of social control with stigmatisation and degradation ceremonies – such as the ritual of the prisoner strip when they enter prison. One of the key results of the secondary deviance process is that the label of deviant becomes a master status, with a person's entire life story being organised around their deviant acts.

Lemert significantly influenced the development of what would become Labelling Theory in the 1960s. His work showed that secondary deviation emerges from a process of reaction and adjustment on behalf of people to the punishing and stigmatising actions of significant others – in Mead's terms, the reference group – such as schoolteachers, parents and law enforcement agencies. An important point Lemert made was that initially individuals – particularly young people – may well engage for only a short time in relatively minor deviant acts that they regard as incompatible with their true selves and their idea of who they are. However, because of the societal response elicited, they may well eventually come to accept their new identities as deviant and move towards a further career in deviance. But the most important contribution which brought Labelling Theory fully into mainstream sociology and criminology was undoubtedly the work of Howard Becker and Kai Erikson.

Becker and deviance as societal reaction

Labelling Theory became an influential view of deviance and crime with the publication in 1963 of Howard Becker's wide ranging and highly influential book *Outsiders*. Working within the framework laid down by Lemert, Becker made three important contributions to Labelling Theory. First, he offered an explicit labelling definition of deviance, arguing that 'deviance is not a quality of the act the person commits, but rather a consequence of the application by others of rules and sanctions to an offender' (Becker, 1963: 9). Becker argues that in the vast majority of cases crime and deviance are a product of the social environment rather than individual psychology and biology. Second, Becker expanded the definition of societal reactions to include the creation and enforcement of social rules. Third, he applied the ideas of symbolic interactionism to describe the process of becoming a marijuana user, developing a deviant culture and initiating a deviant career. Becker provided the first formal labelling definition of deviance. He rejected the conventional views of deviance and crime as individual violations of agreed upon rules or laws on two grounds. First, such a definition falsely assumed that rule violators constitute a homogeneous category. That is, you either are or are not a rule violator and all the people who violate the rules are the same. Second, he argued that the conventional view of rule breaking failed to recognise that deviance is created by society.

Becker (1963: 9) defined deviance explicitly as a social creation in which 'social groups create deviance by making rules whose infraction constitutes deviance, and by applying those rules to particular people and labelling them outsiders'. Becker established the touchstone idea of labelling theory – society creates deviance not by creating the social institutions and structures that cause deviant behaviours but by making rules and labelling people for violating those rules. This implies that deviance is a label and not a behaviour: as Becker (1963: 9) says, 'the deviant is one to whom that label has successfully been applied; deviant behaviour is behaviour that people so label'. Becker's second major contribution to the development of Labelling Theory was his conceptualisation of societal reactions to include rule creation and enforcement. He argued that the process of creating deviance begins not at the point when a person is labelled deviant – for allegedly violating some rule – but rather earlier, when social groups and moral crusaders first create those rules.

According to Becker (1963: 9), 'Social groups create deviance by making the rules whose infraction constitutes deviance, and by applying those rules to particular people and labelling them as outsiders.' Rule creation is often instigated by moral crusaders, who for Becker are typically the upper classes in society who are motivated by humanitarian concerns and preoccupied with the substantive ends, but not necessarily the logistical means, of their crusades. Hence, they tend not to consider how their crusade should proceed and what its effects on others may be. Rather, they focus on the fact that something needs to be done about a social problem. But what moral crusaders do possess is the social position to bring attention to the problem they are concerned with using the mass media. They can marshal support from various interest groups that may have disparate interests in seeing the rule passed. Moral crusades tend to have a natural history, beginning with a broad set of values, deriving specific rules based on those values, and then creating a bureaucratic system to enforce those rules. Hence politicians often end up being moral crusaders, or often appear to start out as such.

Unlike moral crusaders, rule enforcers – lawyers, police, prison guards, security and so on – tend to be more concerned with the bureaucratic imperatives of enforcement than with the actual substantive content of the rules. Becker observed that rules are almost never enforced uniformly to all that fall under their purview, but rather are selectively enforced. Law is more likely to be enforced against members of the lower class or racial minorities, and the reasons for selective enforcement are highly variable, often having to do with organisational and political imperatives. Police may perceive that delinquency is largely a problem of lower-class minorities and view upper-class, white rule violators as good kids having adolescent fun. Labelling theorists were keen to point out that the powerless in society were more susceptible to being labelled than others, even when committing the same rule violations.

It is such considerations which led Becker (1967: 234) to ask in his famous paper, 'Whose side are we on?' Becker was concerned with the need for sociologists and criminologists to recognise that not only is value-free research impossible in the social sciences – we are all guilty of letting our beliefs and values shape our understanding of the social world – but also that it is impossible to not take sides given the inherently unequal nature of the societies we live in. Indeed, a major distinguishing feature of Labelling Theory is that it shows how social control institutions disproportionately label the disadvantaged and powerless as deviant, regardless of their actual behaviour. In this way, although focused around the role of labelling in creating deviance, Labelling Theory became linked to Marxist, Feminist and Critical criminological perspectives, which are discussed in the next two chapters, and which depict society as being segmented into groups disagreeing over values and interests. Laws, for labelling theorists, must be viewed as expressions of one group's political power over others, as more powerful groups can mobilise the law to sanction behaviours that violate their interests or values. All forms of law enforcement as a result are viewed as an expression of the social control of politically weaker groups. Given such circumstances, it is impossible for the social scientist to not take sides and one of the key legacies of the work of Becker and his colleagues is that it serves as a constant reminder of that fact.

Erikson and the social function of crime

Labelling Theory has its intellectual roots in the ideas of both Durkheim and Mead. Indeed, this concern amongst labelling theorists with the role of powerful groups in society exercising power over other groups allows us to examine the functions of deviance for society more closely. For example, Kai Erikson (1962) in his paper on the sociology of deviance asked the very Durkheimian question – what positive functions does deviance serve for a society? Erikson notes that for Durkheim, the punishment of criminals, which requires criminal acts that violate laws, serves two important functions in society. First, punishment reaffirms that moral order of society. Criminal acts violate values, beliefs and morals that we hold dear and thereby threaten the social bonds which hold society together. Were criminals to go unpunished, the strength of our moral beliefs would be undermined – we would cry out, 'where is the justice?' This is why society reacts with outrage and passion in punishing criminals, often doing so in a very public way. In many ways the modern courtroom hearing and sentencing process is as public as the old town square hanging: both exist so people can see the moral order of society at work. This leads to Durkheim's second point, which is that punishment serves to define moral boundaries. Durkheim noted that crime and deviance are not universal but rather are relative to a given society, and therefore, members of society face the problem of distinguishing deviant from normal behaviour. This is done by punishing criminals. Each time an act is punished the line between moral and immoral behaviour is explicitly drawn for all members of society to see. Durkheim held that in a society of saints, with no violence, theft, robbery and so on, crime would still exist, but it would be more a matter of trivial acts of deviance that we would consider as merely being 'bad taste'. Those trivial acts would nevertheless be punished, as this reinforces the moral order and defines moral boundaries.

What this all implies is the idea that a certain amount of deviant behaviour is normal – that is, functional – for society. Erikson notes that Mead argued similarly that deviance serves a social function in that it helps the individual to identify themselves with conventional society. He drew on these ideas to expand labelling theory to include considerations of the social functions of deviance. Erickson noted that labelling entailed a very specific process of selection. Even hardened criminals engage in conventional routine behaviour most of their days, but society singles out 'moments of deviation' – which are small islands of deviance within a sea of conformity – and use them as a measure of what type of person these criminals are. Erikson argued that this selective labelling occurs in a community to define moral boundaries and to develop a sense of shared group identity. It is as much about the public display of what is right and wrong as it is about the actual punishment. Moreover, Erikson notes that the societal reaction to deviance – be it imprisonment or rehabilitation for the criminal – does not seem to reform the criminal, which is their manifest or announced function. Instead it appears to stigmatise the offender, segregate the offender with other deviants, and set up a feeling of distrust within the community. The result is a self-fulfilling prophecy in which deviants return to their deviant ways. Consequently Erikson argued that social reaction to deviance – that is labelling – serves the latent function of providing society with a pool of offenders for defining moral boundaries and reaffirming social solidarity.

This way of looking at how the labelling of deviance serves to enable society to function asks us to consider who we are labelling as deviant, and indeed, where our ideas of deviance come from in the first place. Meanwhile, it also reinforces that we can't ever be anything other than extremely cautious about political leaders who say they want to get tough on the causes of crime and indeed solve the problem of crime altogether – not least of all because the typical outcome of this usually is that the poor, the socially excluded and disadvantaged members of society will be the ones who suffer the most. It is because it brings such matters to the fore that Labelling Theory had such a significant and far-reaching impact on criminology and the sociology of deviance (Chamberlain, 2013).

Several important research studies from the 1970s onwards explored the implications of this for individuals and the ways in which social circumstance and peer groups influenced their sense of self. These include Laud Humphreys, whose 1970 book entitled *Tearoom trade* studied anonymous male–male sexual encounters in public toilets (a practice that was known as 'tea-rooming' in the USA and 'cottaging' in the UK). Humphreys noted that 54 percent of his research sample were heterosexual men, many of whom had long-term partners. He argues that this creates conflict between the private self and the social self for many of the men engaging in this form of homosexual activity, with the result that they are more likely to adopt socially and politically conservative positions on topics when talking to others in social situations. The work of Humphreys led to a burgeoning number of empirical research studies in the US and UK focused on a variety of forms of 'leisure deviancy' (i.e. recreational drug abuse, sex work, smuggling and so on) which the interested reader can explore in Ken Plummer's excellent 2001 book *Documents of life*. Also of particular importance here is the subsequent analysis of delinquent subcultures and moral panics which took place during the 1970s and 1980s, as a result of the work of Stan Cohen. This is a topic we discuss when we examine Cultural criminology in Chapter 8.

However, Labelling Theory possesses clear weaknesses. To say that society is labelling people as deviant seems to be only half the problem. The other half being the behaviour itself and what triggered it before the label of deviant or criminal was first applied. Deviance and criminality cannot be solely a social construct as labelling theorists maintain, can they? This is a particularly pertinent question when, for example, we consider the growing evidence for the importance of biochemical factors in establishing trigger points for certain emotional states which may under certain conditions lead to criminal behaviour, such as feelings of aggression for example. Additionally, if deviance is defined not as the quality of the act but rather the reaction or label of the social group, then how can you explain that deviant and criminal acts are committed by some individuals but not others? Yet the value of the Labelling Theory position is that it reinforces that we don't have to unthinkingly accept the commonplace assumption that certain people are just born bad, or that people choose crime because they feel they will reap certain rewards. As we shall see in the following chapters, the emergence of Labelling Theory signals the beginning of a more critically aware criminology which argues that we must look for the causes of crime in relation to the broader social structures and inequalities that to a certain degree act to shape the choices a person has open to them – a point we will return to in Chapter 6 when we look at Radical criminology.

RESTORATIVE JUSTICE AND BRAITHWAITE'S REINTEGRATIVE SHAMING THEORY

Labelling Theory has had a significant impact over the last 40 years on how criminologists and policy makers view deviance and how society should respond to it (Chamberlain, 2013). One particularly important contemporary development in Labelling Theory, which has influenced calls for moves for a shift towards greater use of restorative justice principles within modern criminal justice systems, has been John Braithwaite's Reintegrative Shaming Theory (2002). The central proposition of Shaming Theory is that crime rates of individuals and groups are influenced directly by processes of shaming. High crime rates result from shaming that stigmatises because rule breakers who are shamed but not forgiven are more likely to become outlaws and to participate in subcultures of crime as a result. This is referred to by Braithwaite as disintegrative shaming, and involves:

- Disrespectful disapproval and humiliation
- Ceremonies to certify deviance but no ceremonies to decertify deviance
- Labelling the person, not just the deed, as evil; and
- Deviance is allowed to become a master trait.

Braithwaite argues that, on the other hand, when rule breakers are shamed but then forgiven and welcomed back to the fold, the unpleasant, punitive experience of being shunned is offset by the pleasant relief of discovering that one is still accepted (that is wanted, cared about and even loved) despite the transgression. This is what Braithwaite called reintegrative shaming. The process of reintegrative shaming confirms that validity of the rules and re-establishes the transgressor's place as a member of society in good standing. This process involves:

- Disapproval while sustaining a relationship of respect
- Ceremonies to certify deviance terminated by ceremonies to decertify deviance
- Disapproval of the evil deed without labelling the persons as evil; and
- Deviance not being allowed to become a master status trait.

Braithwaite's theory was derived from his study of comparatively low crime eastern societies, notably Japan. He argues that systems of punishment that encourage reintegration should experience the lowest crime rates. He suggests that the core problem is that western societies are more individualistic than eastern societies, which he argues tend to be more communitarian and so have more tightly knitted interdependent relationships between family members, work colleagues and local communities. Braithwaite argues that if western criminal justice systems are to adopt a reintegrating shaming approach then they will need to shift the punishment system away from the current court-based system and embed the process of dealing with deviance and criminality within the contexts of family, friends, community and neighbourhoods.

Reintegrative shaming should be community-based and use largely informal systems of control instead of the traditional process of police arrest, court trail and prison punishment. This approach in recent years has developed and become a key restorative justice model within criminology where people with a stake in the specific offence collectively resolve how to deal with the aftermath of the offence and its implications for the future. All parties have the opportunity to have their voices heard about the crime and what needs to be done to restore victims, offenders and communities. This approach can be problematic, and different approaches exist to resolving key issues to do with ensuring victims in particular feel safe and protected as well as that offenders don't see it as an easy option to escape more punitive justice processes such as incarceration. Restorative justice approaches such as reintegrative shaming are undoubtedly becoming increasingly popular in western countries and in doing so they are in no small part reinforcing the continuing contribution of Labelling Theory to studying the problem of crime.

Box 5.6   Key summary points

- Charles Lemert (1951) looked at primary and secondary deviance, defining the former as the act itself and the latter as the social reaction to the act. He argued that the role of criminology was to focus on secondary deviance by agencies of social control, such as the police.
- Howard Becker (1963) built on these ideas to establish Labelling Theory as a major theoretical force by focusing on how the negative labelling of behaviour by moral crusaders and socio-political elites within society is underpinned by social control institutions, such as the police, who together disproportionately label the disadvantaged and powerless within society as deviant and criminal.
- Kai Erikson (1962) extended this analysis to focus on the social function of the labelling and how this serves the latent function of providing society with a pool of offenders for defining moral boundaries and reaffirming social solidarity. Therefore, from this point of view, a crime-free society is impossible as deviance and crime are necessary for ensuring social order.
- Labelling Theory developed out of the ideas of Durkheim and Mead. It is a sociological theory of crime as it argues that no act is intrinsically deviant or criminal. Rather such behaviour is labelled as deviant or criminal as the result of the application of social norms and values advocated by certain interest groups and institutionalised elites within society, i.e. politicians, human rights activists and religious leaders. Although attractive in many ways as it highlights the role of entrenched interests and power and control in oppressing and stifling minority and alternative viewpoints, it can be criticised for failing to adequately account for why some people commit crime while others do not.

(Continued)

(Continued)

- One particularly important contemporary development in Labelling Theory that has influenced calls for moves towards the greater use of restorative justice principles within western criminal justice systems has been John Braithwaite's Reintegrative Shaming Theory (2002). This reinforces the importance of promoting approaches to dealing with the problem of crime which recognise the need to ensure the social stigma that results when a person becomes labelled a criminal by the criminal justice system does not become a key defining feature of how an individual is subsequently viewed by themselves, the people close to them, their local community, or society at large.

Further reading

Becker, H (1963) *Outsiders: studies in the sociology of deviance.* New York: The Free Press.

Becker, H (1967) Whose side are we on? *Social Problems* 14 (3): 234–47.

Braithwaite, J (2002) *Restorative justice and responsive regulation.* Cambridge: Cambridge University Press.

Erikson, K (1962) Notes on the sociology of deviance. *Social Problems* 9: 307–14.

Lemert, C (1951) *Social pathology.* New York: McGraw-Hill.

SELF-STUDY TASKS

1. Write a maximum of 1500 words outlining the key features of Strain Theory, Social Disorganisation Theory and Labelling Theory. How do these theories conceptualise the social nature of crime? Do they supplement or supersede psychological and biological explanations? How do they enable criminologists to gain a deeper understanding of possible factors which may well shape an individual's actions so they are more likely to commit crime?

2. Write a maximum of 1000 words outlining how 'shaming' can be a positive exercise which tackles reoffending behaviour while bearing in mind the needs of both victims and offenders.

6 CRITICAL CRIMINOLOGY, PART 1: MARXIST, PEACEMAKING AND REALIST THEORIES OF CRIME

CHAPTER CONTENTS

CHAPTER OVERVIEW

Chapter 6 introduces and explores the emergence of Critical criminology in the 1960s. It explains how Critical criminologists use core organising social science concepts, such as race, class and gender, to explore deviance and crime, as well as how these are viewed as being both 'identities' and 'social structures'. As social structures, concepts such as race, gender and class contain culturally and historically specific socio-political rules and associated forms of inequality which are institutionalised in a society's organisation and define the forms of social status and relative socio-economic power a group possesses, and so the typical forms of social mobility (or lack thereof) commonly possible to different social groups within the structure of a society. As identities, these concepts tell us something about the expectations a society has concerning the behaviour of its members, and the ways in which people can and do commonly act to construct a sense of personal identity in relation to their gender, their class, or their race. It is a basic principle of Critical forms of criminology that social inequalities present within society shape both definitions of what constitutes deviance and crime as well as the likelihood that a person will be labelled as criminal.

The chapter discusses how early Critical criminology in the form of Marxist criminology emphasised the deterministic nature of social structure through its focus on class, while later Critical forms of criminology, such as Left Realist criminology, tend to emphasise what is called the 'duality of structure'. This stance acknowledges that we are clearly in no small part a product of our social environment as well as that our practical circumstances do act in certain circumstances to constrain and shape our everyday behaviour. But people nevertheless do intrinsically possess agency and free will, and furthermore, certain structures in society can actually act to enhance this agency; for example, equal opportunities and human rights legislation and institutions. This discussion sets the scene for the content of the rest of Chapter 6 as well as that of Chapter 7, which outlines Feminist and Cultural criminological perspectives.

Chapter 6 begins by outlining Marxist criminology. Grounded in the work of Karl Marx and Willem Bonger, Marxist forms of Critical criminology emerged during the late 1960s and early 1970s and focused on the role of the economy and social class in creating and sustaining crime and deviance. This approach promotes the importance of what it views as being a key structural sociological factor – class and class-based struggle – in determining human thought and action, including criminal behaviour. The chapter discusses how, inspired by Marx and Bonger, early Marxist criminologists, such as Richard Quinney and Steven Spitzer, argued that law and order are constituted through the prism of capitalist logic and interest. Crime itself, according to this viewpoint, is a manifestation of class struggle between the powerful bourgeoisie owner of the means of production and the exploited proletariat worker who must sell their labour in order to survive. For Marxist inspired criminologists, such as Stuart Hall, crime occurs because people are brutalised by the conditions of capitalism, and the problem of crime therefore can only be solved by restructuring society.

The chapter outlines the key problems with the Marxist criminological perspective before moving on to explore its influence on contemporary Critical forms of criminology via Peacemaking and Left Realist theories of crime. It discusses how these both argue there is a need to move away from the current punitive mass-incarceration approaches towards the problem of crime, as advocated by many western right-wing political parties as well as Right Realist criminologists, which seem to have come to dominate the popularist political agenda surrounding the problem of crime and how best to address it. This sets the background for exploring Feminist and Cultural forms of Critical criminology in Chapter 7, which focus on the role played by gender and culture in shaping our perceptions and experiences of crime and deviance.

DETERMINISM AND FREE WILL IN SOCIOLOGICAL FORMS OF CRIMINOLOGY

In this chapter we explore the emergence and features of what can be loosely defined as Critical criminology. To begin with, it is important to reflect on its relationship to the theoretical positions outlined in previous chapters. In Chapter 5 we explored the American Chicago School, with its concern for developing the sociological study of deviance and crime. The chapter focused on three key theories of crime – Strain Theory, Social Disorganisation Theory and Labelling Theory – which highlighted the role of social change and anomie, the organisation of city spaces and urban environments, along with the stereo-typing and labelling of human behaviour by socio-cultural elites and interest groups within society, in both shaping and defining certain acts as antisocial and deviant or criminal. This contrasted with Chapters 2–4, where we looked at Classical, Biological and Psychological approaches to the study of crime. Here we noted that whereas Classical criminology emphasised free will and so our personal responsibility for how we act, Biological and Psychological approaches tend to be associated with a more deterministic position which emphasises the impact of factors outside of our direct control on our individual human agency and so the choices we make.

When looking at Strain Theory, Social Disorganisation Theory and Labelling Theory we noted the tendency for these sociological approaches to the study of crime to emphasise the determining nature of social factors, such as the structuring of urban living environments or the labelling of certain behaviours as deviant or criminal by the social group, while at the same time also emphasising the ability of individuals to overcome and even change their circumstances. However, it is important to note that Strain Theory and Social Disorganisation Theory are perhaps more inclined to deterministic explanations for criminal behaviour than Labelling Theory. This is because, although like Strain Theory and Social Disorganisation Theory, Labelling Theory is heavily influenced by the thinking of Durkheim, it is nevertheless fundamentally underpinned by the philosophical tradition of symbolic interactionism and the work of the philosopher Mead, whose view of human beings as creative social actors contrasts somewhat with that of Durkheim who emphasised the role of key socialising forces such as the family, the church, the school and work, in constituting and constraining human beings and their actions.

We encounter the same tensions and differences in this chapter as we look at the emergence of what can be loosely defined as Critical criminology. With Marxist approaches we are emphasising the role of socio-economic factors in the form of class divisions resulting from the mode of production within a capitalistic society, in shaping human behaviour as well as definitions of what constitutes criminal behaviour. In contrast, Peacekeeping and Realist approaches to crime and deviance share much in common with Labelling Theory in emphasising the creative nature of human beings and their free will to choose to act in one way or another and in doing so to overcome their circumstances. Yet it is important to note here that contemporary Critical criminology viewpoints, such as Cultural criminology, tend to emphasise what is called the 'duality of structure'. It is necessary to outline what is meant by this term before moving on to explore the emergence of Marxist criminology. To begin to do this we first must look at how Critical criminology emphasises a conflict view of society.

CRITICAL CRIMINOLOGY: A CONFLICT THEORY OF SOCIETY

Critical criminology encompasses a range of different approaches which have different emphases and nuances and have been categorised under various headings: including, Marxist criminology, Left Realism, Feminist criminology, Peacemaking criminology and Cultural criminology. There is no single way of making a path through these various Critical positions. But we can for the sake of clarity in this chapter explore the development of Marxist criminology and how this transformed into contemporary Critical and Left Realist criminology, while in subsequent chapters we will look at Feminist and Cultural criminology.

A key distinguishing feature of Critical forms of criminology is that they reject utterly and completely the notion that a disinterested and value-free criminology is possible. They by and large embrace the fact that their work is value-loaded because they stand in complete opposition to unequal political, economic and social structures and relationships. As we discussed in Chapter 5, one of the key features of Durkheim's work was that he liked to emphasise order and consensus in society and how group bonds form in and through shared norms and values – hence his focus on deviance and crime as something whose function is to help maintain a sense of common feeling amongst society's members. Labelling Theory by and large shares this approach too as it emphasises how the societal reaction creates consensus amongst groups of people that certain other individuals – the 'outsiders' – are deviant. Critical criminology, in contrast to this, adopts what can be termed a conflict perspective. That is, it sees society as being shaped by conflicts amongst people who have competing self- and group interests. Even though at any one time a society may seem to agree on basic values and goals, such as the individual's right to pursue love, happiness, a rewarding career and fulfilling family life, the existence of scarce resources and the tendency for them to be allocated unequally, frequently mean that someone (or some group) is benefiting at the expense of someone else.

Critical criminologists tend to argue that the key groups at a disadvantage in western nation-states (and some would say worldwide as well) are women, ethnic minorities and the poor and socially excluded. Importantly, they also note that people may not recognise or admit that their interests are in conflict with the interests of others when in fact they are. It is argued that conflict is ubiquitous and historic, and, furthermore, consists of a struggle over three related things: money, power and influence. Those who have more of them try to keep things the way they are. Those who have less of them favour change so that they get a bigger share. The groups with wealth, power and influence are favoured in the conflict precisely because those resources put them in a dominant position. It is the 'have's' rather than the 'have-not's' who make the rules, control the content and flow of ideas and information, as well as design and impose penalties for non-conformity. Sometimes the struggle for resources is blatant and bloody but more often than not it is subtle and restrained.

Of particular interest for Critical criminologists is the fact that mass public protest – both violent and non-violent – is relatively rare, in spite of the presence of large-scale inequality within most western nation-states. Various factors are pointed out as contributing to this. An important idea here, first put forward by the philosopher Karl Marx, is called 'false consciousness'. This is the idea that the dominant group in society is able to promote beliefs and values that support the existing social order to such an extent that the disadvantaged groups actually believe their interests are served by the prevailing social conditions, when in fact they are not. Think here about how you are often told that if you behave yourself and don't get into trouble with the police, or at least not too much trouble to get a criminal record, get a good education and work hard both in your studies and when you get your first job after leaving university, then you will eventually work your way up the career ladder, as well as how this will, in turn, enable you to have the lifestyle you want so you can go on holidays, buy a car, afford to give your children nice things, get a house, and so on. But for Marxist-inspired criminologists what you are being sold here is nothing more than a gilded cage of your own making. You are not being brought up to have a free life. Rather, you are being trained and prepared for a life as a cog in a machine which cares little for you, and indeed, just wants you to keep deluding yourself so it can extract the surplus value of your labour and turn it into a profit for the shareholders of the company you work for. What is more, they will sell this surplus value back to you in the form of consumerist goods and gadgets which in reality you don't need but think you can't survive without because you've been seduced into believing you can't. This is a point we will return to later in this chapter.

CRITICAL CRIMINOLOGY AND THE DUALITY OF STRUCTURE

Critical criminology examines how different forms of oppression, inequality and conflict affect people in everyday life as well as through the lens of crime and law. But it is particularly interested in how structural inequalities evident in a society's class, race and gender structures affect, firstly, participation in crime, secondly, how crime is defined, and thirdly, the making and enforcement of laws. To do this Critical criminologists examine crime relative to social, economic and political structures and forms of inequality, as found in a given society at a particular point in history. When Critical criminologists speak about race, class and gender they use the terms differently from other criminologists, including Classical criminologists, Psychological and Biological criminologists, labelling theorists, or Durkheimian inspired sociologists of deviance. For traditional criminologists race, class and gender tend to be interpreted as characteristics of individuals and are used to identify subjects of study, such as the 'middle class', or 'female victims'. But for Critical criminologists race, class and gender are both personal identities and social structures.

As structures race, class and gender contain culturally and historically specific rules that define (1) the types of power a group possesses, (2) a group's social and economic positions within society and (3) the opportunities for success people from these groups typically possess (Paternoster and Bachman, 2007). As identities, race, class and gender tell us something about the 'social expectations concerning the behaviour of people from different groups, and the ways in which people act to construct themselves, that is their sense of personal identity in relation to their gender, their class, or their race' (Paternoster and Bachman, 2007: 267). So when we label someone as being working class we are defining them as belonging to a particular structural location within the social fabric of a society which tells us something about how it is organised and the forms of inequality which help to define it. This is because this location shapes the opportunities or pathways to success a person belonging to this class typically has at their disposal.

For Critical criminologists we are not all born equal and do not all possess the same level of, or types of, opportunities to enhance our social mobility. We stereotypically expect working-class people to behave in particular ways and possess a life story which is different in several key ways from people who occupy 'higher' class positions as we identify them (and so differentiate them from other social classes) by what type of job they have (and typically can have), what their level of income is likely to be, where they are likely to have grown up and gone to school, who their friends are likely to be, what type of holidays they are likely to go on, how they are likely to dress and spend their leisure time, what illnesses and diseases they are likely to suffer from, what their typical life expectancy is to be, and so on. In summary, the starting point for Critical criminology is that a person's structural location carries with it different forms of behavioural expectations and social opportunities which are built on and reflect social inequalities which arise due to their class, race and gender, as well as help to explain the probability that people located in different structural locations will engage in crime or will be labelled criminal (Chamberlain, 2013).

This then leads us to a key beginning point about Critical criminology in relation to our ongoing discussion about free will and determinism when exploring the causes of crime. Taken as a whole, contemporary Critical criminology viewpoints in particular, such as Cultural criminology, clearly do emphasise structure but they also emphasise human agency and our ability to change our social conditions. Indeed, while early Marxist criminology may well be said to be structurally deterministic, in that it talks about how a society's economic development drives social change, as well as presumes that your class determines your life chances and who you are, subsequent Critical criminological perspectives, such as Left Realism, also emphasise human agency and individual freedom as well as the ability for social structure to enhance this – or in the technical parlance, they recognise the duality of structure. This means that while we are clearly in no small part a product of our social environment and our historical and practical circumstances equally do act to constrain and shape our everyday behaviour, we nevertheless do intrinsically possess agency and free will, and furthermore, certain structures in society are deliberately designed to promote and enhance this agency. We may here think about certain institutional administrative and bureaucratic institutional structures which seek to protect the individual from intimidation on behalf of more powerful social groups or forces, such as equal opportunity or human rights legislation. Structure, in other words, isn't necessarily a bad thing in terms of it limiting our innate human freedom, and furthermore, contemporary Critical criminology arguably reminds us that it is important for criminological theory to recognise the importance of both the positive and negative aspects of determining social structure when studying crime. This is a point we will look at again in this and later chapters, particularly when examining Feminist criminology. But before we do so it is necessary to look at the historical development of Critical criminology through examining the ideas of Karl Marx and the emergence of Marxist criminology in the 1970s.

Box 6.1   Key summary points

- Critical criminology encompasses a range of different approaches which have different emphases and nuances, and which have been categorised under various headings, including Marxist criminology, Critical criminology, Left Realism, Feminist criminology, Peacemaking criminology and Cultural criminology, amongst others.
- These diverse viewpoints share a concern with examining how different forms of oppression, inequality and conflict affect people in everyday life as well as through the lens of crime and law.

(Continued)

(Continued)

- For Critical criminologists core organising social science concepts such as race, class and gender are both identities and structures. As structures, they contain historically located social orders and rules which serve to define the institutionalised forms of socio-political and economic power a group member possesses, as well as the types of opportunities for success and social advancement people from these groups typically have open to them. As identities, they tell us something about the common social expectations concerning the behaviour of people from different groups which are present within a society at different points in time, and so the different ways in which people can and do act to construct a personal sense identity in and through their gender, their class, or their race.
- While early Critical criminology in the form of Marxist criminology emphasised the deterministic nature of social structure, later Critical criminology, such as Cultural criminology, tends to emphasise what is called the 'duality of structure'. This stance acknowledges that we are clearly in no small part a product of our social environment and our practical circumstances do act in certain circumstances to constrain and shape our everyday behaviour, but people nevertheless do intrinsically possess agency and free will, and furthermore, certain structures in society can actually act to enhance agency (for example, equal opportunities and human rights legislation and institutions).

KARL MARX AND WILLEM BONGER: TOWARDS A MARXIST THEORY OF CRIME

The writings of Karl Marx are varied and far-reaching (Elster, 1986). So much so that it is nigh on impossible to summarise them in a brief section. But as our attention is on the contribution of his ideas to the analysis of crime, it is possible to focus on some key points to sensitise ourselves to the main thrust of his ideas, before moving on to explore the influence of these on criminology. Writing in the nineteenth century, Marx was concerned with documenting and commenting upon social processes at work within nation-states across Europe as a result of the rapid economic, socio-political and cultural change brought about by the industrial revolution and the concurrent growth of modern science and technology. For Marx, the story of human history and civilisation is one determined primarily by economic factors, what he referred to as 'the means of production'. The means of production are those things, like land, natural resources and technology, which are necessary for the production of material goods and commodities. He argued that at different points in human history the means of production changed. For example, in the Middle Ages the means of production was based on farming and related land-use, but with growing industrialisation from the early nineteenth century onwards society changed towards a more factory-based economy as large-scale industries developed as a result of technological innovation and advances in modern science as well as civil and mechanical engineering. Additionally, for Marx, what he referred to as the relations of production altered as the means of production changed. The relations of production are defined as the social relationships people enter into as they acquire and use the means of production. So the farmer became the factory worker and the feudal landlord the factory owner, as the means of production changed from the old agrarian land-based model to one based on factory production. In our present society, Marx called the owners of the means of production the bourgeoisie and those who sell their working labour to them the proletariat. One of the key aims of his analysis was to highlight the asymmetrical power relationship which he argued existed between these two groups. He held that the proletariat worker was being exploited by the bourgeoisie and argued throughout his life for social changes to be introduced to rectify this.

Marx did not himself provide us with a definitive theory of crime as part of his broader body of work. But for criminologists a key aspect of Marx's thinking is that different classes are bound in asymmetrical power relationships which are fundamentally exploitative. From this position, laws are created by elite members of society to protect their interests at the expense of others. One of the earliest theorists to apply a Marxist perspective to law and crime was Willem Bonger. In his 1905 book, *Criminality and economic conditions*, Bonger observed that capitalist societies appear to have considerably more crime than do other societies. Furthermore, while capitalism developed, crime rates increased steadily. This is because, under capitalism, Bonger argued, the characteristic trait of humans is self-interested egoism. Given the commercial emphasis on profit maximisation and competition and the fact that social relations are class structured and geared to the economic exchange of goods and services for cash (or 'capital' as both Marx and Bonger referred to it), capitalist societies spawn interclass conflicts as individuals seek to survive and prosper. Interclass conflict is one-sided, however, since those who own and control the means of production are in a position to coerce and exploit the less fortunate. For Bonger, following Marx, criminal law is principally constituted according to the will of the dominant class in order to protect their interests. Crime is a socio-political construct grounded in class-based exploitation.

For Bonger, behaviour threatening the interests of the ruling class is designated as criminal. Since social relations are geared towards competition, profit seeking and the exercise of power, altruism is subordinated to egoistic tendencies: think here of the saying 'charity begins at home'. These tendencies lead, Bonger argued, to a weakening of internal constraint within individuals. Both the bourgeoisie and the proletariat become prone to crime; hence the rise in crimes of the bourgeoisie classes, such as white-collar and corporate crime. But it is the proletariat working class which is subject to further demoralisation precisely because of its inferior exchange position and its exploitation at the hands of the ruling class. Bonger (1905: 195) argued that 'long working hours and monotonous labour brutalize those who are forced into them; bad housing conditions contribute also to debase the moral sense; as do the uncertainty of existence, and finally, absolute poverty, the frequent consequences of sickness and unemployment'. He concluded that the economic conditions of capitalism not only induce egoism but, coupled with a system of law creation and enforcement controlled by the capitalist class, also account for (1) higher crime rates in capitalist societies, (2) crime rates increasing with industrialisation and (3) the working-class character of much 'officially recorded' crime. These three ideas influenced the development of Marxist criminology in the 1970s, with a new generation of scholars encountering Bonger's and Marx's ideas for the first time as a result of new translations and editions of their works.

Box 6.2   Key summary points

- Karl Marx argued that the story of human history and civilisation is one determined primarily by economic factors.
- Marx argued that contemporary society consisted of two main classes, the bourgeoisie and the proletariat, with the former exploiting the latter and society's key governing bodies, including its legal and criminal justice institutions, being designed to serve the vested interests of the bourgeoisie.
- Willem Bonger applied Marx's insights to developing a Critical Marxist form of criminology. Bonger observed that crime rose as western societies became industrialised from the nineteenth century onwards, that capitalist societies appear to have considerably more crime than other types of society, as well as that the crimes committed within them appear to be mostly committed by the working class (or the proletariat in Marx's terms).
- Bonger argued that this was because, under capitalism, the characteristic trait of humans promoted by society's social institutions is self-interested egoism: both people and business are expected to seek profit maximisation while social relations are class structured and geared to the economic exchange of good and services for cash, which creates an inherent potential for conflict.
- For both Marx and Bonger criminal law is principally constituted according to the will of the dominant bourgeoisie class, i.e. property theft.

Further reading

Bonger, W (1905) *Criminality and economic conditions*. London: Sage.
Elster, J (1986) *Karl Marx: A reader*. Cambridge: Cambridge University Press.

MARXIST CRIMINOLOGY: CRIME AS A RATIONAL RESPONSE TO THE CONDITIONS OF CAPITALISM

As a result of the work of Marx and Bonger a key idea running through the emergence of Critical forms of criminology in the late 1960s and early 1970s was that most crime was in fact a rational response to the structure of social life and society's key regulatory and bureaucratic institutions under capitalism. This is not to say that they meant crime was rational in the same sense that Classical criminologists argued. Far from it. Rather, it was argued that crime was a rational means of survival when survival is never guaranteed due to the inherent conflicts and class divisions which exist within capitalist societies.

A key early Marxist criminologist was Richard Quinney, who published *Class, state, and crime* in 1979. Quinney starts with a number of presuppositions. First, to understand the meaning of crime in capitalist society one must take into account how capitalist economics develop. By this, Quinney means that to understand crime in society we should have a sense of the historical evolution of political economy and how it instructs our everyday lives and values. Second, Quinney says it is important to get a grasp of how systems of class domination and repression operate for the benefit of the capitalist class through the vehicle of crime. Here Quinney suggests that law is one weapon in the arsenal of the bourgeoisie to exploit the proletariat and to deflect scrutiny from their own harmful actions.

Quinney writes that ideas about crime and justice are created through human experiences within a capitalist society and therefore the dominant ideology of crime reflects that bias. In other words, like the various Chicago-based sociologists of deviance discussed in Chapter 5, Marxist criminologists view crime and deviance as social constructs, rather than being things which somehow belong to individuals as a result of some aspect of their individual biology or psychology. This leads them to conclude that they must not simply look at the law breakers but the law makers and law keepers too. The Marxist criminologist Steven Spitzer (1975) provides a useful summary of the conditions under which citizens of capitalist societies become candidates for formal social control when they disturb, hinder or simply call into question any of the following:

1. Capitalist modes of appropriating the product of human labour (i.e. those who steal and thieve instead of consuming goods and buying them, so corporations can earn profit)
2. The social conditions under which capitalist production takes place (i.e. those who are unable or unwilling to perform labour)
3. Patterns of distribution and consumption in capitalist society (i.e. those who consume 'illegal substances' such as drugs)
4. The process of socialisation for productive social roles (i.e. children and teenagers who refuse schooling or don't participate in a traditional family life)
5. The ideology that supports the functioning of capitalist society (i.e. revolutionaries and other political deviants)

Source: Spitzer, S (1975) Toward a Marxian theory of deviance. *Social Problems* 12: 638–51.

For Marxist criminologists, notions of law and order and justice are constituted through the prism of capitalist logic and class-based self-interest. Crime itself, according to Quinney, is a manifestation of class struggle. He writes that 'much criminal behaviour is of a parasitical nature, including burglary, robbery, drug dealing, and hustling of various sorts ... the behaviour, although pursued out of a need to survive, is a reproduction of the capitalist system' (Quinney, 1979: 176). For Quinney and other Marxist criminologists, crime occurs because people are brutalised by the conditions of capitalism and the problem of crime therefore can only be solved by restructuring society. It is for this reason that Marxist criminology can be said to promote the importance of a structural sociological factor – class and class-based struggle – in determining human thought and action, including criminal behaviour.

Quinney argued that criminologists must stop claiming to be disinterested social scientists and take the side of the oppressed proletariat. He views criminologists who do not do so as tacit agents of the capitalist state, for the discipline of criminology 'seeks to control anything that threatens the capitalist system of production and its social relations' (Quinney, 1979: 176). What Quinney meant here is that by divorcing the study of crime from the study of class domination criminologists are tacitly involved in reproducing the inequalities caused by capitalism. This is because Marxist criminology argues that the state is a tool used by the bourgeoisie elite to control the poor and protect their own wealth, status and privilege. It is with Marxist criminology that we see the first real call for criminologists to change their focus from predatory street crime, which is by and large committed by the low-paid and often unemployed members of the working classes, towards examining the crimes of the powerful. This led from the early 1980s onwards to a growth in criminological research into white-collar and corporate crime, environmental crime, as well as state crime in the form of the use of genocide, eugenics and torture (Coleman et al., 2009).

Marxist criminology influenced the development of more critical forms of criminology in the USA and Europe from the early 1970s onwards. For example, in their 1973 book *The new criminology*, the UK-based criminologists Ian Taylor, Paul Walton and Jock Young, highlighted the need for criminology to develop as an examination of the crimes of the powerful and the law makers and law keepers. Meanwhile, in his 1978 book *Policing the crisis*, Stuart Hall studied the media reaction to the phenomenon of mugging, which social and political elites tried to present as being imported from American 'street-gang culture', and in doing so he reinforced the socially constructed nature of the concept of crime through highlighting the importance of a key social construct – social class – when analysing deviance and criminality.

Yet Marxist criminology declined in terms of its influence on academic criminological thinking from the mid-1980s onwards. There are several reasons for this, including the fact that the label Critical criminology covers a diverse range of perspectives which emerged out of the conceptual landscape established by early Marxist criminology, such as Left Realism, Feminist, Cultural and Peacemaking criminology. These share in common the recognition of the importance of acknowledging class and economic factors when analysing crime. But they also tend to reject several key aspects of earlier Marxist criminological thinking. Importantly, they reject its emphasis on there being a direct and exclusive relationship between economy and crime. Although contemporary Critical criminology does recognise the importance of the impact of the economy on crime, it is argued that Marxist criminology overgeneralised its importance, and indeed, that there are in fact a range of other factors at work. For example, many Critical and Feminist criminologists strongly feel that certain crimes involving female victims and victims from ethnic minorities, including forms of hate crime, rape and domestic violence, are due to ideological factors relating to patriarchy or institutionalised forms of racism, rather than being rational responses to the class-based inequality caused by capitalist systems (Walklate, 2007).

Marxist criminology was also heavily criticised for holding, firstly, an overly deterministic view of human behaviour and the ability of human beings to exercise free will and change both their behaviour and their circumstances, and secondly, an overly romantic view of the working-class criminal and having a concurrent tendency to excuse their behaviour on the grounds of the fact that they are exploited by a ruling elite (Coleman et al., 2009). Furthermore, it is generally held by later Critical criminologists that Marxist criminology oversimplifies society into essentially two groups of 'have's' and 'have-not's', not least of all because the idea that a small band of powerful people, who are in collusion with each other, somehow run society and determine the destinies of us all is rather wide of the mark and arguably somewhat the stuff of bad Hollywood movies. It is important to remember here the key position of the conflict paradigm: that society is made up of a number of competing groups operating in conflict with each other, not just two. Finally, another key criticism of Marxist criminology is that its proponents seemed to argue that a Critical socialist revolution is the only solution to society's many social problems, including crime. Yet more pragmatic criminologists pointed out that this oversimplified matters and that they would probably achieve more lasting social change from working with the existing system and making incremental changes within it.

Box 6.3   Key summary points

- Influenced by the work of Marx and Bonger, a key idea running through the emergence of Critical Marxist forms of criminology in the late 1960s and early 1970s was that most crime is a rational means of survival when survival is never guaranteed due to the inherent conflicts and class divisions which exist within capitalist societies. In his book *Class, state and crime* Richard Quinney (1979: 176) writes that 'much criminal behaviour is of a parasitical nature, including burglary, robbery, drug dealing, and hustling of various sorts'.
- Marxist criminologists view crime and deviance as social constructs, rather than as things which somehow belong to individuals as a result of some aspect of their individual biology or psychology.

(Continued)

(Continued)

- Marxist criminologists argued that by divorcing the study of crime from the study of class domination criminologists are tacitly involved in reproducing the inequalities caused by capitalism. They are challenging the idea that criminology can be a disinterested social science and conclude that criminologists must not simply look at the law breakers, but the law makers and law keepers as well.
- Marxist criminology was criticised for possessing an overly deterministic view of human behaviour and an over-romantic view of the working-class criminal. It was also criticised by Critical and Feminist criminologists who argued that certain crimes involving female victims and victims from ethnic minorities, including forms of hate crime, rape and domestic violence, are due to ideological factors relating to patriarchy or institutionalised forms of racism, rather than responses to the class-based inequality caused by capitalist systems.

Further reading

Coleman, R, Sim, J, Tombs, S and Whyte, D (2009) *State, power, crime.* London: Sage.

Quinney, R (1979) *Class, state and crime.* London: Longman Group.

Spitzer, S (1975) Toward a Marxian theory of deviance. *Social Problems* 12: 638–51.

Taylor, I, Walton, P and Young, J (1973) *The new criminology: for a social theory of deviance.* London: Routledge.

Walklate, S (2007) *Imagining the victim of crime.* Maidenhead: McGraw-Hill and Open University Press.

PEACEMAKING CRIMINOLOGY

Peacemaking criminology grew out of the thinking of the social psychologist Harold Pepinsky and the Marxist come Critical criminologist, come Peacemaker, Richard Quinney, who together in 1991 published *Criminology as peacemaking.* They discuss how advanced capitalist countries like the USA and the UK have high crime rates and consistently come top of the league for possessing the most recorded violent crime worldwide. As well as how in both the USA and the UK, like in many other western nation-states, the use of imprisonment has increased year on year since the beginning of the nineteenth century (a trend which has continued into the twenty-first century). Pepinsky and Quinney also discuss how this trend for mass incarceration and penalism is heavily racialised, with one out of every three African American men in the USA between the ages of 20 and 29 becoming involved in some way with the criminal justice system (Chamberlain, 2013). As a result, they argue that there is much evidence that western liberal-democratic capitalist countries have shifted towards being 'penal states'. Yet they note that long-term prison sentences and other harsh sentences and sanctions are not making the city streets, people's homes, or their intimate relationships any safer.

Reiman and Leighton (2012) argue that this extreme harshness is seen by many criminologists as being a right-wing conservative social experiment which has clearly failed. In response to this ongoing crisis they contend it is now time for politicians, criminal justice officials and members of the general public to recognise that the USA, UK and other punitive penal states, such as Russia, are going about things the wrong way. However, there are many conflicting answers to the question of what can be done about crime and its control. Some people – who as we shall discuss in the next section are called Right Realists – continue to call for a criminal justice system that is even more punitive than the current one. One benefit of claiming that the system is not harsh enough is that no matter how harsh it becomes, there is no way of proving that it isn't harsh enough. If getting harsher does not seem to have any important effect on crime, there is always room for people to start to assert that we need to get harsher still. Peacemaking criminologists, in contrast, contend that critical change is needed if we are to find a solution to crime problems.

Peacemaking criminologists see crime as being only one of many different types of violence – such as war, racism and sexism – which contribute to human suffering. Coming to the fore in the 1990s, and gaining momentum ever since, Peacemaking criminology is informed by a mixture of eastern meditative thought, penal abolitionism, feminism and Marxism. The basic principles of Peacemaking criminology have been outlined by Pepinsky and Quinney (1991) as follows:

1. Crime is suffering, and crime can only be eliminated by ending suffering.
2. Crime and suffering can only be ended through the achievement of peace.
3. Human transformation will achieve peace and justice.
4. Human transformation will occur if we change our social, economic and political structure.

For Peacemaking criminologists, the current criminal justice system is a failure because it is rooted in the very problem it is ostensibly trying to eliminate – violence. Populist penal discourses such as a 'war on crime' or a 'war on drugs' or a 'war on gangs', and indeed all other wars, are based on the assumption we can stamp out, push back, eliminate or somehow eradicate crime, using violence. Thus, for example, many people believe crime can be stopped by using even harsher sentences, even for relatively minor antisocial behaviour. When this doesn't work they argue that we must increase the penalties further. Peacemaking criminologists do not believe we can end violence with violence. One key area which Peacemaking criminology has influenced is the field of restorative justice, which focuses on decreasing the role of the state in responding to crime and increasing the involvement of personal, familial and community networks in repairing harm caused by crime. Like Braithwaite's reintegrative shaming approach discussed in Chapter 5, Peacemaking criminology focuses on how victims, offenders and communities must sit down together and work through the impact of crime and what can be done; the emphasis being on perpetrators facing up and taking personal responsibility for what they have done. As a result of this, it has been argued that Peacemaking criminology is overly idealistic and utopian, while it also has been criticised for not being a testable theory which can concretely guide criminal justice policy. Yet even if Peacemaking criminology ultimately proves ineffectual, its first axiom of research ethics is 'do no harm' and compared to the war on crime perspective that is currently in fashion, Peacemaking is clearly superior.

Box 6.4   Key summary points

- Peacemaking criminology was first articulated by the social psychologist, Harold Pepinsky and the Marxist criminologist, Richard Quinney.
- Peacemaking criminology argues that the problem of crime cannot be solved by continuing to follow the punitive populist Right Realist approach which arguably dominates the contemporary political agenda in regard to the problem of crime.
- Peacemaking criminology has been criticised as being too idealistic in advocating that victims, offenders and local communities must sit down together and work through the impact of crime and what can be done about it.

Further reading

Pepinsky, HE and Quinney, R (1991) *Criminology as peacemaking.* Bloomington: Indiana University Press.
Reiman, J and Leighton, P (2012) *The rich get richer and the poor get prison.* Harlow: Pearson.

LEFT AND RIGHT REALIST CRIMINOLOGY

Left Realist criminology developed in the late 1980s and early 1990s, originating in the writings of the British criminologists Jock Young and Roger Matthews (Matthews and Young, 2003). Taking the lead from Marxist criminology, Feminist criminology as well as the ideas of Strain and Labelling theories of crime, Left Realists view capitalist free-market societies such as western states like the UK and US and Europe as being inherently criminogenic as they possess deep-seated social inequalities. Yet Left Realism developed out of an academic critique of Marxist criminology, which Left Realists refer to as Left Idealism, alongside the emergence of a more populist punitive approach to crime in the UK and US, which Left Realists refer to as Right Realism (Matthews and Young, 1992).

Right Realism grew out of a critique of Strain Theory and Labelling Theory, which informed much of criminal justice policy in the USA and UK during the 1970s and 1980s. These approaches, it was argued, ignored the victim of crime and were too closely tied up with left-wing politics and the viewpoint that an expansion of state welfare to promote equality of opportunity could reduce crime. The realist tag, which is shared by both Left and Right forms of realism, results from the view that the state should set itself clear and doable targets to deal with crime. Key proponents of Right Realism were James Wilson and Richard Herrnstein, who in their 1985 book *Crime and human nature* tried to construct a biosocial approach to crime, based on the Classical criminological concept of free will outlined in Chapter 2, which they combined with Eysenck's social-psychological theory of criminality discussed in Chapter 3, which argued that the biological basis for crime lies in the human nervous system.

Wilson and Herrnstein argued for the need for criminologists, politicians and criminal justice practitioners to be pragmatic and to begin with two key facts as they saw them; firstly, that some people are just born to be criminals (a conclusion they drew from the work of Eysenck); and secondly, that some people may wander into committing crime as a result of social deprivation and being brought up in urban areas which have high levels of drug use, alcohol abuse, domestic and interpersonal violence. In summary, they held that deterministic biological and sociological factors did play a role in influencing some members of society to commit crime, but at the same time that in all but the most extreme instances people did so as a result of exercising their own free will and engaging in rational decision-making behaviour. From this beginning they drew the conclusion that it was impossible to solve the problem of crime – how could it be if some people were just born criminal? – consequently, they argue that society has to prioritise becoming more effective in managing the problem of crime. Furthermore, they hold that this can be achieved by being more punitive and using a mixture of welfare reform and social conditioning to reinforce that committing crime is wrong and people must take personal responsibility for their actions. It was held that society must take a tough stance on criminals and criminality, primarily by putting more people in prison.

This viewpoint appealed to right-wing conservative political parties in both the USA and Europe as it allowed them to acknowledge social deprivation as a factor in creating crime but nevertheless required people take personal responsibility for their actions as they are held to be by and large operating under their own free will. Right Realists advocated the Broken Windows and zero tolerance policing approaches to situational crime prevention discussed in Chapter 5 as a key means by which to tackle antisocial behaviour and urban decay. While the behaviour of some individuals was held to be influenced by biological and psychological factors it was argued that there was a need for medicalised treatment programmes for mentally disordered offenders, persistent repeat offenders, paedophiles and drug abusers.

Left Realists emerged to reject the Right Realist position with its popularist punitive approach to the problem of crime. Matthews and Young (2003) argued that just because criminalising and locking up more people appeals to the mass of people and politicians, it doesn't mean it is the right thing to do. They argued against the position that biological factors drive some people to crime and were heavily critical of Eysenck's social-psychological theory of criminality discussed earlier. However, they accepted the Right Realist argument that Strain Theory, Labelling Theory and Marxist forms of criminology had all perhaps focused too much on the offender and by and large paid little attention to victims of crime. Left Realism accused Marxists in particular of being 'Left Idealists' because they held a romantic view of the working class and a utopian vision that crime could be eradicated. In contrast, Left Realism, like Right Realism, is pragmatic about the problem of crime, holding that it will in all likelihood remain a key feature of human civilisation for the foreseeable future. Hence they shift the focus onto looking for a realist solution to the problem of crime, but in a politically left-leaning way. This is because Left Realists retain a concern with the damage done by the crimes of the powerful – i.e. corporate and state crime – but the bulk of their theoretical and empirical work is focused on street crime and hard police tactics to deal with it, such as stop and search powers, alongside the abuse of women in intimate relationships by violent men (Young, 1994).

Left Realists retained a Marxist concern with class, but also added race and ethnicity, gender and sexuality to the study of Critical criminology, as well as focusing their attention on tackling right-wing politicians and draconian criminal justice policies that, they argue, harm people at the bottom of the social ladder and preclude the creation of a society based on class, race, ethnic and gender equality. The task Left Realists set themselves was to seek to advocate reform in the criminal justice system while at the same time seeking to protect the public. A central concern for Left Realists is how they can work in and against the state to bring about social change. Essential to this exercise is the concept 'the square of crime'. The square of crime is a reminder that crime is the result of a number of forces and that intervention to prevent it must therefore take place at different levels to be effective. The four key factors are, first, the state, principally the capacity of its front-line agents such as the police and legal system to label individuals and groups as offenders. Second, is the victim, whose voice must be clearly heard if crime is to be solved. This is particularly the case with gendered and racial violence. Third, is society, through which the various sources of control are exercised and whose various parts – such as the media, professional groups, victim rights organisations and local communities – must all play a positive role in tackling crime. Fourth, are the offenders themselves, who they are, how many they are, what type of crime they do, and so on. Left Realists argued that only by involving all four parts of the square of crime as partners in the process will crime prevention and control serve to minimise crime in a significant and positive fashion.

Left Realism stresses the importance of partnership and rejects punitive and exclusory criminal justice practices, including trends for mass incarceration as advocated by Right Realists. One of the key influences of Left Realism on contemporary criminal justice policy is its concern with social exclusion and victimisation. This stance somewhat influenced in the UK the 1998 Crime and Disorder Act of the New Labour government. This sought to tackle the problem of domestic violence, low level social disorder and antisocial behaviour while also developing programmes and initiatives to tackle social deprivation and repeat offending behaviour. Within this context Left Realist principles were used to advocate the need to ensure the voices of victims and offenders are heard. However, the New Labour agenda and Left Realism were criticised by Feminist criminologists for not going far enough in addressing domestic violence and gendered crime. Meanwhile Left Realists themselves argued that the crime and justice agenda of the New Labour government was limited by the fact that it by and large advocated a more punitive criminal justice system operating in line with Right Realist principles (Matthews and Young, 2003). It was certainly the case that social-structural factors, such as class, race and gender, were much less emphasised in the political discourse of the time surrounding law and order. Left Realists were particularly critical of this aspect of the New Labour government agenda. This critique of the Right Realist leaning political landscape has continued since the Conservative–Liberal Democrat Coalition government came into power in 2010.

A key factor underpinning the ongoing criticism of Anglo-American governmental policy by Left Realists is that, like Right Realists, the main political parties of the left (i.e. the Labour Party in the UK and the Democrat Party in the US) and the right (i.e. the Conservative Party in the UK and the Republican Party in the US) have conceptualised the link between social inequality and crime in a manner which runs counter to the key concept of 'relative deprivation'. Left Realists argue that crime is rooted in the social conditions a person lives in and that crime is closely connected to deprivation, i.e. high levels of unemployment, welfare dependency, poor life expectancy. However, they reject the idea that factors such as poverty and unemployment can be seen as directly responsible for crime. Rather, it is argued that social deprivation will only lead to crime when it is experienced directly by an individual as involving a sense of relative deprivation. A person experiences relative deprivation when they feel deprived in comparison to other people, or when their expectations are not met in some way. It is not the fact of being deprived as such, but the relative feeling of deprivation in relation to others which is important. The concept of relative deprivation has been important in the development of contemporary Critical criminology with Left Realism practitioners using it to explore how people become involved in crime, as both victims and perpetrators (Matthews and Young, 2003). Left Realism has had significant impact on the thinking of Critical forms of criminology, such as Cultural criminology. However Left Realism is not beyond criticism. In particular, it has been criticised by Right Realists for being too utopian and idealistic in advocating a criminal justice process based on partnership, particularly when it comes to the relationship between an offender and their victim.

Box 6.5   Key summary points

- Left Realist criminology developed in the late 1980s and early 1990s, originating in the writings of the British criminologists Jock Young and Roger Matthews, in response to the populist punitive discourse of Right Realism which advocates mass incarceration and a heavily punitive 'zero tolerance' approach to the policing of offending behaviour and prosecution of criminal activity.

(Continued)

(Continued)

- Right Realism was first developed in the 1980s by James Wilson and Richard Herrnstein, who critiqued Strain Theory and Labelling Theory which had informed much of criminal justice policy in the USA and UK during the 1970s and 1980s, particularly in relation to youth offending. Wilson and Herrnstein constructed a biosocial approach to crime based on the Classical criminological concept of free will combined with Eysenck's social-psychological theory of criminality.
- Two core Left Realist concepts are 'the square of crime' and 'relative deprivation'. The square of crime requires the offender, their victim, the criminal justice system and society at large be viewed as partners in the criminal justice process and the detection, punishment and prevention of crime. The concept of relative deprivation recognises that it is not indicators of absolute deprivation, such as poverty and unemployment, which cause people to engage in crime, but rather it is when they feel deprived in comparison to other people, or when their expectations are not met in some way.
- While Right Realism can be criticised for being overly draconian and punitive, Left Realism can equally be criticised for being overly utopian – particularly when it advocates that offenders and victims must be viewed as equals in the criminal justice process. Feminist criminologists, amongst others, have argued that this is heavily problematic in the context of addressing interpersonal forms of violence, such as domestic abuse for example.

Further reading

Matthews, R and Young, J (2003) *The new politics of crime and punishment.* London: Willan Publishing.

Wilson, JQ and Herrnstein, RJ (1985) *Crime and human nature: the definitive study of the causes of crime.* New York: The Free Press.

Young, J (1994) *The exclusive society: social exclusion, crime and difference in late modernity.* London and Thousand Oaks, CA: Sage.

SELF-STUDY TASKS

1. Write a maximum of 400 words outlining the key features of Critical criminology and how it has developed over the last 30 years into a range of contemporary Critical criminology perspectives which share in common a concern with structural inequality in terms of class, race and gender.
2. Critically evaluate in no more than 500 words the argument that Marxist criminology concentrated too much on the crimes of the powerful and over-romanticised working-class criminality by seeing it as a response to structural inequalities present in contemporary western nation-states.
3. Prepare a short 15-minute PowerPoint presentation which outlines and critically contrasts the key features of Left and Right Realist criminology.

7 CRITICAL CRIMINOLOGY, PART 2: FEMINIST AND CULTURAL CRIMINOLOGY

Chapter 7 examines two key Critical criminological perspectives: Feminist and Cultural criminology. The chapter outlines how these two Critical traditions reinforce the importance of paying close attention to the interaction of social factors such as gender, class, race and culture, in shaping a person's involvement with crime, as victim and offender, as well as societal responses to crime. In doing so the chapter highlights how both Feminist and Cultural criminology reject, firstly, the positivist paradigm which holds that crime can be known and explained only through the scientific method, and secondly, that people who break the law are somehow psychologically, biologically or morally defective. Rather, emphasis is placed on the structuring of social action in and through the categories of class, gender and race and ethnicity, while at the same time advocating 'the duality of structure'. This concept highlights how just as human agency and free will can be shaped and constrained by a society's governing institutions, they can be designed to promote our ability to act and combat social inequalities (i.e. through promoting anti-discriminatory practices to tackle sexism, racism and homophobia). The chapter concludes by discussing how Cultural criminology brings to the fore the role of both contemporary culture and the news media in representing crime, as well as highlighting the need to pay close attention to the emotional aspects of criminality.

CRITICAL CRIMINOLOGY AND FEMINIST AND CULTURAL THEORIES OF CRIME

In this chapter we continue our examination of the development of Critical criminology through looking at the emergence of Feminist and Cultural theories of crime. The previous chapter discussed how Critical criminology encompasses a range of different approaches which have different emphases and nuances, and which have been categorised under various headings: including Marxist criminology, Left Realism, Feminist criminology, Peacemaking criminology and Cultural criminology. It was also noted that these diverse viewpoints reject the positivist assertions of Classical, Biological and Psychological theories of crime covered in Chapters 2–4, alongside early sociological theories of deviance outlined in Chapter 5, that criminal behaviour can be solved in a value-neutral manner and following the methodology of the natural sciences. Furthermore, it was discussed how although Critical forms of criminology often disagree with each other they nevertheless share a concern with examining how different forms of oppression, inequality and conflict affect people in everyday life as well as through the lens of crime and law. This is because for Critical criminologists the core organising social science concepts, such as class and gender, are held to be both personal identities and social structures. As social structures, they contain culturally and historically specific rules which are institutionalised in the broader forms of the organisation of a society and serve to define the socio-economic status of a group and so the types of social opportunities members typically have open to them. As identities, they tell us about common social expectations concerning the behaviour of people from different groups which help to shape how people construct a sense of personal identity.

In this chapter we will examine how gender and culture act to shape and constrain human behaviour, including behaviour labelled as deviant or criminal. In doing so we will note how Feminist and Cultural theories of crime often highlight the deterministic nature of social structures, typically in the form of patriarchal relations and gendered socio-cultural ways of life which inherently discriminate against women. Yet we will also highlight how these perspectives also tend to emphasise the duality of structure. This is because they do acknowledge that we all clearly are in no small part a product of our social environment and that our practical circumstances do act in certain circumstances to constrain and shape our everyday behaviour. But at the same time they also reinforce that we nevertheless do possess agency and free will, and furthermore, certain structures in society can actually act to support and promote our agency and capacity to exercise free choice: for example, equal opportunities and human rights legislation and associated legal institutions such as the European Court of Human Rights, which was set up under the Council of Europe, currently has 47 member states, and enforces the European Convention on Human Rights. The extent to which such structures achieve their goal of promoting social equality, opportunity and justice is an area of continuing concern for many Critical criminologists, particularly when it comes to tackling at a broader institutional and socio-cultural level gender-based oppression and violence, such as, for example, rape as a weapon of war, domestic abuse and human trafficking.

THE FEMINIST CRITIQUE OF 'MALESTREAM' CRIMINOLOGY

It is a truism in the criminological study of deviance and crime that gender is a good predictor of the likelihood that an individual will engage in criminal behaviour. In short, men generally commit more crime and women generally commit less crime (Chamberlain, 2013). Yet it is arguable that criminology as a discipline did not get to grips with the gendered nature of crime until the emergence of Feminist criminology in the 1970s. This is not to say that crimes committed by women were before this time ignored by criminologists. Rather, what is of note is that mainstream criminology arguably reflected the broader social and cultural mores of the time which Feminist criminologists argued were discriminatory and served to promote a biased and negative view of women in general, let along female offenders. It is not too hard to see why they argued this point. Chapter 3 explored early approaches to crime, including the early

Biological criminology of Lombroso. As was discussed, Lombroso viewed criminals as evolutionary throwbacks who could be identified by atavistic stigmata present in their physical features. A key problem Lombroso faced was that, if men are superior to women, as demonstrated by their enhanced capacity for reason and moral action, and the criminal type is an evolutionary throwback, how come the vast majority of criminals were male?

In his 1895 book the *Female offender* (Lombroso, 1895), which was the first text ever written on women and crime, Lombroso put forward the idea that women had failed to reach the same evolutionary stage of development as men, and on his scale, white men were at the top and black women at the bottom. Lombroso argued that women in general, because they were not as well developed as men, had failed to evolve a moral sense and so would often lie and cheat. This Lombroso deduced from the fact, as he saw it, that women often lied about when they menstruated and about how much they masturbated, frequently had sexual frenzies and were subject to strong overwhelming passions for material goods and physical pleasures. Furthermore, he argued, they could be highly cruel to children and men who they professed to love. Hence, for Lombroso, they had a greater propensity for crime than man in general, but because they lacked reason and intelligence, as well as generally lacked the atavistic markings of Lombroso's criminal man, then clearly they were being held in check by their natural feminine inbred subservience to men. 'Rational man', in other words, held 'emotional women' in check. However, Lombroso recognised that because of evolution some women would develop more muscular strength and intelligence, and were 'born criminals, monsters, who belong more to the male than to the female sex, combining the worst aspects of womanhood – cunning spite and deceitfulness – with the criminal inclinations and callousness of men' (Lombroso, 1895: 152–3).

Although he didn't agree with all of Lombroso's ideas and research, William I Thomas certainly agreed that women were inferior to men. In his 1923 book *The unadjusted girl* (Thomas, 1923) he argued that this was as much a social and cultural as a biological fact. Thomas recognised that there had been matriarchal female-led societies as well as famous female leaders throughout human history. But he concluded that over time as societies became more complex women had been more and more relegated to the home making role, primarily due to their reproductive and maternal childcare role. For Thomas, women have a great desire for respect in the eyes of others, they are most concerned with what people think of them, and this can drive them to seek social respectability. However, some amoral women use their sexuality to get what they want. In *The unadjusted girl* he made the argument that as societies became more complex and women became increasingly more independent, entering the world of work, and less subject to social control through being kept in the home making role, their engagement in deviance and crime increased.

Thomas felt that both men and women were not suited to monogamous relationships. But women had been forced into them more than men because of their relegation to the home sphere and now, as society progressed through the early part of the twentieth century, they were experiencing more social freedoms. The result of this was that as they were no longer tied to the home they encountered more and more opportunities to act deviantly and criminally. Furthermore, Thomas held that their pent up sexual energy was finding release in deviant and even criminal acts; hence they were engaging in more drug use, having more illegal abortions, prostituting themselves for money, and generally committing more low level crime out of their wish for excitement and new experiences.

Thomas argued that women needed to be better controlled by men to stop their wanton desires, need for new experiences and increasing criminal behaviour from taking over their personalities. Like Thomas, Otto Pollak saw that women were coming more and more into the criminal sphere as society gradually changed and became freer during the twentieth century. In *The criminality of women* (Pollak, 1950) he argued that the real level of female crime was underreported. He argued that this was because their crimes are harder to detect and because the police are less likely to proceed with charges against women. This was the first development of what became known as the 'chivalry hypothesis': that women are let off crime by men precisely because they are women.

Pollak attributed the lower visibility and detection of female crime to their cunning and deceitful ways. He thought their willingness to fake sexual orgasm, hide their periods and have sexual frenzies showed that women are inherently deceitful. He also argued that for most of their lives women are subject to emotional, physiological and psychological imbalances due to having to experience menstruation, pregnancy and menopause. All of this he felt contributed to making them deceitful, vengeful and full of a mixture of anger and passion likely to reveal itself in deviance and criminality – albeit, as he saw it, a low level 'attention seeking' kind of crime such as shoplifting and minor drug and alcohol-related offences. He also claimed that some women deliberately sought out professions such as nursing, being a housemaid or teacher, which enabled them to commit crimes that were difficult to detect, such as stealing money or abusing children.

Taken together, the work of Pollak, Thomas and Lombroso reinforces that underpinning criminological thinking regarding gender and crime up until the 1960s was a view of women which was fundamentally contradictory. They were portrayed as calculating, deceitful monsters on the one hand, yet on the other hand, they were seen as being most suited to caring for children and staying at home to be safely looked after by men. By modern standards, such viewpoints can be quite legitimately accused of being misogynist. Yet it is important to remember that in many ways their work reflected broader social norms and values of the time concerning men and women, their respective makeup, as well as their roles within society in general and the family in particular. This was certainly the criticism made by the emerging second wave feminist movement of the mid-1960s onwards, which sought to challenge at a broader ideological level entrenched sexism.

Furthermore, the very idea that theories that explain male deviance and criminality can also be used to explain female deviance was challenged by the emergence of Feminist criminology. It was argued that mainstream criminology was, in fact, 'malestream' criminology, with the analysis of female offenders being limited to a handful of studies and gender and crime staying firmly off the criminological agenda. For example, the Feminist criminologist Carol Smart argued in her 1977 book, *Women, crime and criminology*, that:

> ... in comparison with the massive documentation on all aspects of male delinquency and criminality, the amount of work carried out on the area of women and crime is extremely limited. (Smart, 1977: 23)

It is important to acknowledge that several different strands of feminist thought emerged from the 1960s onwards which influenced the development of Feminist criminology; including Liberal Feminism, Marxist or Socialist Feminism, Radical Feminism and Black Feminism, to name but a few. There is not enough space in this chapter to explore either the emergence or key features of each of these feminist positions, not least because over the last two decades Lesbian, Disabled and Postmodern forms of feminism have also emerged to internally challenge these viewpoints and in doing so have helped to turn Feminist criminology into a highly complex field of study. Interested readers should see Walklate (2007) for more detail. For the purposes of this chapter suffice it to say that all these feminist standpoints share in common a concern with the marginalisation of women, as both perpetrators and victims, within criminological thinking and practice, as well as view this state of affairs as being symptomatic of broader gender-based inequalities present within contemporary society.

The concept of patriarchy lies at the centre of this analytical concern. Patriarchy means 'rule of the father' and it is held that the relegation of women to the private home sphere, centred around family life, is supported by cultural norms and values which seek to promote male power over women on the basis of their respective biological and reproductive roles; and what is more, these gender-based inequalities have over the course of human history become institutionalised within society's governing and regulatory institutions, including its criminal justice system. This is a point that we will return to throughout this chapter.

Over the last four decades Feminist criminology has engaged in a political project of seeking to address the gendered nature of crime, particularly violent and sex crime. The 2011/12 Crime Survey of England and Wales (CSEW) shows that there were 2.1 million violent incidents in England and Wales with 3 percent of adults victimised (Home Office, 2013a). The number of violent incidents has halved from its peak in 1995 when the survey estimated over 4.2 million violent incidents. Yet although overall crime is declining, gender-based violence and sex crime have stayed relatively static, and indeed, are held by most criminologists to be grossly underreported. For example, research shows that female victims of domestic violence are likely to be physically assaulted over 30 times before reporting an incident to the police (Chamberlain, 2013). The 2011/12 CSEW shows that 31 percent of women had experienced some form of domestic abuse (emotional, psychological, financial, physical) since the age of 16. These figures are equivalent to an estimated 5 million female victims of domestic abuse based on UK population figures. Furthermore, government statistics show that approximately 85,000 women are raped on average in England and Wales every year, over 400,000 women are sexually assaulted each year and 1 in 5 women (aged 16–59) has experienced some form of sexual violence since the age of 16 (Home Office, 2013b). Yet only 15 percent of serious sexual offences against people 16 and over are reported to the police and of the rape offences that are reported, fewer than 6 percent result in an offender being convicted of this offence (Home Office, 2013b).

These figures act as an important reminder that criminologists, Feminist and otherwise, have much left to do if they are to address the problem of violent and sex crime. Feminist criminology has been at the forefront of contemporary efforts to address gendered crimes such as domestic violence. In doing so they have advocated the need to provide victims with appropriate welfare support services to help them break the cycle of abuse, such as safe houses and refuges, while at the same time seeking reforms in the criminal justice system to ensure such women are protected from violent partners (Walklate, 2007). As an ongoing emancipatory political project, feminist scholarship has undoubtedly done much over the last five decades to highlight that while the majority of crime in general is done by men against men, certain types of crime are nevertheless gendered, with women continuing to suffer sexual and physical abuse in their homes, as well as sexism and misogyny in the public spheres of work and leisure. Yet in addition to seeking to help female victims of crime, Feminist criminology has also cast light on the question of why female involvement in crime seems to be increasing.

In the last decade the number of women in prison has doubled. In 2013 there were 85,340 people in prisons and young offender institutions in England and Wales. The male prison population is 81,374 and the female prison population is 3966 (Ministry of Justice, 2013a). It is clear from the crime statistics that although there are many more male prisoners than there are female, women offenders are capable of all types of crime, even those which transgress traditional conceptualisations of feminine nurturing characteristics, such as sexual offences against children. But perhaps most importantly the statistics show that in the last 10 years in the UK women's involvement in crime increased in the areas of violence against the person, robbery, fraud and forgery and criminal damage (Home Office, 2013a). This trend for women committing more crime isn't isolated to the UK. It seems to be the case that women in western nation-states are generally committing more crime. For example, in the US research has shown that in 1980 women comprised 20 percent of arrests for index crimes and only 13 percent of arrests for drug crimes. Index crimes are defined as murder, rape, robbery, street assault, burglary, grand larceny and car theft. Yet by 2008 women comprised over 30 percent of arrests for index crimes and almost 20 percent of arrests for drug crimes (Corman et al., 2010). The next section of this chapter looks at explanations why this may be the case, as put forward by Feminist criminologists.

- Early criminological examination of women and crime up until the 1950s was informed by the work of Cesare Lombroso, William Thomas and Otto Pollak. This by and large reflected the patriarchal socio-cultural norms and values of the time, which by today's standards would be judged as being sexist and misogynistic. Women were held to occupy a subservient role to men within society. They were expected to adhere to strict social norms regarding their behaviour and to stay in the private sphere of family life, focusing on their reproductive and home life roles. As a result, female offenders were held to be 'doubly deviant' on the basis that they were not just violating the rule of law when committing a crime but also socio-cultural norms regarding appropriate feminine behaviour.
- Over the last five decades Feminist criminology has engaged in a political project and advocated the need to address forms of gender-based violence and sexual abuse, such as domestic violence. It emerged against the background of feminism evolving as a social movement in the mid-1960s. It criticised mainstream criminology for failing to develop theories of female offending behaviour which did not solely rely on patriarchal thinking and empirical data which had emerged as a result of studying juvenile and/or adult male offenders. As a result, an emerging body of research into the female experience of crime as both victim and offender started to appear from the mid-1960s onwards.

Further reading

Lombroso, C (1895) *The female offender.* London: Fisher Unwin.
Pollak, O (1950) *The criminality of women.* Philadelphia: University of Pennsylvania Press.
Smart, C (1977) *Women, crime and criminology.* London: Routledge and Kegan Paul.
Thomas, WI (1923) *The unadjusted girl: with cases and standpoint for behaviour analysis.* Boston: Little Brown.
Walklate, S (2007) *Imagining the victim of crime.* Maidenhead: McGraw-Hill and Open University Press.

MARXISM AND FEMINIST CRIMINOLOGY

Given that Marxist criminology emerged during the same period of time in the 1970s it should perhaps come as no great surprise that early Feminist criminology of the period was influenced by the work of Marxist criminologists outlined in Chapter 5. However, this was a two-way process. Indeed, one of the key feminist contributions to Marxist thinking in the 1970s was the incorporation of a second aspect of social structure into theorising about the causes of crime in addition to class: namely, gender (Carlen, 1988). Specifically, this is what Messerschmidt (1986: ix) refers to as 'the relations of reproduction'. In the 1986 book *Capitalism, patriarchy and crime* Messerschmidt argues that all societies need people to produce offspring in order to maintain the human species and continuation of the nation-state. Consequently, people collectively organise into relations of reproduction in order to satisfy these needs and it is argued that in capitalist societies these organisations take the form of patriarchal gender relations. Here the male appropriates labour power and controls the sexuality of the female. Therefore, according to this viewpoint, the subjugation of women as a group to men as a group is entwined with class domination and the masculine gaze is levelled at all women regardless of where they are located in the class ladder.

Marxist-inspired Feminist criminologists like Carlen and Messerschmidt endeavoured to show how interlocking class and gender relations affect both criminal behaviour and the organisation of the criminal justice system. So the difference between male and female offending behaviour noted earlier in this chapter is partly explained by this position in terms of a lack of female opportunities for legitimate and illegitimate activities which results from the fact that women are subordinate to men and relegated to the private sphere of home life. In short, it is argued that women would engage in more crime if they could but they have less opportunity for crime than men do. This, it is held, explains why women are increasingly becoming involved in criminal activity as they have come to have more opportunities to commit crime over the last 40 years as they have gradually become more able to enter the public sphere of work and leisure. This, in turn, is a result of the fact that cultural expectations have changed and patriarchy has been challenged as a result of the activities of the feminist movement since the 1960s (Walklate, 2004).

Furthermore, it is held as a logical extension of this position that women from the lower end of the class spectrum – i.e. the unemployed and the working classes – are more likely to engage in crime precisely because they are more likely to suffer from class-based discrimination and social inequality. It is argued that this provides an additional incentive base from which criminal behaviour arises. This position is congruent with the Marxist criminological view, outlined in Chapter 5, that members of the working-class proletariat are more likely to become involved with the criminal justice system, as both victims and offenders, precisely because they suffer from inequality, exclusion and poor social mobility. The emphasis of Marxist forms of Feminist criminology on patriarchy, class, inequality and blocked opportunity influenced, firstly, the development of the economic marginalisation thesis, and secondly, the development of power/control theory. The chapter will outline power/control theory before discussing the economic marginalisation thesis.

Box 7.2   Key summary points

- Feminist and Marxist forms of criminology critiqued how crime was viewed and researched by mainstream criminology from the early 1970s onwards and this lead to much reflection by criminologists on the role of gender and class in structuring an individual's experience of crime, as both perpetrator and victim.

(Continued)

- Marxist-inspired Feminist criminology contributed to the development of contemporary forms of Critical criminology through highlighting the importance of focusing on, firstly, how some forms of violent and sex crime such as domestic violence appear to be inherently gendered crimes, secondly, that men and women at the lower end of the social class ladder are more likely to become involved in the criminal justice system, and thirdly, that female offending appears to have increased over the last several decades.

Further reading

Messerschmidt, JW (1986) *Capitalism, patriarchy and crime.* Totowa, NJ: Rowman and Littlefield.

Walklate, S (2004, 2nd edn) *Gender, crime and criminal justice.* Cullompton: Willan Publishing.

THE GROWTH OF FEMALE OFFENDING: POWER/CONTROL THEORY, THE LIBERATION OPPORTUNITY THESIS AND THE ECONOMIC MARGINALISATION THESIS

Over the last 40 years research has documented the differential socialisation of sons and daughters within families to such a degree that it is a truism that fathers and mothers treat their sons and daughters differently, often without realising it, and in doing so socialise their children into different gender roles. Furthermore, a number of researchers have also shown that social class is a mediating factor in gender socialisation. It has been found that parents from poorer and lower social class backgrounds are more rigid in socialising their children according to traditional gender roles when compared to parents from the higher end of the class spectrum (Walklate, 2004).

John Hagan and his colleagues (Hagan et al., 1990) postulated that differences in male and female youth offending rates are a direct result of this differing socialising process. However, he also grounds his theory in the premise that power relations within the family are derived from power relations in the public sphere and that these are gendered. For Hagan, therein lies the relationship between class relations, gender and offending behaviour. He writes:

> ... that particular form of structural criminology that we propose here, power-control theory, argues that to understand the effects of class position in the workplace on crime and delinquency it is important to trace the way that work relations structure family relations, particularly relations between fathers and mothers, and in turn, relations between parents and their children, especially mothers and daughters. (Hagan et al., 1990: 1025)

Hagan identifies that the gendered division of labour present within the traditional family model of westernised industrial societies, such as the UK and US, places the husband-father outside of the private sphere of family life and in the public sphere of paid labour; in short, he is the family breadwinner. In contrast, the wife-mother remains at home to care for the household and children. In effect, she becomes an ever present agent of socialisation in the family home from which the children learn their respective gender roles as they develop, particularly in their first years before school. Tacitly accepting this gendered division of labour, indeed in many ways actively reproducing it through her interaction with her children, the mother imposes different social controls and expectations on her sons than daughters.

Hagan focuses on how in the traditional family arrangement daughters are expected to become wives and mothers and are therefore socialised by their mothers to be domestically focused even if they expect them to seek and maintain some form of paid work as they grow up. Hence, daughters become like their mothers, domesticated, controlled and unlikely to become involved in antisocial and criminal acts. Sons, on the other hand, are subject to less direct maternal control, are expected to go out into the world and take risks, and consequently, are more likely to engage in antisocial and criminal behaviour. Hagan argued that the traditional patriarchal family form is most common in lower-class households.

In contrast to this patriarchal family is the egalitarian family. Here both parents work outside of the home. A key result of this is the lessening of maternal control over children. This is particularly important in relation to the role of the daughter. In these homes both parents are dominant and equal. Hagan's research showed that in such homes, both parents share positions of equal dominance in the family, with the result that daughters' behaviour tends to parallel sons'. The result is that they are more likely to take risks and become involved in delinquent and criminal behaviour; particularly alcohol-related delinquency and low level minor theft such as shoplifting. A key critique of power/control theory is that although Hagan did not directly state so, it nevertheless seems to be the case that what is being argued is that women's liberation and female employment is causing daughters to engage in antisocial activity and crime (Walklate, 2004). However, for many criminologists, power/control theory reinforced the need to focus on the intersection of economic inequality, gender and crime, with the result that the economic marginalisation thesis has come to represent a powerful force in contemporary Feminist criminology.

The relationship between gender and crime and changes therein, with the empirical data seeming to suggest that female offending has increased, has been linked by criminologists to the presence of increased opportunities in society for women over the last 100 years. That is, as women became more liberated from their home and family roles, greater opportunities for crime have presented themselves, both in the workplace and in society at large. To a certain degree, such a conclusion appears to be logically consistent with the position that men and women are equal. Indeed, the Feminist criminologist Freda Adler, in her 1975 book *Sisters in crime*, argued that an increase in female offending behaviour should be expected and in doing so she put forward what became termed as the 'liberation opportunity thesis'. Adler argued that women were becoming more masculine in their character and attitude as they entered the workplace in increasing numbers and that this, combined with the presence of greater opportunities for crime as a result of entering the public sphere, caused the increase in female antisocial behaviour and offending.

The liberation opportunity thesis has been criticised for failing to acknowledge that the types of crime women seem to engage in, such as fraud, shoplifting, prostitution and drug-related crime, are all often referred to by criminologists as 'survival crimes'. Survival crimes have an economic focus based on providing an income and typically do not involve the offender being physically violent to another person. For example, Mullins and Wright (2003) investigated burglary and conducted research with men and women who had been convicted of this crime. They found that while men often reported they stole to enable them to abuse drugs or alcohol, women were more likely to report they were using the money they made from burglary to take care of their children. For instance, one female respondent stated that:

> 'I needed money, cause I need a roof over my head, food to eat, things for my baby ... cause I needed nappies and I was broke and, you know, my hours had been cut and I didn't have the money to pay rent plus to get the baby what it needed, you know, it's gonna be cold soon, I need winter clothes for my kid.' (Mullins and Wright, 2003: 835)

It could be argued that the participants in Mullins and Wright's research were rhetorically self-justifying their criminal behaviour. But for Feminist criminologists, statements like these provided evidence for the feminisation of poverty and as a result what they termed the economic marginalisation thesis.

The economic marginalisation thesis argues that in contemporary societies such as the UK and US, many women may well no longer be tied to the home making and mothering roles, as well as to seem to enjoy greater personal independence and improved economic and social positions in society than they did several generations ago. It might also be the case that women are more and more engaging in employment-related crimes, which they arguably couldn't engage in before, such as fraud and embezzlement. Nevertheless, it is important to note that much of the work they do is low-paid and part-time as well as that they are more likely to be subject to unemployment, be dependent on welfare benefits, suffer from poverty and, most importantly, the harmful effects of male criminality, i.e. domestic violence. Such considerations reinforce the fact that a great number of women are economically marginal, possessing far less real economic power than their male counterparts, as well as that this marginality has an effect on the intersection of the negative features of class and gender. This state of affairs reinforces how:

> ... women offenders tend to be poor, [as well as] ... members of minority groups, and have truncated education and spotty employment histories. These [are] precisely the women whose lives were largely unaffected by the gains, such as they were, of the essentially white, middle-class women's rights movement. (Chesney-Lind, 1987: 12)

The economic marginalisation thesis reinforces the importance of paying attention to class when analysing gender and crime. As with men, young female offenders and adult women in prison are more likely to come from lower socio-economic groups than higher ones. However, of course, this is not to say that all women (or men for that matter) who belong to economically and socially marginalised groups in society commit crime. Or that middle-class teenage girls or professional career women in their thirties don't commit crime and find themselves in trouble with the police. Far from it. But this state of affairs arguably reinforces the need to address offending behaviour through social policy and employment and education initiatives, rather than becoming overly focused on retribution and punishment. Certainly, the economic marginalisation thesis has led over the last two decades to a substantial body of work looking at how women are treated by the criminal justice system (Walklate, 2004). However it is open to the criticism that, as with Feminist criminology in general, it arguably possesses a highly restricted conception of men and the male criminal. This is a point we will touch on in the next section, which examines the contemporary influence of both feminist and masculinity studies on the criminological study of crime.

Box 7.3   Key summary points

- Since the 1970s a key feature of Feminist criminology has been the exploration of why female offending has risen as a result of female liberation from the private sphere of home and family life, with more and more women entering the public spheres of work and leisure.
- Power/control theory focuses on the role of the differential socialisation of young women and men in working-class and middle-class families, along with the growing economic independence of middle-class women, in shaping anti-social behaviour and criminal behaviour amongst teenage girls. Power/control theory has been heavily criticised by Feminist criminologists for seeming to equate an increase in antisocial and offending behaviour amongst young women with greater female liberation from the traditional feminine home maker and mothering roles.
- The liberation opportunity thesis argues that as men and women become more equal in society it should come as no surprise that as more and more women enter the public spheres of work and leisure female offending will increase as greater opportunities for crime present themselves.
- The economic marginalisation thesis argues that the liberation opportunity thesis does not account for the fact that class and gender intersect, with women frequently being economically dependent on social welfare and/or economically marginalised into low-paid and poor status part-time employment; which keeps them economically dependent upon male employment. It is argued that the increase in female crime is a result of working-class women in particular being more likely to commit 'survival crimes', such as petty theft, as a result of their economical marginalisation and the need to provide for their family.

(Continued)

(Continued)

Further reading

Adler, F (1975) *Sisters in crime: the rise of the new female criminal.* New York: McGraw-Hill.
Chesney-Lind, M (1987) *Girls' crime and women's place.* Honolulu: University of Hawaii Press.
Hagan, J, Gillis, AR and Simpson, J (1990) Clarifying and extending power-control theory. *The American Journal of Sociology* 95 (4): 1024–37.
Mullins, CW and Wright, R (2003) Gender, social networks and residential burglary. *Criminology* 41 (3) 813–40.
Walklate, S (2004, 2nd edn) *Gender, crime and criminal justice.* Cullompton: Willan Publishing.

FEMINISM, MASCULINITY STUDIES AND CONTEMPORARY CRITICAL CRIMINOLOGY: HIGHLIGHTING THE IMPORTANCE OF GENDER, RACE AND CLASS

The emergence of Feminist criminology over time led to a reassessment within criminology of how masculinity is viewed. From around the late 1980s onwards criminology turned its attention to the question of why crime is predominately a male activity. As already discussed, many Feminist criminologists argue that the concept of patriarchy demonstrates how all men have power over women. However, some criminologists criticised this idea as they felt men cannot be so easily placed into a single category in this manner. In short, it was argued that men are not a homogeneous group, and indeed, that men have different types of masculine experience and enact masculinity in different ways, not all of which actively seek to subordinate women. An important concept relating to this analysis is hegemonic masculinity.

This concept was first put forward by Connell (1995), in her book *Masculinities*, who argued that hegemonic masculinity is the dominant cultur-ally approved yardstick against which men create and define themselves as men and distance themselves from women, as well as just as importantly subordinate other forms of masculinity, such as homosexuality or 'new men' who are in touch with their emotions and feelings. Indeed, Connell argued that within western nation-states a particular form of hegemonic masculinity has emerged to cultural dominance which subordinates homosexuality and other forms of masculinity in favour of an idea of what it is to be a man based around competitive individualism, independence, aggression, a capacity for violence and heterosexuality. Hence men, to be 'real men', must avoid all things feminine, restrict emotions severely, show toughness and aggression, exhibit self-reliance, strive for achievement and social status, and actively engage in homophobia.

But it does not mean that all men act this way all the time or that there is not a multiplicity of ways to enact 'maleness'. Yet this particular form of hegemonic masculinity provides a framework in which most men can locate their sense of self, 'do' gender, and construct a masculine identity in social situations, both with other men and with women. This position led to the growing recognition within criminology that for many men, crime serves as a resource for doing gender: the aggressive risk-taking behaviour often associated with acts of criminality, both violent and otherwise, signifies to others and the perpetrator that they *are* men as this is how men should act. Additionally, Critical criminologists such as Messerschmidt (1997, 2004) pointed out that in addition to gender and class, it is important to pay close attention to the interaction of race and ethnicity.

Messerschmidt (1997) agreed with Connell that cultural expectations about gender and what it is to be a man can lead some young men, in the right social circumstances, to use crime to show that they are men in the eyes of both themselves and others. But Messerschmidt was also concerned with looking at how class and race intersect with gender in relation to masculinity and crime and exploring how working-class white and black males in inner-city areas from poor and disruptive family backgrounds can become more marginalised if for various reasons they don't achieve, or choose to reject, forms of masculinity and associated social statuses and rewards linked with academic achievement. Instead, they might construct their masculinities around acts of antisocial behaviour and physical aggression, involvement in gang-related activity, as well as the use of racist and homophobic language and actions, all of which are designed to demonstrate toughness and physical power.

Messerschmidt found from talking to young men that the material and economic rewards of crime were often secondary to an attempt in their eyes to prove their maleness to themselves and others by enacting the culturally dominant western hegemonic form of masculinity noted by Connell. Importantly, he also found that young men of colour can suffer from the same masculine pathway as young working-class white males, but that their involvement is also heavily influenced by the historical legacy of discrimination against black and Asian groups, which disproportionately subject ethnic groups to the social and economic disadvantages that tend to breed violence (DeKeseredy, 2011).

What is being pointed out here is that young working-class male involvement in crime, regardless of colour, which arguably is the dominant social problem for contemporary criminologists, the criminal justice system and society as a whole, isn't simply a result of the biology or psychology or free will of the male offender, but rather, is due in no small part to an intersection between social deprivation and discrimination with a hegemonic form of masculinity which rewards aggressive behaviour and is arguably endemic throughout the cultural fabric of society as a whole as the dominant idea of what it should be to be a man. Indeed, Messerschmidt subsequently did some life history research with girls who engage in violent assault and concluded that both teenage boys and girls – white and black – seek to display themselves and acts of violence in masculine ways (Messerschmidt, 2004). This reinforces the importance for contemporary Critical criminology to focus on the complex and nuanced relationships which exist between class, gender, race and crime (Feilzer and Hood, 2004).

It is undoubtedly the case that class-, gender- and race-based inequalities permeate western nation-states and criminal justice systems. The Asian male prison population in the UK grew by 261 percent between 1985 and 2009, while the last 10 years have seen a gradual increase in the number of Middle Eastern and Eastern European offenders entering the UK criminal justice system (May, 2010). Criminological research has repeatedly shown over the last four decades that ethnic minority groups and individuals from working-class backgrounds are disproportionally overrepresented in the criminal justice system; that black, Asian and mixed-raced youths are more often subject to formal criminal justice processes and frequently get higher penal tariffs than their white counterparts; as well as that young female offenders are similarly often treated more punitively than their male counterparts (white or otherwise) while at the same time often being the victims of gender-based violence (Maguire et al., 2012).

However, we must be careful to not overemphasise the deterministic nature of social structure – be it conceptualised in the form of class, race or gender – in shaping our sense of personal identity or the exercise of our freedom of choice and action. Contemporary Critical criminological forms of scholarship, of which Feminist criminology is one strand, emphasise that human beings and their actions are not wholly determined by the environment in which they live and indeed that social structures in the form of society's institutions (i.e. its schools, churches, political and regulatory bodies and so on) can act to promote human agency as well as tackle inequality and gender- racial- and class-based forms of discrimination (DeKeseredy, 2011). For example, it has been argued by Feminist criminologists that the problem of domestic violence needs to be addressed as part of the personal and sex education curriculum at both primary and secondary school levels (Walklate, 2004).

Box 7.4   Key summary points

- Criminologists concerned with masculinity and crime have highlighted how Feminist criminology up until the 1990s seemed to promote a highly limited view of masculinity, treating men as a homogeneous group who collectively benefit from the presence of patriarchal ideology within society. Rather it is argued that men have different types of masculine experience and enact masculinity in different ways, not all of which actively seek to subordinate women.
- An important development within contemporary Critical criminology, which is grounded in the emergence of Feminist and Marxist criminology with their respective concerns for gender (male and female) and class, has been the advent of viewpoints which highlight the importance of race in shaping an individual's experience of crime, as both victim and offender.

Further reading

Connell, R (1995) *Masculinities.* Cambridge: Polity Press.
DeKeseredy, WS (2011) *Contemporary critical criminology.* London: Routledge.
Feilzer, M and Hood, R (2004) *Difference in discrimination?* London: Youth Justice Board.
Maguire, M, Morgan, R and Reiner, R (2012, 5th edn) *The Oxford handbook of criminology.* Oxford: Oxford University Press.
May, T (2010) *Statistics on race and the criminal justice system.* London: Ministry of Justice.
Messerschmidt, JW (1997) *Crime as structured action: gender, race, class, and crime in the making.* Thousand Oaks, CA: Sage.
Messerschmidt, JW (2004) *Flesh and blood: adolescent gender diversity and violence.* Lanham, MD: Rowman and Littlefield.

CULTURAL CRIMINOLOGY

Cultural criminology emerged in the 1990s and is influenced by an eclectic mix of themes and ideas centred around examining links between popular culture, style and criminality, with the goal of understanding the meanings and emotions associated with the lived experience of crime and the criminal act, against the backdrop of a concern with social control and the role of the media in representing crime and criminality in different ways. To achieve this it has drawn on a range of different ideas and perspectives to examine the topic of culture, emotions and crime, some of which we have already covered, including Left Realism, feminism, anomie and Strain Theory, symbolic interactionism and Labelling Theory. It is also heavily influenced by cultural studies, media studies and film studies. Cultural criminology emphasises the creative social actor who gives meaning to their existence themselves every day of their lives and does not presume that social structures such as class, race or gender, either together or individually, create criminality and deviance or the societal reaction to them (DeKeseredy, 2011).

Two particularly intellectually important starting points for understanding Cultural criminology are subcultural theory and the concept of moral panic. Chapter 5 discussed the emergence of symbolic interactionism and Labelling Theory. Amongst other things, the chapter discussed the development of Strain Theory and the work of Merton and his argument that criminal behaviour was an outgrowth of strains that people experience because of their particular positions in the structure of a society. Many criminologists used the work of Merton to study a particular form of criminal behaviour – gang delinquency. One of these, Albert Cohen, took exception to Merton's depiction of criminal behaviour being essentially a rational reaction undertaken to achieve a desired end or goal, i.e. to relieve the feeling of strain. Although Cohen felt this may be the case with some types of crime, he recognised that this did not apply to most of the activities of delinquent gangs of young men he saw on the streets of Chicago around him, who he noted tended to come from lower-class neighbourhoods.

In his book *Delinquent boys: the culture of the gang* (1955) Cohen summarised his research into various youth gangs. He identified five interrelated characteristics which he argued were intrinsic to lower-class delinquent gangs and together comprise a delinquent subculture. Firstly, *non-utilitarianism*: Cohen agreed with Merton that people steal because they want things for some reason but he also found that often people in gangs stole for the hell of it, just because it was fun and came attached with a sense of profound satisfaction, glory and prowess, for gang members. Importantly, Cohen is identifying here that crime is an emotional event not just a rational choice or a product of social deprivation. Yes, people often stole because they needed money or food, but they also stole for fun and the mere excitement and thrill of stealing. Cohen noted that this was often the main reason behind acts of deviance and crime by gangs of young people. Secondly, *maliciousness*: Cohen noted that much gang delinquency and antisocial behaviour was just plain mean and caused problems for the people living in neighbourhoods. Indeed, he found that acts of vandalism were often done by gang members for the thrill of making others unhappy. Thirdly, *negativism*: Cohen noted that gangs had their own codes and values and rules for behaviour, and these often were the polar opposite of what they perceived as being the dominate culture of a society. Indeed, he argued that a delinquent subculture takes its norms from the larger culture but turns them upside down. Fourthly, *short-run hedonism*: Cohen argued that most gang members were into short-term fun, with young people seeking immediate gratification, with little regard for long-term gains and losses. Fifthly, *group autonomy*: Cohen argued that gang members resist any kind of restraint on their behaviour except from that imposed informally by gang members, so they seek to defy the authority of parents, teachers and other agents of social control, such as the police.

Cohen argued that gang membership was a response to the strains young people experience when they are confronted and judged. He felt that the dominant culture of the time was middle-class and argued that this consisted of values such as delayed gratification, self-control, ambition, academic and occupational success, good manners and a respect for property. He argued that middle-class parents exert pressure on their children to abide by these values; however, the socialisation of working-class children was, he argued, more relaxed. And the key problem Cohen noted was that once lower-class children enter school behavioural problems can start because schools are institutions governed by middle-class values. They are therefore at a disadvantage and if they can't achieve social status from academic or other related means, such as through participation in sports, they experience status frustration. This was particularly a problem for boys. If they couldn't achieve a masculine role through status attainment by doing well at school academically or in sports and so on, then they might express their frustration by being aggressive towards others. Consequently, a delinquent subculture could be seen as a lower-class boys' collective response and solution to the problem of status frustration, as since they cannot acquire status by conforming to middle-class values, they reject them and create their own, against which they can be judged by their peers. So in a gang they can prove their masculinity and raise their status, especially if they excel at delinquent activities.

Cohen's analysis was highly influential and led to a number of studies being subsequently published over the following decades into youth subcultures and gangs. Subcultures were defined, following Cohen, as smaller, more localised and differentiated structures, which are to varying degrees related to larger cultural networks, i.e. working-class culture in Britain can be defined against other class subcultures, such as middle-class culture, as well as English culture more broadly. A number of studies focused on deviant and rule breaking youth subcultures such as mods and rockers, punks and goths, ravers and emos, from the 1950s onwards. One particularly important subcultural analysis was conducted by Stan Cohen, who was concerned with the subculture of mods and rockers (Cohen, 1973). Cohen was concerned with how a subculture was a particular way of life which expresses certain meanings and values in the fields of work, leisure and education. He argued that subcultures, particularly youth subcultures, are often in tension with each other, while the dominate culture and the media played a key role in mediating and resolving perceived threats to society posed by unruly youths. In his now classic book *Folk devils and moral panics* (1973) Cohen argued that the media played a key role in representing young people as a social problem and their behaviour as a moral panic. Cohen (1973: 9) argued that a moral panic occurs when '[a] condition, episode, person or group of persons emerges to become defined as a threat to societal values and interests'. This threat is then used to justify an overly punitive approach to dealing with the problem of deviance and crime, while also affirming the norms and values of dominant cultural groups.

Influenced by the work of Albert Cohen and Stan Cohen, Cultural criminology emerged in the 1990s to focus on the role of the mass media in representing transgressive behaviour in order to analyse how crime has become a cultural concept which is loaded with popular cultural references and influences. From this perspective, contemporary society is media saturated. Global electronic communication systems have made time and space much more immediate than they have been: with a click of a mouse or push of a button we can access a whole range of live events as they happen around the world via the internet or TV. As a result, the world is now awash with constantly changing information, images and signs. One dimension of this is the cultural meanings attached to such things as crime, criminals, deviance, heroes and monsters. We consume crime via a range of media-driven formats, such as TV dramas, video games and movies. While on a day-to-day level we live through a constant barrage of new images concerned with the problem of crime as we consume 24-hour news. These meanings are produced, reproduced, circulated, reshaped, absorbed or rejected, in a variety of complex and continuous processes of interaction and interpretation involving a range of information sharing technologies, including news channels, social networking sites and daily newspapers. Each day via the mass media individuals enjoy their 15 minutes of fame or infamy; violent criminals are transformed and romanticised into lovable rogues and celebrities; and whole communities and sections of society are stigmatised as the barbarians at the gate, while exploited migrant labour is recast as a threat to the British way of life.

In this frenzy of media images and signs, where the mass media are the mediators of reality as we perceive it, the distinction between fact and fiction dissolves. Hollywood and Croydon, or Moss Side, or Toxteth, are worlds apart, and yet they interconnect in new ways every day, scripting each other's behaviours as they enter the hyper-reality of the globalised multi-media, multi-platform, network. Hence, instead of seeking the causes of crime, which is seen as a futile task, Cultural criminologists turn their attention to the ways in which representations of crime and criminals are socially constructed by the mass media and reproduced in the form of textual images and sound bites. The concern, then, is with how the media choose to focus on particular crimes and criminals in particular ways, create moral panics and folk devils, and amplify the deviancy of the events they present us with. So every act of deviance, crime or social unrest signifies that British society is on the brink of collapse, is morally bankrupt and in terminal decline. We are all surrounded by violent gangs of teenagers, drunken and threatening weekend drinkers, paedophiles and sex offenders, as well as terrorists and criminal kingpins. They lurk around every corner, waiting for their chance to strike.

Hence Cultural criminology focuses on how social order and control is maintained through the promotion of a culture of fear, while it emphasises that cultural meanings arise as interactional processes, in which individuals play an active and creative role, in creating and responding to deviance and crime. Cultural criminologists, such as Ferrell et al. (2004), emphasise the agency of the individual, and since people create meaning and culture every day through their interaction, they prefer to use qualitative ethnographic research methods to gather data, looking at how the cultural meaning of crime, deviance and transgression amongst those involved in such events is created and shared in the moment as they happen. So a Cultural criminologist would argue we can only explore and understand crime by actually going out and being there as it is committed by people, rather than just sitting at home and watching it on TV. They also emphasise criminal and deviant behaviour in terms of the emotion, thrill and excitement. This is because Cultural criminology is heavily influenced by the work of Katz (1988) on the sensual attractions to crime.

Towards a criminology of the emotions

In the 1988 book *Seductions of crime* Katz (1988) explores the relationship between doing crime and the emotional states of the offender. He is looking then at the compulsions and seductions which are felt by people as they engage in criminal activity and which draw them into pursuing what he calls criminal projects. He argues that it is necessary to understand crime through the eyes of the people doing it and what it feels for them when they do it. He examines a range of crimes, including murder, robbery, gang violence and burglary, and finds that offenders feel what he calls a family of emotions, which include humiliation, righteousness, arrogance, ridicule, cynicism, defilement and vengeance, to name but a few. He says that the closer we look at crime and the relevant emotions attached to it, the more we can see how people emotionally respond to deviance and crime, delighting in being deviant, taking pride in having a bad reputation, enjoying taking vengeance on somebody who they feel did them wrong. Katz argues that, from the offenders' perspective, the emotional attraction proves to be the most fundamentally compelling when the offenders sees themselves as enacting transgressions, deviant acts or simply breaking the law, in order to overcome a personal challenge in their own existence. Indeed, he often writes as if the offender undergoes an almost uplifting spiritual experience of self-overcoming when they commit crime.

Crime is, then, a self-project which some people do to escape from mundane, everyday, routine, boring life. Crime embodies a creative exploration of emotional worlds. It 'expands the possibilities of the self … [and] … ways of behaving that previously seemed inaccessible' (Katz, 1988: 73). This focus on the emotionality of sneaky thrills – such as shoplifting, graffiti painting, joyriding and drug use – is also discussed by Lyng (1990), who argues that people flirt with danger and perform 'edgework' – that is do potentially dangerous activities such as sky diving and tombstoning – for the emotional high they get when they survive the leap. For Cultural criminologists, we all like our sneaky thrills. Presdee (2000) explores this in his carnival of crime thesis. He is concerned with the broader criminalisation of everyday life in which 'everyday responses to modern, highly commodified, society become themselves defined as criminal' (Presdee, 2000: 15). Presdee's main concern is with how it is a crime to be many things, 'including poor, young, disadvantaged, to fail and even at times to be creative' (Presdee, 2000: 162). He argues that much of the crime occurring in society, especially relating to social disorder, is a product of the fact that the existing relationships of production within society force us to lead two separate lives. Our first life is our official life, and is characterised by formal education and the world of work and so imposed social order, which provides us with the means to sustain our physical existence. In contrast, our second life is where we live out our fantasies and obtain emotional fulfilment. It runs counter to the sense of alienation caused by what he calls the rhythms of production in the first life. In doing so it seeks to restore some meaning to our lives and personal control over our existence. During the course of living out this second life, which Presdee calls our 'carnival of leisure', he says the boundaries of social order are frequently crossed, leading us into what he calls the 'carnival of crime'. We can, in effect, consume crime during our leisure activities, not just through our diet of entertainment, but also when the commoditisation of excitement that characterises much of our leisure time is taken just that one step further; while the arrival of new technologies has transformed how we consume and participate in crime. Indeed, in Presdee's view, the internet has become a safe site for the second life of people where they can test society's boundaries if they need to as it provides an environment 'where we can enjoy in private immoral acts and emotions', ranging from internet pornography to illegal file sharing and computer hacking (Presdee, 2000: 64). While in the context of applying such ideas at a broader level, Moore and Measham (2012) explore the recreational use of drugs in the context of second life activity, detailing as they do so how part of the sneaky thrills of such activity often lie in the fact that it allows the user to enter and consume a second life world of everyday criminality which is often highly divorced from the rest of their life.

Critiquing Cultural criminology

Cultural criminology is concerned with a range of activities, such as body modification, joyriding, sadomasochist clubs, raving, drug use, gang rituals, the internet, festivals and extreme sports, to name but a few. It also argues that boredom, resulting from experiences of alienation and anomie in the media-saturated world we live in, and the search to live out a second life to escape from it, can provide the basis of forms of crime and deviance. As Ferrell (2004: 294) says, 'so while some die a day at a time, others seek to overturn organized boredom ... with a spray can'. It is certainly the case that this focus on the emotionality of crime has done much to reinvigorate contemporary Critical criminology through enabling it to better address the practical problem of how best to tackle the social inequalities which permeate the everyday lived experience of crime; as both victim and offender. However, Cultural criminology has been heavily criticised for its heavy focus on high profile crime, social deviants and moral panics, and in doing so seemingly trying to create a criminology exclusively made up of 'nuts, sluts and perverts ... [and] ... the exotic, the erotic and the neurotic' (Adler and Adler, 2003: 79).

It certainly does seem to be the case that Cultural criminology over-stylises crime and makes it feel attractive and everyday – when reading the work of key Cultural criminologists such as Ferrell it can feel like you are locked into a Hollywood version of crime, deviance and social order. This is somewhat ironic given Cultural criminology's take on the commodification of crime. Also, and perhaps most importantly, Cultural criminology arguably overemphasises 'the cultural' at the expense of social-structural factors, such as gender and class-based inequalities. Therefore it can and does often detach individuals from background factors such as poverty, education and politics. Yes, it does talk about alienation and capitalism, but because it refuses to look at the causes of crime, it really can't explain how cultural experiences are situated within broader social-economic conditions. While it arguably also avoids issues to do with harm and morality and, like Marxism, can paint an over-romanticised picture of the criminal behaviour of the socially excluded working classes. Perhaps the key problem with Cultural criminology is that its focus on the criminals' self-reported lived experience of their crimes can lead to the victims' lived experience being displaced from the centre of the narrative. Indeed, it is important to recognise that Katz's (1988) work on the emotionality and seductions of crime does not include crimes such as sex killings and sexual assaults, and this is precisely because of the need to prioritise bringing to the foreground the victim's experience and voice when analysing such crimes.

Box 7.5   Key summary points

- Cultural criminology emerged in the 1990s and is influenced by an eclectic mix of themes and ideas centred around examining links between popular culture, style and criminality, with the goal of understanding the meanings and emotions associated with the lived experience of crime and the criminal act, against the backdrop of a concern with social control and the role of the media in representing crime and criminality in different ways. To achieve this goal Cultural criminology draws on a range of different ideas and perspectives to examine its topic of culture, emotions and crime, including Left Realism, feminism, anomie and Strain Theory, symbolic interactionism and Labelling Theory.
- The focus of Cultural criminology on the emotionality of crime has done much to reinvigorate contemporary Critical criminology by enabling it to better address the practical problem of how best to tackle the social inequalities which permeate the everyday lived experience of crime; as both victim and offender. However, Cultural criminology has been heavily criticised for its heavy focus on high profile crime, social deviants and moral panics, and in doing so seemingly trying to create a criminology exclusively made up of 'nuts, sluts and perverts … [and] … the exotic, the erotic and the neurotic' (Adler and Adler, 2003: 79). It also can be accused of displacing the victim from the centre of criminology.

Further reading

Adler, PA and Adler, P (2003) *Constructions of deviance: social power, context, and interaction*. Belmont, CA: Wadsworth.

Cohen, AK (1955) *Delinquent boys: the culture of the gang*. Glencoe, IL: The Free Press.

Cohen, S (1973) *Folk devils and moral panics*. St Albans: Paladin.

Ferrell, J (2004) Boredom, crime, and criminology. *Theoretical Criminology* 8 (3): 287–302.

Ferrell, J, Hayward, K, Morrison, W and Presdee, M (eds) (2004) *Cultural criminology unleashed*. London: Cavendish/Glasshouse.

Katz, J (1988) *Seductions of crime*. New York: Basic Books.

Lyng, S (1990) Edgework: a social psychological analysis of voluntary risk taking. *American Journal of Sociology* 95 (4): 851–86.

Presdee, M (2000) *Cultural criminology and the carnival of crime*. London: Routledge.

8 POSTMODERN CRITICAL STANDPOINTS AND THE CRIMINAL LIFE COURSE

CHAPTER OVERVIEW

The chapter explores the development of the contemporary Critical criminological concern with the life course of offending behaviour. It begins by outlining how

(Continued)

(Continued)

Critical criminological positions encompass a range of differing approaches, all of which have their own particular emphases and nuances, and furthermore, they have been categorised under various headings, including Marxist criminology, Radical criminology, Left Realism, Feminist criminology, Sociological criminology or the Sociology of Deviance, Peacemaking criminology and Cultural criminology, to name but a few. This chapter then discusses how influencing the development of Critical standpoints in criminology and the emphasis on the duality of structure has been the rejection of positivism and the emergence of postmodern sensibilities. This leads on to discuss how postmodernist anti-realist viewpoints accord equal validity to all perspectives and voices. This position is congruent with contemporary Critical criminology perspectives, such as Cultural criminology, as well as qualitative research methodologies. It has led to the development of an increasing focus within criminology over the last three decades on narrative and biographical life story forms of qualitative research as part of a broader concern with tracing the life course of offending behaviour.

The chapter then discusses how the development of Life Course criminology is not solely bound up with the postmodern narrative turn within Critical forms of criminology. Indeed, Life Course criminology can arguably trace its roots back to the early Chicago School discussed in Chapter 5. The chapter highlights how Life Course criminology focuses on tracing over time the life trajectories and stories of criminals. As well as that it is viewed as an integrated theory of crime in that it seeks to incorporate both developmental biological-psychological and social factors within its analysis of the criminal career trajectory from youth delinquency to adult offending. The chapter then explores two influential Life Course theories: Moffitt's Dual Taxonomy (1993) and Sampson and Laub's Age Graded Stability and Change Model (1993).

After outlining these respective theories, the chapter concludes by highlighting that research does seem to show that institutions, such as the family, school, employment and so on, have differing capacities to modify criminal trajectories at different stages in the life course. It is suggested that during the early years family relationships are important in shaping behaviour, however as children grow direct parental impact lessens and peer groups and social institutions such as schools become more important, while in adulthood schools and parents both take a backseat to jobs and spouses as primary mechanisms for social control. As a result Life Course criminologists often argue for the value of implementing a broad range of preventive school and penal system based interventions to promote a change in the criminal career trajectory. However, it is noted that this approach is often at odds with the more punitive Right Realist youth crime agenda of most western societies of the last three decades, which has seen an increase in juvenile punishment and incarceration rates worldwide.

INTRODUCTION: CRITICAL CRIMINOLOGY REVISITED

This chapter builds on the material covered in previous chapters to examine the impact of postmodernism on contemporary criminology as well as the emergence of a life course perspective, which is a somewhat relatively new way of thinking about how an individual's life is determined through the occurrence of certain life events, including their experience of deviant and criminal acts, both as victim and offender. Previous chapters have historically traced the development of criminology as a discipline by examining the emergence in western societies over the last 200 years of rational choice, psychological, biological and sociological theoretical approaches to examining the causes of crime. In doing so, the chapters reinforced the value of acknowledging the role of psychological and biological factors in influencing human behaviour, particularly when examining topics such as the care and treatment of mentally disordered as well as violent and sex offenders, while at the same time emphasising the central role of society in both creating and shaping responses to the problem of crime. Indeed, contemporary academic criminology is arguably dominated by a critical concern with issues of social diversity, power and inequality when it comes to addressing the highly complex and multilayered problem that is crime (Young, 2011).

The historical development of Critical criminological positions discussed from Chapter 6 onwards readily attests to the fact that it is a highly complex area of the criminological corpus. It certainly encompasses a range of differing approaches, all of which have their own particular emphases and nuances, and furthermore, they have been categorised under various headings – Marxist criminology, Radical criminology, Left Realism, Feminist criminology, Sociological criminology or the Sociology of Deviance, Peacemaking criminology and Cultural Criminology, to name but a few (Radzinowicz, 1999). There is no single way of marking out a clear path through these various critical positions. However, we can for the sake of clarity say that a key distinguishing feature of Critical forms of criminology is that they reject utterly and completely the notion that a disinterested and value-free criminology is possible, and indeed, they by and large embrace the fact that their work is value-loaded, for they stand in complete opposition to unequal political, economic and social structures and relationships. Critical forms of criminology are therefore politically engaged and focus attention on the role played by broader socio-structural factors, such socio-economic and gender-based inequalities, rather than viewpoints that emphasise biological and psychological developmental factors, in shaping how a person responds to being labelled a criminal and seeks to manage a 'spoiled identity' (Young, 2011). This is because underpinning the various Critical criminology positions is a shared point of view which rejects the emphasis placed by situational crime prevention perspectives and rational choice models of crime and criminality on the individual social actor as the source and cause of crime and criminality. Rather, although they by and large accept that people indeed do choose to engage in deviance and crime, Critical criminological viewpoints emphasise the role played by prevailing social circumstances and conditions in shaping the actions of both law makers and law breakers (Chamberlain, 2013).

Up until the 1960s mainstream criminological thinking was heavily influenced by the work of Durkheim, who adopted a functionalist position regarding how societies operate and who therefore saw that crime was useful for society. One of the key features of Durkheim's work was that he liked to emphasise order and consensus in society and how group bonds form in and through shared norms and values. Therefore, Durkheim focused on deviance and crime as something whose function is to help maintain a sense of common feeling amongst society's members by enabling the mass of people – i.e. lawful citizens – to identify with each other and create common social ties and bonds, through differentiating themselves from the law breakers. Labelling Theory, which emerged from the Chicago School of the sociology of deviance in the 1960s, by and large shares this approach as it emphasises how the societal reaction to acts of crime creates consensus amongst groups of people that certain individuals are deviant. However, as Chapters 6 and 7 outlined, Critical criminology first emerged in the 1960s and 1970s under the banner of Marxist and then Feminist criminology. Both of which, in contrast to Labelling Theory and functionalist viewpoints, adopt a conflict perspective when examining society in general and the problem of crime in particular. That is, they see society as being shaped by conflicts amongst people who have competing self- and group interests. Even though at any one time a society may seem to agree on basic values and goals, such as the individual's right to pursue love, happiness and a rewarding career and family life, the existence of scarce resources and the tendency for them to be allocated unequally, means that someone (or some group) is benefiting at the expense of someone else.

Indeed, Critical criminologists tend to argue that the key groups at a disadvantage in western nation-states (and some would say worldwide as well) are women, ethnic minorities and the poor and socially excluded. Yet people on the losing end may not recognise or admit that their interests are in conflict with the interests of others, when in fact they are. It is argued that conflict is ubiquitous and historic, and furthermore, consists of a struggle over three related things: money, power and influence. Those who have more of them try to keep things the way they are; those who have less of them favour change so that they get a bigger share. The groups with wealth, power and influence are favoured in the conflict precisely because those resources put them in a dominant position. For Critical criminologists it is 'the have's' rather than 'the have not's' who make the rules, control the content and flow of ideas and information, and design and impose penalties for non-conformity. Sometimes the struggle for resources is blatant and bloody, but more often than not it is subtle and restrained. Various factors are pointed out as contributing to this. An important idea here first put forward in the 1970s by Marxist criminology was the notion of 'false consciousness'. This is the view that the dominant group is able to promote beliefs and values that support the existing social order to such an extent that the disadvantaged groups actually believe their interests are served by the prevailing social conditions, when in fact they are not. Think here about how you are often told that if you behave yourself and don't get into trouble with the police, or at least not too much trouble, and get a good education and work hard both in your studies and when you get your first real job after leaving university, then you will eventually work your way up the career ladder, and this will in turn enable you to have the lifestyle you want: so you can go on holidays, buy a car, afford to give your children nice things, get a house, and so on. Whether or not we might find this an attractive proposition, for Marxist criminologists what you are being sold here is nothing more than a gilded cage of your own making. This is because you are not being brought up to have a free life controlling your own labour and its benefits. Rather, you are being trained and prepared for a life as a cog in a machine which cares little for you, and indeed, just wants you to keep deluding yourself so it can extract the surplus value of your labour and turn it into a profit for the shareholders of the company you work for. What is more, these companies you work for are so interconnected and globalised that they sell the surplus value they extract from you back to you in the form of consumerist goods and gadgets, which in reality you don't need but think you can't survive without because you've been seduced into believing you can't.

As the 1970s and 1980s progressed Critical forms of criminology began to systematically examine how different forms of oppression, inequality and conflict affect people in everyday life, as well as in the sphere of crime and law. They were particularly interested in how structural inequalities evident in a society's class, race and gender structures affect, firstly, participation in crime; secondly, how crime is defined; and thirdly, the making and enforcement of laws. To do this, they examined crime relative to social, economic and political structures and forms of inequality, as found in a given society at a particular point in history. For example, Critical criminologists of a Marxist viewpoint, such as Richard Quinney (1979), argued that most crime is a rational response to the structure of social and cultural life and its associated key regulatory and bureaucratic institutions, which he held emphasised free-market economics. Crime, in other words, is a means of survival in a society within which survival is never guaranteed due to the structural inequalities that permeate it as a result of an underpinning emphasis upon free-market competition as the basis for westernised ways of life. For Quinney, any analysis of western criminal justice and legal systems must take into account how its fundamentally capitalist economic structure developed and is organised to protect the interests of certain groups who benefit most from this state of affairs. This is a point which led him to also conclude that crime is a social construct and criminologists must therefore not simply look at the law breakers, but the law makers and law keepers too.

It is important to note that when Critical criminologists speak about race, class and gender they use the terms differently from other criminologists, such as Classical criminologists, Psychological and Biological criminologists, labelling theorists, as well as Durkheimian inspired Sociological criminologists. For these other criminologists key concepts such as race, class and gender tend to be interpreted as characteristics of individuals and are used to identify subjects of study, such as the 'middle-class', or 'female victims'. But for Critical criminologists, race, class and gender are at the same time both identities and structures. As structures, race, class and gender contain culturally and historically specific rules that define (1) the types of power a group possesses, (2) a group's social and economic positions within society and (3) the opportunities for success people from these groups typically possess. As identities, race, class and gender tell us something about the social expectations concerning the behaviour of people from different groups, and the ways in which people act to construct themselves – that is, their sense of personal identity in relation to their gender, their class, or their race. So 'middle-class' defines a location in the social structure, which in turn defines the types of power persons can access and wield, their opportunities or pathways to success, and the forms of oppressive conditions which they control or which control them. But 'being middle-class' also defines behavioural expectations, and we expect middle-class people to behave in particular ways. We identify middle-class people by what job they might have, what their income is likely to be, how they dress, where they went to school, and so on. In short, the starting point for Critical criminology is that a person's structural location carries with it different forms of access and opportunities and different behavioural expectations, and from this point of view, these differences are evidence of inequality and these inequalities help explain the probability that people located in different structural locations will engage in crime or will be labelled criminal.

This leads us to a key point about Critical forms of criminology concerning notions of free will and determinism in relation to the choice of the individual to engage in crime. Early forms of Critical criminology, such as Marxist criminology, tended to be overly structurally deterministic, in that they emphasised how economic factors can drive social change and as a result tended to presume that your class determines your life chances and who you are. Clearly such a position can be criticised for being overly reductionist as not every sphere of human relations is reducible to economic factors. As a result, critical positions that emerged from the 1990s onwards, such as Cultural criminology and Peacemaking criminology, emphasised agency and individual freedom. This shift in emphasis is seen as necessary to ensure that Critical criminology does not lose sight of the fact that not every person who is subject to a socially determined factor, such as poverty or racial inequality, chooses to commit crime. Indeed, most contemporary Critical criminological viewpoints recognise what can be termed 'the duality of structure'. Meaning that they focus on the fact that people clearly are a product of their social environment, which does constrain and shape their behaviour, how they think, as well as the opportunities they have open to them in a given social situation. This can be seen in the common patterns of human behaviour and shared life experiences which operate on a day-to-day level all around us. However, people do nevertheless possess agency and free will, and furthermore, certain structures in society can actually act to enhance agency. For example, we may here think about certain institutional bureaucratic structures which seek to protect the individual from intimidation on behalf of more powerful social groups or forces, such as equal opportunity or human rights legislation. Structure, in other words, isn't necessarily a bad thing, and furthermore, contemporary Critical criminology reminds us that it is important to recognise the importance of both the positive and negative aspects of structure and agency when studying crime and deviance (Young, 2011).

Box 8.1   Key summary points

- Critical criminological positions encompass a range of differing approaches, all of which have their own particular emphases and nuances, and furthermore, they have been categorised under various headings: including Marxist criminology, Radical criminology, Left Realism, Feminist criminology, Sociological criminology or the Sociology of Deviance, Peacemaking criminology and Cultural criminology.
- Critical criminologists adopt a conflict perspective when examining society in general and the problem of crime in particular. That is, they see society as being shaped by conflicts amongst people who have competing self- and group interests.
- For Critical criminologists, core analytical concepts, such as race, class and gender, are at the same time both identities and structures. As structures race, class and gender contain culturally and historically specific rules that define (1) the types of power a group possesses, (2) a group's social and economic positions within society and (3) the opportunities for success people from these groups typically possess. As identities, race, class and gender tell us something about the social expectations concerning the behaviour of people from different groups, and the ways in which people act to construct themselves, that is their sense of personal identity in relation to their gender, their class, or their race.
- Earlier Critical standpoints, such as Marxism and Feminism, can be accused of being too deterministic when it comes to analysing the impact of social factors on individual behaviour, including behaviour labelled as deviant and criminal. However, contemporary Critical criminological viewpoints recognise what can be termed 'the duality of structure' – meaning that they focus on the fact that people clearly are a product of their social environment, which does constrain and shape their behaviour, how they think, as well as the opportunities they have open to them in a given social situation. This can be seen in the common patterns of human behaviour and shared life experiences which operate on a day-to-day level all around us. However, people do nevertheless possess agency and free will, and furthermore, certain structures in society can actually act to enhance agency, i.e. legislation to promote equal opportunities.

Further reading

Chamberlain, JM (2013) *Understanding criminological research: a guide to data analysis*. London: Sage.
Hogg, R (2002) *Critical criminology: issues, debates, challenges*. London: Willan Publishing.
Quinney, R (1979) *Class, state, and crime*. London: Longman Group.
Radzinowicz, L (1999) *Adventures in criminology*. London: Routledge.
Thalia, A (2008) *The critical criminology companion*. Sydney: Hawkins Press.
Young, J (2011) *The criminological imagination*. Cambridge: Polity Press.

POSITIVISM AND REALISM, POSTMODERNISM AND ANTI-REALISM

A key factor influencing the development of Critical standpoints in criminology and the emphasis on the duality of structure has been the rejection of positivism and the emergence of postmodern sensibilities. Positivism was discussed when Biological criminology was discussed in Chapter 3 and Psychological criminology in Chapter 4. Positivism adopts a philosophical stance of realism as it assumes there is an objective reality that exists independently to human beings and emphasises the need for a researcher to engage in systematic observation and experiment in a value-neutral and dispassionate manner in order to discover underlying causal laws of behaviour. Criminologists working in the Biological and Psychological traditions by and large utilise this approach to inform policy making through focusing on obtaining statistical evidence of 'what works' in relation to a range of criminal justice policy initiatives, interventions and crime reduction strategies. These include prison administration, community-based crime prevention, rehabilitative diversion schemes for youth and adult offenders with mental health problems, domestic violence programmes, as well as interventions to tackle alcohol and substance abuse related crime (Sherman, 2012). Meanwhile, a general bias within contemporary criminology towards positivism, in the form of both experimental and survey-based research, can be deduced from examining the methodology adopted by empirical research studies published in leading criminology and criminal justice journals (Kleck et al., 2006). However, this bias is slightly more prevalent in the US than other western societies. For example Tewksbury et al. (2010) undertook a detailed content analysis of leading academic journals. They found that only 5.7 percent of published articles in American criminology and criminal justice journals (*Criminology, Criminology and Public Policy*) relied on qualitative data and analysis compared to 27.2 percent in leading international journals (*British Journal of Criminology, Australian* and *New Zealand Journal of Criminology* and *Canadian Journal of Criminology*).

The findings of Tewksbury et al. (2010) reinforce the preference for quantitative criminology in America but they also demonstrate more generally the relatively heavy emphasis placed internationally on quantitative methods within criminology, at least in terms of published research in leading academic journals. This is perhaps to be expected. The use of large-scale survey methods to capture snapshots of criminal activity and the victim experience of crime, alongside the dynamics of criminal justice processes and outcomes, is tightly bound up with the emergence of criminology as a discipline during the nineteenth century, as well as the contemporary development of policy-oriented criminology as it has sought to generate a statistical evidence base from which to influence governmental practice (Young, 2011). Statistical information on crime patterns were first gathered in Europe in the nineteenth century by early Neoclassical and Biological criminologists as well as in the early part of the twentieth century in

American criminology by researchers and academics working in Chicago (Knepper, 2007). As the twentieth century progressed, governments internationally recognised the value of systematically collecting statistical information to inform decision-making and policy development. The practical utility of the information provided by victim surveys, police operational statistics, court sentencing outcome data, crime reporting patterns in urban and rural areas, alongside a wealth of other criminal justice outcome data, has been held by some to reinforce the validity of the viewpoint that the methods of the natural sciences are appropriate for understanding crime and criminality, and furthermore, for making both these social constructs amenable to governmental manipulation and control (Sherman, 2012). Survey-based criminology enables the large-scale collection of descriptive statistical information (i.e. the prevalence of burglary) as well as the use of analytical statistics where correlation tests are applied to two or more variables (i.e. if a person has been a victim of burglary in relation to whether they live in an urban or rural area) in order to test a hypothesis (i.e. that people in rural areas are less likely to be victims of burglary than their city dwelling counterparts). Survey-based criminology typically distributes questionnaires and/or conducts survey interviews with a target sample from a larger study population. More recently, the internet and modern mobile technologies have made electronic and online surveys possible (Chamberlain, 2013).

For all the positive impact of such approaches, many Critical criminologists argue that their discipline cannot adopt the methods of the natural sciences to identify underlying causal patterns at work when crime occurs; often because they feel uneasy about the positivist distinction between facts and values. This perhaps can be most clearly seen in the experimentalist viewpoint that it is the role of criminology to produce facts to advise policy makers without considering the values at play in the governmental decision-making process (Sherman, 2012), while it is arguable criminology must not be limited to the research questions suggested by the social control priorities of the governmental project. To argue otherwise denies it the ability to operate independently and if need be, focus its attention on the state and its crime control agencies when their actions engender harm. Furthermore, criminology encounters problems when it tries to promote evidence-based decision-making under the guise of a social-scientific cloak of objectivity and neutrality, not least of all because there is no such thing as an 'ideology-free zone' (Knepper, 2007: 9). Indeed, underpinning wariness of positivism of much of contemporary Critical criminology is postmodernism, with its anti-realist undertones, which has been hugely influential in the intellectual development of politically engaged Marxist, Feminist, Realist, Cultural and Sociological forms of criminology.

The realist position appears commonsensical: as we go about our everyday lives we typically assume the world around us existed before we were born and indeed will continue to exist after we die. What is more, human beings who live, work and play together tend to possess shared values and beliefs about the nature of the world in which they live which guide how they interact with each other, in part because these shared values and beliefs are internalised by individuals from a young age through the processes of socialisation. Furthermore these objectively and materially confront us on a day-to-day basis as external 'social facts' in the form of social organisations and institutions which embody communally shared values and ideals that act to channel individual human behaviour in socially acceptable ways.

But realism has been increasingly challenged over the last few decades by the rise of anti-realist postmodern positions. Postmodernism is an intellectual movement which highlights the contingent nature of human knowledge, holding that accounts of the world are social constructions which do not exist independently of the social actor and the language they use to describe the world around them (Silverman, 2007). The intellectual heritage of postmodernism lies in the traditions of idealist and relativist western philosophy. This suggests we cannot know anything about the so-called 'real world', rather everything we experience is mediated through mental and linguistic constructs. Due to its relativistic take on the nature of human knowledge the postmodernist anti-realist viewpoint accords equal validity to all perspectives and voices. In doing so it often also denies that any one ethical position can be privileged over another. This is a state of affairs some individuals find difficult to accept. As although they may recognise the historically situated and socially constructed nature of human beliefs and values it is also possible to argue that moral absolutes do exist in the social world, particularly in regard to what constitutes appropriate behaviour towards other individuals given the embodied nature of the shared human condition. Hence varying points of extreme exist in the anti-realist postmodern position. Some stress the socially constructed nature of social reality. They acknowledge the active role played by individuals within this process without doing away with the idea that social reality exists externally to the individual and constrains their behaviour. Others insist that the social world does not exist independently of the social actor and the language used to describe it. For example Potter (1996: 98) argues, '[the world] … is constituted in one way or another as people talk about it, write about it and argue it'. Whether one agrees with their arguments or not, anti-realist positions bring to the fore the idea that researchers present their own interpretation of the social world rather than a definitive account of it (Chamberlain, 2013).

Narrative and life story research within criminology

This anti-realist postmodern emphasis on rejecting objectivity and value-free research is congruent with Critical criminology perspectives as well as qualitative research methodologies, which has led to the development of an increasing focus within criminology over the last three decades on narrative and life story qualitative research (Chamberlain, 2013). Many narrative criminologists readily acknowledge that their work is driven by a personal ethical and political commitment to improving the individual and social conditions of socially excluded and stigmatised groups. Such a stance is argued to be particularly important when dealing with sensitive topics, such as domestic violence for example. Consequently Clandinin and Connolly (2000) talk about 'living the story' with research participants so a researcher works collaboratively in a participatory fashion with both individuals and communities to engender social change.

One only needs to look at the 'true crime' section of any high street bookshop to realise the popularity of life stories and insider accounts of criminal life. Within academic criminological research narrative biographies and life stories tend to focus on critical incidents or significant turning points in a life. These are used to explore an individual's relationship to crime from their own point of view while also bringing to the fore broader social-structural issues, such as for example social mobility and class-based inequality, racism and hate crime, as well as patriarchy and gender-based violence. Hence Critical criminologists have used victim narratives to explore issues such as rape (Bletzer and Koss, 2006), childhood sexual abuse (Staller and Nelson-Gardell, 2005) and domestic violence (Walklate, 2004). In addition to using offender's narratives to explore the dehumanising nature of prison life (Morgan, 1999), the female experience of imprisonment (Peckham, 1985), life on death row (Sarat, 2001), why people reoffend (Nellis, 2002), organised crime (Warshow, 1970), drug trafficking (Ross and Richards, 2002), subcultures, drug use and dance music (Wilson, 2007) and youth gang membership (Venkatesh, 2008). Prison autobiographies provide a rich vein of stimulus to the criminological imagination as they search for insight into the causes of offending behaviour, how individuals cope with long-term imprisonment, as well as desistence from crime (Hoskison, 1998; Evans and Wallace, 2008).

Part of the attractiveness of the narrative biographical and life story approach for many criminologists is that it seeks to invert the traditional power relationship between the researcher and researched through requiring they take a back seat and allow a person to tell their own story in their own words in a free flowing manner. This reinforces the politicised nature of the criminological project (Chamberlain, 2013). While as the next section of this chapter discusses, this shift towards recognising the value of narrative and life story has arguably also contributed to a renewed emphasis within criminology on the trajectory of an offender's criminal career during their life. The rest of this chapter examines the Life Course approach to the criminological study of crime.

Box 8.2   Key summary points

- A key factor influencing the development of critical standpoints in criminology and the emphasis on the duality of structure has been the rejection of positivism and the emergence of postmodern sensibilities.
- Positivism is influential in Biological and Psychological forms of criminology. It adopts a philosophical stance of realism as it assumes there is an objective reality

(Continued)

(Continued)

that exists independently to human beings and emphasises the need for a researcher to engage in systematic observation and experiment in a value-neutral and dispassionate manner in order to discover underlying causal laws of behaviour.

- In contrast to positivism, postmodernism is an intellectual movement which is anti-realist as it highlights the contingent nature of human knowledge, holding that accounts of the world are social constructions which do not exist independently of the social actor and the language they use to describe the world around them.
- The intellectual heritage of postmodernism lies in the traditions of idealist and relativist western philosophy. Due to its relativistic take on the nature of human knowledge the postmodernist anti-realist viewpoint accords equal validity to all perspectives and voices. This is congruent with Critical criminology perspectives as well as qualitative research methodologies, which has led to the development of an increasing focus within criminology over the last three decades on narrative and life story forms of qualitative research as part of a broader concern with the life course of offending behaviour.

Further reading

Austin, S (2001) *When the state kills: capital punishment and the American condition*. Princeton, NJ: Princeton University Press.

Bartels, L and Richards, K (2011) *Qualitative criminology*. Annandale, NSW: Federation Press.

Bennett, J (1981) *Oral history and delinquency: the rhetoric of criminology*. Chicago: University of Chicago Press.

Bletzer, KV and Koss, MP (2006) After-rape among three populations in the southwest: a time for mourning, a time for recovery. *Violence Against Women* 12 (1): 5–29.

Chamberlain, JM (2013) *Understanding criminological research: a guide to data analysis*. London: Sage.

Evans, T and Wallace, P (2008) A prison within a prison: the masculinity narratives of male prisoners. *Men and Masculinities* 10 (4): 484–97.

Goody, J (2000) Biographical lessons for criminology. *Theoretical Criminology* 4 (4): 473–98.

Hoskison, J (1998) *Inside: one man's experience of prison*. London: John Murray.

James, J (2004) American prison notebooks. *Race and Class* 45 (3): 10–20.

Kleck, G, Tank, J and Bellows, JJ (2006) What methods are most frequently used in research in criminology and criminal justice? *Criminal Justice Education* 17 (2): 503–25.

Knepper, P (2007) *Criminology and social policy*. London: Sage.

Peckham, A (1985) *A woman in custody: a personal account of one nightmare journey through the English penal system*. London: Fontana.

Potter, J (1996) *Representing reality: discourse, rhetoric and social construction*. London: Sage.

Searle, C (1999) *The quality of qualitative research*. London: Sage.

Sherman, LW (2012) *Experimental criminology*. London: Sage.

Silverman, D (2007) *A very short and fairly interesting introduction to qualitative research*. London: Sage.

Tewksbury, R, Dabney, D and Copes, H (2010) The prominence of qualitative research in criminology and criminal justice scholarship. *Criminal Justice Education* 21 (4): 297–322.

Venkatesh, S (2008) *Gang leader for a day.* London: Penguin.

Walklate, S (2004, 2nd edn) *Gender, crime and criminal justice.* Cullompton: Willan Publishing.

Ward, T and Marshall, B (2007) Narrative identity and offender rehabilitation. *International Journal of Offender Therapy and Comparative Criminology* 51 (3): 279–97.

Warshow, R (1970) The gangster as tragic hero. *The immediate experience: movies, comics, theatre and other aspects of popular culture.* New York: Atheneum.

Young, J (2011) *The criminological imagination.* Cambridge: Polity Press.

LIFE COURSE CRIMINOLOGY

The development of Life Course criminology is not solely bound up with the postmodern narrative turn within Critical forms of criminology over the last three decades. Indeed, Life Course criminology has a long history in criminology. It arguably can trace its roots back to the early Chicago School discussed in Chapter 5, while it has developed utilising both qualitative and quantitative research methods, particularly in the USA. Certainly, the collection of longitudinal quantitative and qualitative data is one of the hallmarks of Life Course criminology given its focus on tracing over time the life trajectories and stories of criminals. It is also viewed as an integrated theory of crime in that it seeks to incorporate both developmental biological-psychological as well as social-psychological factors within its analysis of criminal careers, particularly the trajectory from youth delinquency to adult criminality (Wright et al., 2015). The Life Course perspective can best be conceptualised as viewing life events in the context of life stages, turning points and pathways, all of which are embedded in social institutions; specifically, the family, the school, the workplace, the penal system and so on (Pager, 2003). Its primary concern is with the fact that the majority of crime in western nations is committed by youth offenders between the ages of 16 and 25 and that desistence from crime as a person ages is common to all offenders regardless of any similarities or differences in their early childhood experiences (Young, 2011). The rest of the chapter will explore how Life Course criminologists have explored the interaction of these elements in the production of a criminal career by examining two influential theories: Moffitt's Dual Taxonomy (1993) and Sampson and Laub's Age Graded Stability and Change Model (1993).

Moffitt's Dual Taxonomy

Life Course criminology begins with a simple axiom: that an adult criminal career by and large requires childhood antisocial behaviour yet not all antisocial children become antisocial adults or offenders. It is exploring why this is the case, why the life trajectory of some young people and not others leads to an adult criminal career, which led Terri Moffitt (1993) to argue that the pattern of offending behaviour over time is characterised by stability or change. Moffitt argues that they are two groups of offenders and they need to be treated differently. The first group, which Moffitt calls life course persistent offenders, are repeat adult offenders who have exhibited a range of antisocial behaviours from a young age, including biting and hitting other children as toddlers, being disruptive in classrooms as young children, getting into drinks and drugs as adolescents, stealing and starting fights as teenagers, and finally, as adults committing crimes ranging from fraud to violence and sexual abuse. Moffitt (1993: 680) argues that 'if some individuals' antisocial behaviour is stable from pre-school to adulthood, then investigators are compelled to look for its roots early in life, in factors that are present before or soon after birth'. Moffitt argues that what she calls 'neuropsychological deficits' are key to understanding persistent antisocial and criminal behaviour throughout the life course. These are developmental psychological problems and disorders which affect an individual's ability to exert self-control over behavioural impulses and to consider the consequences of actions, and which have been associated as key risk factors in predicting antisocial and aggressive behaviours (Pager, 2003). In contrast to this group, whose antisocial and criminal behaviour is a relatively constant feature of their life course from youth to adulthood, Moffitt's second group, who she believes describes most young people, are those who are well behaved at a young age, but get into trouble during adolescence or their teenage years, but desist from such behaviour once they enter adulthood. Perhaps unsurprisingly, Moffitt calls these adolescent limited offenders. Moffitt explains that this group suffers from a tension during their teen years whereby adult behavioural rules – particularly in relation to sexual activity and the consumption of goods, alcohol and drugs – appear attractive to them. Indeed, informal social sanctions from peers and reference groups may encourage such behaviour even when formal socio-cultural rules clearly do not. This state of affairs leads some generally rule-abiding teenagers into episodic delinquent behaviour as an adaptive behaviour to cope with this tension and socially demonstrate their peer group memberships. Moffitt argues that as these youths transition into adulthood the need to transgress somewhat naturally diminishes. This certainly makes some sense. After all, a 15-year-old may well wish to emulate the behaviour of an 18-year-old, but by the time they reach their mid-twenties there is very little difference between their socially sanctioned behaviour and that of a 30- or 40-year-old.

At the heart of Moffitt's theory lies a biologically grounded developmental psychological model of criminal behaviour which holds that the life course of a small proportion of adult offenders demonstrates that the roots of their offending behaviour leads back not only into their childhood but the fact that they possess neuropsychological defects, such as attention deficit hyperactivity disorder, which affect their ability to empathise with others, see the consequences of their actions and exert self-control over their behaviour. Research does seem to indicate that a relationship exists between neuropsychological defects and persistent offending behaviour amongst men (Raine, 2005). However, this is dangerously close to stating that a distinct biological criminal type exists which separates these individuals from the larger youth offending group. This is a position which is somewhat at odds with the Critical criminologist standpoint regarding the politicised and value-laden nature of definitions surrounding what constitutes transgressive, deviant and criminal behaviour and what does not (Young, 2011). Furthermore, it is argued that Moffitt's developmental theory is arbitrary in its cut-off between youth and adulthood, and most importantly, does not adequately account for the importance of parental style, attachment and social bonds in influencing the development of a young person's ability to see the consequences of their action and exercise self-control (Hirschi and Gottfredson, 1995).

Hirschi's Social Control Theory

The social psychologist Travis Hirschi has been critical of Moffitt's theory and argued instead for the importance of social bonds when analysing youth delinquency and offending behaviour in his Social Control Theory (SCT) (Hirschi, 1969; Hirschi and Gottfredson, 1995). This asks the question 'why do people not break the law?' to which it replies 'because of social bonds'. In other words, SCT assumes that people are free to break the law in any number of ways but certain controls stop them. Hirschi (1969) argues that these controls are located in the social bonds which tie individuals together and engender law-abiding behaviour. He defines four types of bond, stating that 'elements of social bonding include attachment to families, commitment to social norms and institutions (school, employment), involvement in activities, and the belief that these things are important' (Hirschi, 1969: 16). Importantly, SCT hypothesises that the presence of these four social bonds helps to prevent criminal behaviour and encourage lawful behaviour. Each of the four bounds can be operationalised into variables against which it is possible to obtain empirical data. Hirschi (1969) provides empirical data from over 4000 informants between 12 and 17 years old. He operationalised and tested his four concepts – 'attachment', 'commitment', 'involvement' and 'beliefs' – and doing so showed that rule-breaking behaviour and delinquency did seem to occur in children from families with poor emotional ties between children and parents ('attachment'), when children felt they did not have much to lose from not meeting expectations surrounding participation in educational study ('commitment'), as well as perhaps did not invest much personal time and energy in organised social activities such as sports or other leisure pursuits ('involvement'), and finally, did not seem to have recognised the value of rules to regulate behaviour amongst people ('beliefs'). Since Hirschi's original formulation SCT has been subject to further empirical study and although by no means conclusive the evidence does seem to tentatively support the theory, although it has been criticised for its tendency to focus on young male offenders (Chamberlain, 2013). However, SCT has been influential in Life Course criminology by providing the basis for the work of Sampson and Laub (1993), who in their critique of Moffitt (1993) extended the applicability of SCT to include adult offenders, as is discussed in the next section of the chapter.

Sampson and Laub's Age Graded Stability and Change Model

SCT heavily influenced the work of Sampson and Laub (1990, 1993). They are critical of Moffitt's focus on either stability or change. Indeed, they argue that the life course of the offender is dynamic in that it consists of both elements. This is because they are concerned with the possibility of intervention to deter individuals from repeating criminal behaviours. For Sampson and Laub (1993) the key question is what factors affect the offending trajectory of individuals and they provide an answer with their age graded model of informal social control. They begin by expanding SCT to include adult behaviour and argue that having quality social interactions and bonds with others determines the impact and strength of informal social controls on an individual and so their willingness and ability to exercise self-control over their actions. That is, if the bonds are high quality and emotionally rewarding then self-control increases and antisocial and criminal behaviour lessens. The stronger the bond, the stronger the informal social control, which in turn increases an individual's potential to change and follow a non-criminal trajectory. Put simply, the weaker the social bonds the more likely there will be continuity in offending behaviour, while the stronger the social bonds the more likely a reduction in offending behaviour will occur.

Particular institutions of formal social control, such as school, employment and family, each change throughout the life course in their ability to affect an individual's behaviour due to the formal and informal social bonding opportunities they provide (Sampson and Laub, 1990). Indeed, it is suggested that the ability of certain institutions to control criminal or conforming behaviour is dependent on age graded variability as an individual moves from youth into adulthood. In other words, their impact in deterring antisocial and criminal behaviour is in flux and changes over time and is dynamic rather than continuous. Therefore, although delinquent and criminal behaviour can and does often exist with much continuity from youth into adulthood, Sampson and Laub (1993) assert that social bonds in adulthood (including school, family, peers and community relations) can explain change and why offending behaviour often ends as a young person enters adult life, with specific life events within the trajectory of a life course influencing behaviour. A meaningful shift in bonds created by, for example, achieving for the first time academic or sporting success at school, getting that first job, meeting a life partner, getting married and becoming a parent, are common key turning points and transitions in the life course, and so can redirect an individual's criminal pathway. As a result,

Sampson and Laub argue for the need for criminologists to engage with mixed-method quantitative and qualitative longitudinal research in order to explore what effect the varying ties to particular institutions at different stages in the life course have on the capacity to modify criminal trajectories (Sampson and Laub, 1993).

Targeted Life Course interventions

The age graded model makes sense as evidence does suggest that during the early years family relationships are important in shaping behaviour; however as children grow direct parental impact diminishes and peer groups and social institutions such as schools become more important, while in adulthood schools and parents both take a backseat to jobs and spouses as primary mechanisms for social control (Wright et al., 2015). The research of Sampson and Laub (1993) does allow for a rethink in terms of crime prevention policy. For example, school-based interventions to deter and address antisocial behaviour and youth delinquency prior to formal involvement in the criminal justice system have been advocated to increase social bonds and reinforce trajectories away from a criminal career. This could be achieved by changing educational environments and working cultures to reduce the negative labelling and stigmatisation of young people, better tailored job training to individual needs, wider sporting and extra-curricular activities, as well as providing counselling, relationship advice and sexual health services (Benson, 2013).

In relation to the criminal justice system, the situation is undoubtedly more complex. Most prolific young offenders possess a range of problems and issues which make it difficult to prescribe a one-size-fits-all approach to the problem of youth crime: including trauma and aggressive behaviour resulting from being a victim of childhood neglect or physical or sexual abuse; a lack of opportunity and social mobility; substance and alcohol abuse problems; high levels of disengagement from educational pathways; poor communication and life skills; dysfunctional family relationships; a lack of positive male and female role models; a distrust of authority figures; and finally, feelings of isolation and social exclusion (Millie et al., 2005). For Andrews and Andrews (2003) repeated experience shows that the complex needs of young offenders mean that targeting social bonding activities, such as sports and athletics, must be embedded within professionally-led counselling, mentoring, life skills training and educational programmes, to support young people to change their offending behaviour and connect with a pathway to work.

However, such approaches to dealing with antisocial, delinquent and criminal behaviour – be they located in the school or the prison – are often at odds with the broader, more punitive Right Realist youth crime agenda which has dominated western societies over the last 30 years or so, with the result that we have seen an increase in juvenile punishment and incarceration rates worldwide (Young, 2011). Nevertheless, for its proponents, Life Course criminology offers realistic and humanistic opportunities for developing crime prevention policy, with interventions being targeted to suit need at particular key points in the life course (i.e. on release from prison), and its influence on criminal justice practitioners, particularly those who work with youth offenders, is undoubtedly growing (Benson, 2013). This is not least because the emphasis of Life Course criminology on collecting statistical and life story data to trace the impact of significant life events and social bonds on offending behaviour by and large chimes with practitioners' day-to-day professional experience of 'what works' when working with offenders to achieve lasting positive change in their lives.

Box 8.3   Key summary points

- Life Course criminology focuses on tracing over time the life trajectories and stories of criminals. It is also viewed as an integrated theory of crime in that it seeks to incorporate both developmental biological-psychological as well as social-psychological factors within its analysis of criminal careers, particularly the trajectory from youth delinquency to adult criminality.
- The Life Course perspective can best be conceptualised as viewing life events in the context of life stages, turning points and pathways, all of which are embedded in social institutions – specifically, the family, the school, the workplace, the penal system and so on. Its primary concern is with the fact that the majority of crime in western nations is committed by youth offenders between the ages of 16 and 25 and that desistence from crime as a person ages is common to all offenders regardless of any similarities or differences in their early childhood experiences.
- Two influential Life Course criminological theories are Moffitt's Dual Taxonomy (1993) and Sampson and Laub's Age Graded Stability and Change Model (1993).
- At the centre of Moffitt's (1993) theory lies a biologically grounded developmental psychological model of criminal behaviour which holds that the life course of a small proportion of adult offenders demonstrates that the roots of their offending behaviour lead back not only to their childhood but the fact that they possess neuropsychological defects, such as attention deficit hyperactivity disorder, which affect their ability to empathise with others, see the consequences of their actions and exert self-control over their behaviour. Research does seem to indicate that a relationship exists between neuropsychological defects and persistent offending behaviour amongst men (Raine, 2005). However, the eminent social psychologist Travis Hirschi has been critical of Moffitt's theory and argued instead for the importance of social bonds when analysing youth delinquency and offending behaviour in his Social Control Theory (SCT) (Hirschi, 1969).
- Sampson and Laub (1990, 1993) emphasise social bonds and note that particular institutions of formal social control, such as school, employment and family, each change throughout the life course in their ability to affect an individual's behaviour due to the formal and informal social bonding opportunities they provide. Sampson and Laub argue for the need to engage with mixed-method quantitative and qualitative longitudinal research in order to explore

what effect the varying ties to particular institutions at different stages in the life course have on the capacity to modify criminal trajectories. The resulting research does suggest that during the early years family relationships are important in shaping behaviour, however as children grow direct parental impact lessens and peer groups and social institutions such as schools become more important, while in adulthood schools and parents both take a backseat to jobs and spouses as primary mechanisms for social control.

- Life Course criminology is growing in popularity amongst both academics and criminal justice practitioners. Some Critical criminologists have highlighted that this approach is often at odds with the more punitive Right Realist youth crime agenda of most western societies for the last three decades, which has seen an increase in juvenile punishment and incarceration rates worldwide.

Further reading

Andrews, J and Andrews, G (2003) Life in a secure unit: the rehabilitation of young people through the use of sport. *Social Science and Medicine* 56 (3): 531–50.

Benson, M (2013, 2nd edn) *Crime and the life course.* London: Routledge.

Hirschi, T (1969) *Causes of delinquency.* Berkeley: University of California Press.

Hirschi, T and Gottfredson, M (1995) Control theory and the life course perspective. *Studies in Crime and Crime Prevention* 4 (2): 131–42.

Millie, A, Jacobson, J, McDonald, E and Hough, M (2005) *Anti-social behaviour strategies: finding a balance.* London: The Policy Press.

Moffitt, TE (1993) Adolescence-limited and life-course persistent antisocial behaviour: a developmental taxonomy. *Psychological Review* 100 (4): 674–700.

Pager, D (2003) The mark of a criminal record. *American Journal of Sociology* 108 (5): 937–75.

Raine, A (2005) Neocognitive impairments in boys on the life course persistent antisocial path. *Journal of Abnormal Psychology* 114 (1): 38–49.

Sampson, RJ and Laub, JH (1990) Crime and deviance over the life course: the salience of adult social bonds. *American Sociological Review* 55 (5): 609–27.

Sampson, RJ and Laub, JH (1993) *Crime in the making: pathways and turning points through life*. Cambridge, MA: Harvard University Press.

Wright, JP, Tibbetts, SG and Daigle, LE (2015) *Criminals in the making: criminality across the life course.* London: Sage.

SELF-STUDY TASK

Write a maximum of 750 words outlining the emergence of Life Course criminology over the last three decades as well as why the concepts of stability, change, social bonds and turning points are important to understanding why not all antisocial and delinquent youths become adult offenders.

9 REFLECTING ON THEORIES OF CRIME, THEORIES OF HUMAN NATURE: CRIME IN THE AGE OF THE ENTERPRISING RISKY CITIZEN-SUBJECT

CHAPTER OVERVIEW

Chapter 9 concludes our analysis of the historical development of criminological theory outlined in the previous eight chapters. It explores how underpinning the study of crime over the last 200 years has been a growing rationalisation, scientisation and medicalisation of the topic. This is because governing elites have sought to make the problem of crime ever more manageable and controllable as western nation-states have become ever more complex and technologically advanced. It argues that contemporary shifts noted by criminologists in criminal justice systems internationally towards a more risk-adverse culture of state surveillance and actuarial forms of justice are in reality bound up with broader global socio-political changes brought about from the shifting conditions associated with late or high modernity. In doing so, the chapter critically reflects on the different ways in which the causes of crime are conceptualised by the theories discussed in the preceding chapters and how they each make differing assumptions about what it means to be human, and so what causes people to act as they do, including behaviour labelled as deviant and criminal. As a result, the chapter concludes our discussion of criminological theory by arguing that the student of criminology must remain ever mindful of the need to ensure they approach the topic with a willingness to adopt a critical stance towards popularist viewpoints to the problem of crime. For these often advocate a highly punitive 'just desserts' solution when it comes to dealing with deviant behaviour. Yet history shows that no matter how justifiable such approaches may at first appear, ultimately punitive solutions to the problem of crime are self-defeating, because they are based on a view of human nature and behaviour which is highly restrictive, and most importantly, which only a minority of people are able to conform to.

INTRODUCTION

Taken together the previous chapters have reinforced three key points. Firstly, that crime and a preoccupation with its causes and the ways in which it can be stopped are a topic with a historical legacy which stretches back to the birth of modern human civilisation. Secondly, that underpinning the different ways in which the causes of crime are conceptualised are differing assumptions about human nature and so what it means to be human. And thirdly, that a key feature of the study of crime over the last 200 years or so has been the growing rationalisation, scientisation and medicalisation of the topic. This chapter reflects on the consequences of this state of affairs for the contemporary study of crime. Its aim in doing so is to conclude our discussion of criminological theory by reinforcing how the student of criminology must remain mindful of the need to ensure they approach the topic with a willingness to adopt a critical stance towards popularist discourse surrounding the problem of crime and suggested solutions concerning how best to deal with it. Indeed, this is particularly pertinent in today's age of mass surveillance and risk, as underpinning the contemporary popularist discourse surrounding crime is a particular politicised view of human nature, which, as we will discuss, many Critical criminologists would argue is a highly limited view of what it means to be human. It is important to remember, therefore, that crime policy and practice take place within a broader set of shifting social conditions. In short, the criminal justice system and its aims, structure, process and outcomes are all bound up tightly with the nature of the society within which they operate. Therefore, before looking more closely at the forms of human nature assumed by differing theories of crime, it is necessary to first trace the broader social conditions within which contemporary criminological discourse has emerged. To this end, the next section focuses on the shifting broader social context and the changes brought about since the nineteenth century by the Enlightenment movement, tracing as it does so the emergence and re-emergence of the political-philosophical ideas of liberalism against the background of the risk-saturated conditions of high modernity. This helps to establish a necessary historical background against which to subsequently explore developments within the criminal justice system and theories of crime and human nature.

FROM MODERNITY TO HIGH MODERNITY

As was discussed in previous chapters, the broad intellectual movement known as the Enlightenment involved a complex array of social, economic, political, technological and cultural processes. It produced a very different form of social life than had existed in Europe up until the seventeenth century. Indeed, it completely changed how citizens of European nation-states viewed their place in the world. For example, for the first time we see the growth of democratic ideals and notions surrounding social equality and opportunity. So we start to see the gradual rejection of traditional social hierarchies which were built around the social structure of the serf/lord relationship which had dominated much of the social world until this time. This is why this period in human history is sometimes referred to by social scientists such as Polanyi (1967) as the Great Transformation. We certainly are talking here about a complex and far-reaching form of social change. But for the sake of clarity we can break down the birth of modernity into three key interrelated processes.

First is the Enlightenment itself. What we have here is the re-emergence of the idea from classical Greece that the scientific method can be a valid source of human knowledge and a concurrent belief in the ability of reason and practical experiment to describe, explain and change the world around us. The idea of progress is bound up with this. Prior to this time people by and large lived their lives out in a set cyclical way, very much in tune with the natural seasons of the world. But with the re-emergence of science we see the growth of the idea that human beings can change the world around them and indeed control it to their satisfaction. This directly challenged traditional orthodoxies of the God-given order of the natural and social worlds, with monarchs at the top and serfs at the bottom. So we start to see sustained attempts at mass social transformation, such as the French Revolution or the American War of Independence. Secondly, and related to the scientific progress bound up with the Enlightenment, is a rapid process of urbanisation and industrialisation. Here we see how gradual technological advances led to what was called the industrial revolution, with work opportunities increasingly shifting from rural farming areas to urban factories as a result of scientific progress enabling the mass production of goods. Here, of course, we also start to see urban over-crowding, and so problems such as poverty and disease, which of course led to the early development of public health medicine (White, 2001). Thirdly and finally, tied up with the scientific progress of the Enlightenment, social reform and rapid industrialisation is the growth of capitalism and free-market eco-nomics. In short, we see the beginnings of liberalism as a particular economic and political philosophy that believes in the need to set limits on the role of the state in the governance of society.

Liberalism and possessive individualism

Liberalism is a critique of state reason which seeks to set limits on state power (Peters, 2001). But not only does liberalism have a particular view of the role of the state, it also has a particular view of the nature of the individual. The concept of possessive individualism lies at the heart of classical liberalism (Macpherson, 1962). This first emerged in the seventeenth and eighteenth cen-turies, through the works of a variety of writers, such as Thomas Hobbes, John Stuart Mills, Adam Smith, Thomas Locke, Jeremy Bentham and Herbert Spencer. Macpherson (1962) argues that for these thinkers the individual and their capabilities prefigure the circumstances into which they are born. In short, individuals' talents and who they are owe nothing to society, rather they own themselves, and as such are morally and legally responsible for themselves alone. In this viewpoint, the individual is naturally self-reliant and free from dependence on others. They need only enter into relationships with others because they help them pursue their self-interests and pleasures. Bound up with this viewpoint is the belief that society is a series of market-based relations made between self-interested subjects who are actively pursuing their own interests. It was argued that only by recognising and supporting this position politically and economically will the greatest happiness for the greatest number be achieved.

A key problem with this view of the individual is that it tends to ignore or underplay the value of existing social structure and inequalities therein. Indeed, a very real problem here is that individual members of society do not start their lives equally. This fact led social reformers in the nineteenth and twentieth cen-turies to advocate changes in working conditions, poor relief and public health. A huge literature was produced by social activists of the time, such as Henry Mayhem, linking inequality and poverty to disease and death (White, 2001).

Furthermore, contra the ethos of liberalism, after the financial crash of the 1920s economists such as John Maynard Keynes tended to argue for a strong interventionist role for the state in regulating the market, protecting working and living conditions, as well as promoting public health. Adopting Keynesian economics to control the tendency of capitalism to operate in boom and bust cycles formed an important part of the foundation of the post-Second World War welfare state in the UK. However, as the twentieth century progressed sociologists began to notice that significant technological and socio-cultural changes were occurring in the makeup of states, particularly from the 1960s onwards, while the rate of change rapidly intensified as the 1980s progressed. The birth of the personal computer and the rise of the mobile phone reinforced that the way people were living their lives and relating to one another and the world around them was gradually being fundamentally reorganised. There also seemed to be a distinctive shift towards more diverse, pluralistic and multicultural populations within western nation-states as a result of a rise in immigration due to the increasing availability of cheap international transport and advances in communication technologies. Such considerations led some to conclude that the processes of modernity had intensified and led to a period in human history characterised by an intense feeling of personal uncertainty to such a degree that we had entered the age of high modernity. It signalled the emergence of the risk society.

The rise of the risk society

For many social scientists the re-emergence of liberalism from the 1980s coincided with a general social shift towards the conditions of late or high modernity. We certainly live in an increasingly interconnected, technologically advanced, globalised world where events and happenings occurring on the other side of the globe are immediately available for personal consumption (and arguably therefore immediately impact on the socio-cultural and economic-political spheres). For social theorists such as Beck (1992) and Giddens (1990, 1991, 1999) a key defining feature of modern society – or late or high modernity as they call it – is that there has been 'a social impetus towards individualisation of unprecedented scale and dynamism ... [which] ... forces people – for the sake of their survival – to make themselves the centre of their own life plans and conduct' (Beck and Beck-Gernsheim, 2002: 31). Both Beck and Giddens argue that as capitalist-industrial society gives way under the tripartite forces of technology, consumerism and globalisation, there is a categorical shift in the nature of social structures, and more importantly, the relationship between the individual and society. Here key sociological categories which have traditionally structured society increasingly lose their meaning. Hence categories such as race, gender and class, for example, increasingly no longer serve to restrict a person's social opportunities or define who they are as individuals to the extent they once did. Furthermore, as working conditions change, and the technology and communication revolutions continue apace, more than ever before individuals are required to make life-changing decisions concerning education, work, self-identity and personal relationships, in a world where traditional beliefs about social class, gender and the family are being overturned.

Now for many social theorists this state of affairs has led to a concern with dangerousness and risk entering centre stage within society's institutional governing apparatus, alongside individual subject-citizens' personal decision-making process (Mythen, 2004). One of the key risk theorists, Giddens (1990), talks about two forms of risk: external and manufactured risk. Put simply, external risks are those posed by the world around us and manufactured risks are created by human beings themselves. In essence, as Giddens explains, it is the difference between worrying about what nature can do with us – in the form of floods, famine and so on – and worrying about what we have done to the natural world via how we organise social life. But of course it is not that simple. Risk theorists argue that throughout human history societies have always sought to risk-manage threats, hazards and dangers. But these management activities have by and large been concerned with natural external risks, such as infectious diseases and famine.

However, in today's technologically advanced society, individuals are seen to be both the producers and minimisers of manufactured risk (Giddens, 1990). That is, within the conditions of high modernity, risks are seen to be solely the result of human activity (Mythen, 2004). Hence manufactured risk takes over. Even events previously held to be natural disasters, such as floods and famine, are now held to be avoidable consequences of human activities that must be risk-managed (Lupton, 2011). Society's governing institutions and expert bodies need to become ever more collectively self-aware of their role in the creation and management of risk (Beck and Beck-Gernsheim, 2002). For the individual, meanwhile, uncertainties now litter their pathway through life to such an extent that it appears to be loaded with real and potential risks. So they must seek out and engage with a seemingly ever growing number of information resources, provided by a myriad of sources, as they navigate through their world. In the risk society '[we] find more and more guidebooks and practical manuals to do with health, diet, appearance, exercise, lovemaking and many other things' (Giddens, 1991: 218).

Of course, this state of affairs links in with the possessive liberalism view of the individual being responsible for themselves, and indeed, risk theorists such as Giddens and Beck talk about how we can see that since the 1960s and 1970s there has been a growing cultural and political discourse of rights and responsibilities emerging which seeks to regulate the individual while also arguing for the need for greater personal freedom. This leads us into another key feature of high modernity which is arguably central to the study of crime. Namely, that within the risk society a sense of growing (perhaps even mutual) distrust characterises the relationship between the public and experts (Giddens, 1999). At the same time, a pervasive and seemingly increasingly necessary reliance on an ever growing number of experts appears to be a key feature of the individual's personal experience of everyday life (Mythen, 2004). Interestingly, it was argued that this established the conditions for the public to challenge elitism and expert forms of knowledge. For under such changing social conditions expert authority can no longer simply stand on the traditional basis of position and status, not least because an individual's growing need to manage risk and problem solve their everyday life, to make choices about who they are and what they should do, mean that personal access to the technical and expert knowledge of the elite becomes more urgent than ever before. Furthermore, the development of mass information sharing tools, such as the mobile phone, personal computer and the internet, means that knowledge and expertise is no longer the sole preserve of those elite few who have undergone specialist training. As Giddens (1991: 144–6) notes: 'technical knowledge is continually re-appropriated by lay agents. … Modern life is a complex affair and there are many "filter back" processes whereby technical knowledge, in one shape or another, is re-appropriated by lay persons and routinely applied in the course of their day-to-day activities. … Processes of re-appropriation relate to all aspects of social life – for example, medical treatments, child rearing or sexual pleasure.'

There is then a tension between experts and citizens, between those in power and those who are not, and this can perhaps most clearly be seen in relation to modern technological advancements, particularly in relation to the rise of surveillance technology. After all, surveillance is essential to the task of identifying and managing and controlling risk – not least because under the neoliberal social conditions associated with high modernity it is by their ability to successfully manage risk that the state legitimises its governing activities. Bound up with this, as we shall now turn to discuss, is the need for law-abiding citizens to allow the surveillance of their everyday life to become a normalised feature of everyday existence.

The risk society as the surveillance society

One of the key academics who have looked at the growth of surveillance in modern society is Lyon (1994, 2001). Lyon (2001: 33) defines the surveillance society as 'a situation in which disembodied surveillance has become societally pervasive'. He goes on to say that the 'precise details of our personal lives are collected, stored, retrieved and processed every day within huge computer databases belonging to big corporations and government departments. This is the "surveillance society"' (Lyon, 1993: 3). Lyon argues that there are two faces to surveillance: care and control. That is, on the one hand the growth of surveillance technology enables us to more successfully manage risk and so care for ourselves and our social groups, but on the other hand, it also enables governments and state agencies to monitor and control populations, particularly for signs of potential threat and risk. Hence social sorting is a central feature of the application of surveillance technology at all levels. For surveillance possesses a classificatory imperative related to the ability to socially sort activities, peoples and events. This renders it as a medium of power to control and risk-manage citizens so their behaviour reflects dominant social, cultural and common-sense norms and values. Furthermore, for risk theorists, it is no coincidence that western states such as America and the UK suffer from endemic forms of surveillance. This is because, as Lyon notes, the rise of the surveillance society may be traced to modernity's impetus to coordinate and control. Surveillance technology certainly is rooted in modernity and the rise of the modern nation-state and a concurrent increase in the bureaucratic institutional organisation. For Giddens (1990: 321), surveillance is bound up with the growth of modernity, for 'surveillance is fundamental to social organization of all types, the state being historically the most consequential form of organization, but nevertheless being only one organization among many others'.

The work of Foucault (1979) has been very instructive in helping social scientists trace the historical development of the growth of surveillance. Foucault analysed historical penal documents from which he tied the development of modern surveillance to the punishment practices established in modern European prisons from the early eighteenth century onwards. His analysis reveals that during this period punishment shifted from the public spectacles of torture and execution, what Foucault calls exercises of monarchical power, to the techniques of what he terms 'soul training', which were mastered in the new prison regimes emerging at the time under the aegis of the Enlightenment revolution. These, he holds, were geared towards the production of obedient and docile individuals, who, in line with the Enlightenment pursuit of engendering positive social change through the application of reason, were held to be redeemable, if handled correctly, and hence ultimately able to contribute to society in some small way, that is if they are punished correctly with a view to changing their behaviour. Foucault termed this process carceral punishment, in that it heralded a constant surveillance of inmates under a new kind of power, namely disciplinary power, which over time, he argued, was gradually replacing monarchical power.

Foucault argues that as the nineteenth century progressed the prisons of Europe bore witness to the development of a form of spatial and temporal control over prisoners via hierarchies of classification and control which sought to discipline both body and mind. Amongst other things, Foucault uses the daily prison timetable of routines to illustrate his points: each prisoner's daily routine followed a set series of disciplinary practices, ranging from washing, to eating, to working and exercising, from the time they woke up in the morning until the time they went to sleep at night. He traces how guards and doctors kept ledgers of events and behaviours to enable the sharing of information. In this way, he argues, prisoners were subject to normalising judgements concerning right and wrong behaviour, which were orchestrated by guards and newly emerging professionals, including doctors, psychiatrists, sociologists and criminologists, all of whom observed, recorded, collated and categorised knowledge of inmate behaviour. Deviation from the norm was thus identified, recorded and corrected, often using the fruits of early scientific research and experiment.

For example, the results of human anatomy dissections, particularly from the nineteenth century onwards, were used by some early penal experts, notably Lombroso, whose early Biological criminology was discussed in Chapter 3, to identify how some criminals were a distinctive human-type who were abnormal biologically to law-abiding citizens, and hence needed to be subject to particular disciplinary regimes.

For Foucault the surveillance gaze was asymmetrical as those subject to it were unable to challenge or resist it. The sense one gets from reading Foucault is that acts of resistance may well be possible in some limited sense, but for obvious reasons ultimately power lies with those doing the surveying. The fact that surveillance utilised the fruits of emerging modern sciences, such as medicine and the social sciences, to justify its practices, alongside the fact that it was by and large enacted on the poor and socially excluded, contributed significantly to this state of affairs. In short, the form of surveillance in place within the confines of the prison walls operated through the panoptic principle – where the few (guards, doctors and a growing range of penal experts) could exercise control over the many (the prisoners). This ensured a new kind of legitimate authority which sought a more intensive, constant, efficient and somewhat automatic functioning of power and control over those individuals subject to its gaze. As we shall discuss in more detail shortly, it is this form of power that Foucault argues has stayed with us. Indeed, he holds it was gradually dispersed throughout society from the mid-nineteenth century onwards. But for the moment it is important to note that the development of the modern prison from the mid-eighteenth century onwards acted as a laboratory within which a range of experts and penal reformers experimented to identify how best to monitor, regiment, train and correct individual behaviour, and furthermore, they drew on the emerging fruits of modern science to help them achieve their goals. Yet it must be recognised that these events are not to be viewed negatively: Foucault notes that many of the new regimes introduced were born out of good intentions and a growing belief that individuals were not fundamentally flawed and indeed could be rehabilitated. Additionally, as Foucault is particularly concerned to point out, what is important about this shift towards the exercise of a more disciplinary form of power is that it is deliberately designed to encourage prison inmates to conduct self-surveillance in regulating and disciplining their own behaviour.

For Foucault, panoptic power and the forms of expertise and unverifiable surveillance this gave rise to, do not end at the prison walls. Rather, this distinctly modern form of corrective disciplinary surveillance gradually came to operate outside the prison as a new instrument of social control which would 'insert the power to punish more deeply in the social body ... [as it pursued] ... the utopia of the perfectly governed society' (Foucault, 1979: 198). Indeed, he argues that by the end of the nineteenth century we can see it operating across society's social institutions, including schools, military institutions, hospitals, asylums, governing bodies and even worker factories. Hence, for Foucault, surveillance is a tool for ensuring obedience which proliferated throughout a range of social institutions. In a very real sense, then, the disciplinary society is the surveillance society. For in such a society, according to Foucault, the judges of normality are everywhere. We live in a society of the teacher-judge, the doctor-judge, the social-worker-judge. In this sense, the thrust of modern surveillance is conjoined with the generation of knowledge used to normalise individual bodies, gestures, behaviours, aptitudes and attainments. Accordingly, what once constituted a drive to control illegalities and crime became applicable to a whole range of behavioural contexts in which 'the norm' reigns supreme and surveillance offers the possibility of countering many different forms of deviance, wherever it occurs.

Panoptic surveillance for Foucault is about whether an individual is behaving as they should in accordance with a social rule. For him, modern surveillance sites – such as the school, the workplace and the town centre shopping complex – aid the maintenance of social well-being and order. Hence they encourage a docile citizenry who are self-inspecting, self-judging and self-correcting in relation to predominant social expectations and norms. We will discuss in more detail shortly how these expectations and norms are bound up with the neoliberal form of the enterprise self – that is, the responsible subject-citizen who adheres to certain expectations of who they are and should be, as based around free-market processes and ideals relating to the production and consumption of services and goods – in order to explore how this has impacted on the ways in which governing frameworks operate. As a result, it is important at this point to turn to consider the dispersal of discipline in more detail.

The dispersal of discipline

For Foucault, surveillance is tied to the development of a distinct method of social control – disciplinary power – by which the organisational and social control apparatus of the modern nation-state in western societies has gradually evolved over the last 200 years into its present form. In essence, the risk-saturated social conditions associated with the surveillance society means it is by definition also a normalising society in which the norm of discipline and the norm of regulation intersect. Contemporary reforms in governing bodies are firmly linked to ongoing developments surrounding the need to engender self-surveillance and self-control on behalf of subject-citizens as western neoliberal democratic states continuously seek to minimise risk and maximise profit. In exploring this point further it is useful to examine the work of Cohen (1985).

Cohen used Foucault's insights to explore how surveillance generates new practices of social control as communication and information technologies develop throughout the twentieth century and in doing so shape the management of deviance via the introduction of various social engineering initiatives, including community-based social interventions, indeterminate sentencing for offenders and the mentally ill, neighbourhood watch schemes and private security firms, as well as more recently, the growth of CCTV cameras. For Cohen, these initiatives reinforced how the dispersal of discipline has adapted to changing social circumstance ever since it emerged from the prison gates. Indeed, Cohen notes that there has been a move towards informal, private, communal controls outside of the mechanisms of the state: in other words just as disciplinary control moved from the prison to the hospital, to the military yard, to the school and to the factory, it has over time moved from being located firmly within what can be defined quite broadly as the governing apparatus and into everyday areas of social life. This process is a somewhat logical outcome of the fact that a key feature of discipline is that it requires all individuals to engage in self-regulation and inspection, not just those who deviate from the norm. Cohen notes that a key outcome of this expansionist process is that it widens the net of the formal system of control by bringing about an increase in the total number of deviants getting into the system in the first place. Related to this, new types of deviants are created as a thinning of the mesh of the net of social control occurs as it expands in this manner, with the result that we see an increase in the overall level of intervention, including in more traditional forms of institutionalisation such as prisons and psychiatric detention, but also in community sentencing and treatment programmes as well. Here both old and new deviants become subject to surveillance and control in new ways, including electronic tagging, forced treatment orders and drug and alcohol abuse programmes (Cohen, 2010).

According to Cohen the dispersal of discipline as a method of social surveillance and control throughout contemporary society during the twentieth century brings with it a blurring of the previous boundaries between the public and the private, as well as formal and informal forms of control. This results in more people getting involved in the control problem of risk identification and management. Accordingly, modern surveillance technology heralds the beginning of a more insatiable processing of deviant groups which is undertaken by new experts in new spatial settings, i.e. the computer software engineer and the CCTV operator working with facial recognition software in a city-centre control room. Such processes are bound up with a general intensification in profiling to identify and manage risk. As Bogard puts it in relation to policing, 'if your skin colour, sex, age, household area, matches the computer profile each officer carries while on duty, you're a target, whether you have actually done anything wrong or not' (Bogard, 2007: 97).

Cohen highlights that it is important to remember that although the features of the process may have changed over time the most fundamental fact about what is going on is that it is much the same as what went on historically. For, like Foucault before him, Cohen traces the bedrock of surveillance to an insatiable governmental need to control a population via classifying and ordering it. Citizens must be identifiable and knowable so they can be handled appropriately with state intervention into their lives occurring as needed, both directly and indirectly by agencies of social order ranging from the school and the prison to the workplace and the hospital, in order to maintain discipline and social control. This process, it is argued, may well have existed for as long as human civilisation, but it was consolidated in the nineteenth century with the emergence of rational, scientific, knowledge, which dramatically expanded our ability to analyse and predict human behaviour and change the natural and social world to our liking. Additionally, it is important to remember that part of the attraction of the promise of scientific knowledge is that it is heralded as value-neutral and objective and therefore is trusted by the mass of people, even if the people who use it are not. It is this need to classify in order to analyse, predict and control, that has continued to the present and is woven into the minutia of social life, bringing with it new forms of expertise without which it is assumed we can no longer function as parents, travellers, consumers, workers or sexual beings. Hence, as Giddens (1991) notes, we become increasingly reliant on a day-to-day level on a mixture of specialised expert knowledge and self-help manuals, as modernity intensifies and progresses into the risk-saturated social conditions associated with high modernity.

Resisting the surveillance assemblage

For Cohen, as a cornerstone of modern social control, surveillance now operates right outside the formal punitive system of social control, i.e. the criminal justice system. It has become more and more dispersed throughout society to such a degree that it is now present within consumer culture, social welfare and communities, as well as everyday family life. For Cohen, inclusionary social control – the use of supervision of offenders in the community – as well as exclusionary social control – such as the use of prisons – will over time merge to reinforce each other and expand even further into every aspect of society. Also he thinks we are increasingly going to see pre-emptive forms of surveillance to spot and halt deviance at an early stage. There is certainly evidence to suggest that there is a trend for criminal justice agencies as well as health and social care professionals to focus on profiling risky citizens – that is those who are a danger to themselves or others – in order to prevent deviance in the form of physical violence, domestic violence, sexual abuse and terrorism. Consequently, the value of the work of Foucault and Cohen arguably lies in the fact that they bring to the fore the idea of panoptic control and its dispersion throughout society. This, in turn, introduces us to the important idea of an unseen observer – perhaps the core icon of modern Big Brother surveillance imagery – and how it pursues relentlessly, via the innovative use of constantly improving surveillance technologies, the classification of bodies, thoughts, gestures and actions, all with the goal of maintaining social order and managing risk.

Although the value of such insights must be acknowledged, it is also clearly useful to reflect on how human resistance happens under such panoptic forms of control. Foucault famously downplayed human agency. He felt that in the face of the combined forces of language, other people and the governing machinery of the state, individuals possessed very little room to manoeuvre and express resistance. So, in some respects, does Cohen. There is undoubtedly some obvious truth in both Foucault's and Cohen's tendency to downplay resistance in favour of focusing on compliance, as by and large the vast majority of everyday social interaction does serve to maintain social order and the agencies of social control are always at hand to deal with individuals who do not conform. However, there is equally truth in the assertion that a key defining feature of human beings is the capacity to resist and pursue social change – for example, the growth of modern information and communication technologies, particularly mobile phone technology, which has undergone a revolution over the last decade, offers us an avenue through which to explore the possibility of resistance. Lyon (2001), for instance, discusses resistance in relation to the growth of surveillance technology developments such as biometrics, cyber surveillance and identity cards. Here he notes how although state surveillance practices have expanded and intensified over recent decades, nevertheless the internet and mobile communication technologies allow citizens to turn the tables and survey powerful elites within society. This is an important point, because the impression you can get from authors such as Foucault and Cohen is that this is all a one-way street, with people being subject to panoptic power in a one-directional form.

The work of Haggerty and Ericson (2006) is extremely instructive here. They argue that in the late twentieth and early twenty-first century surveillance has proliferated and generated greater social visibility. That is, one of the key features of the surveillance society is that citizens can no longer hide and go off the grid: they are tagged and tracked via various means of social sorting as they journey from birth into everyday adult life and onto old age and death (Lyon, 2001). Yet, in tune with the risk society, Haggerty and Ericson note how contemporary surveillance transforms social hierarchies, rendering them less rigid as people from all social backgrounds and groups – elite and not so elite – are now under surveillance, not least because we all run the danger of becoming risky subjects. Furthermore, they say this is because of the rise of the surveillance assemblage, which they say encompasses the advances and extension in information and data gathering we have witnessed so far. This assemblage is what they term rhizomatic: that is, it is the result of unforeseeable offshoots, interconnections and dispersed flows of data globally across borders and institutions. One way of thinking about this idea is the viral adverts one now finds on the internet for a range of products and services, including movies, holidays and personal grooming products, which seem to emerge of their own accord.

In terms of looking at individuals and their information, Haggerty and Ericson talk about how nowadays it is difficult for people to maintain their anonymity under the surveillance gaze due to the rise of communication and mobile technology. So they talk about the disappearance of disappearance and equality through technology, with different social groups of individuals being subject to the surveillance assemblage at different times and places for different ends. For example, police can and do survey and record protestors and their conduct and likewise protestors survey and record the police – both these acts of surveillance can and have led to members of the public and the police becoming subject to legal processes. The idea of the surveillance assemblage, then, runs against the views of surveillance as a necessary top-down tool of the powerful, which is evident in the institutionally fixed conceptions of panoptic surveillance. This new surveillance, gathered around the use of techniques such as the internet and mobile phones, allows for the scrutiny of the powerful by both institutions and the general population. There are a number of related consequences of this view of surveillance. First, privacy may be ending for more and more social groups, but that privacy is being traded by subjects for benefits, services and rewards offered by surveillance bodies – such as for example when we allow supermarkets to gather information on us via supermarket loyalty cards in return for better deals and targeted vouchers and such like. This also shows how surveillance is increasingly being rationalised around seduction. In other words, the acceptance of surveillance as part of our lives is greater not because of any directly oppressive or coercive reason, as associated with more traditional panoptic power, and institutionalised in the form of the prison, but rather because we have become seduced to conform to the pleasures of consuming goods offered by the corporate bodies which survey our everyday shopping habits.

Secondly, the assemblage allows for greater, expandable mutability as surveillance regimes intended for one purpose find themselves used for another. This is evident in the use by the police of non-police databases for fighting and preventing crime and terrorism; such as financial, educational, media or insurance organisational surveillance records pertaining to individual behaviours and habits when they are suspected of being terrorists. Thirdly, the assemblage's supposed rhizomatic nature is arguably underpinning an as yet unfinished democratisation of surveillance. This is because the panopticon – where the few see the many – is being supplanted gradually over time, or at least joined up with another, equally pervasive surveillance medium – the synopticon. In a world in which surveillance now enables the scrutiny of the demeanour, idiosyncrasies and foibles of powerful individuals it is no longer merely the case that the few see the many, as in panoptic power, but rather the many come to see the few, which is synoptic power.

There can be no doubt that Haggerty and Ericson's view of surveillance has taken into account current technological advances and its increasing multi-media character, as well as its ability to enable groups to engage in resistance. The growth of mass media and digital and internet forms have transformed the surveillance landscape and created what some call 'the viewer' society. Here collective phenomena such as reality TV shows highlight how people have come to accept surveillance and even revel in the spotlight. While perhaps most importantly, the many – in other words the watching public – are encouraged to watch and judge the few – celebrities, politicians, VIPs, the notorious and the criminal. The key question we need to ask ourselves is, of course, if this apparent turning of the tables is indeed happening and the growth of surveillance technology across society not only enables the greater surveillance of the population, but also the rhizomatic levelling of traditional social hierarchies. Whereas Foucault claimed that people were self-governing when they were part of the panoptic society, could it perhaps be said that in today's society by watching the few we establish shared norms and values, lifestyles and our understanding of the world around us and our place in it? Could synoptic surveillance actually simply be an extension or transformation of panoptic forms of disciplinary power? And perhaps most importantly, just how are non-compliance and resistance dealt with under the constantly shifting social conditions of the risk society? The next section considers such matters in relation to contemporary trends in the criminal justice system.

Box 9.1 Key summary points

- It has been argued that the rapid social changes which have occurred in the last 30 years have led to a change towards the social conditions associated with late or high modernity where the identification and management of risk becomes of paramount concern when it comes to governing populations.
- Underpinning this shift is the re-emergence of neoliberalism, at the heart of which lies a view of human nature which stresses possessive individualism.
- Social theorists and criminologists have argued that the increased emphasis placed on surveillance and risk management provides new opportunities for governing elites to control and discipline populations as well as for members of society, in turn, to resist such processes.
- It is argued that this state of affairs had led to changes in the way crime is managed within western societies.

Further reading

Barry, A, Osborne, T and Rose, N (1996) *Foucault and political reason*. London: University College London Press.
Beck, U (1992) *Risk society: towards a new modernity*. London: Sage.
Lyon, D (2001) *Surveillance society: monitoring everyday life*. London: Sage.
Macpherson, CB (1962) *The political theory of possessive individualism*. Oxford: Clarendon Press.
Mythen, G (2004) *Ulrich Beck: a critical introduction to the risk society*. London: Pluto.

THE NEOLIBERAL ENTERPRISE FORM AND THE CRIMINAL JUSTICE SYSTEM

The preceding section of this chapter highlighted that there has been a profound shift in 'the nature of the present' (Rose, 1992: 16) and the way '[we] come to recognise ourselves and act upon ourselves as certain kinds of subject' (Rose, 1992: 161). This is due in no small part to the re-emergence of liberalism and the growing ascendancy of the concept of the enterprise self throughout all spheres of modern social life (Gordon, 1996). For example, Burchell (1996) argues that neoliberalism's dual advocacy of the self-regulating free individual and the free market has led to 'the generalisation of an "enterprise form" to all forms of conduct' (Burchell, 1996: 28). Enterprise – with its focus upon energy, drive, initiative, self-reliance and personal responsibility – has assumed a near-hegemonic position in the construction of individual identities and the government of organisational and everyday life. Enterprise has assumed 'an ontological priority' (du Guy, 1996: 181). Consequently, as Burchell (1993: 275) notes: 'one might want to say that the generalization of an "enterprise form" to all forms of conduct – to the conduct of organisations hitherto seen as being non-economic, to the conduct of government, and to the conduct of individuals themselves – constitutes the essential characteristic of this style of government: the promotion of an enterprise culture'.

Although it is sometimes argued that liberal societies seek to govern by consent, liberal mentalities of rule nevertheless seek to promote good citizenship by discursively constructing and promoting subjective positions for subject-citizens to occupy in relation to the forms of the enterprise self. Typically, this is associated with a bundle of characteristics such as energy, resilience, initiative, ambition, calculation, self-sufficiency and personal responsibility (Rose, 1999). For the world of enterprise valorises the autonomous, productive, self-regulating individual, who is following their own path to self-realisation, and so it requires all society's citizens to 'come to identify themselves and conceive of their interests in terms of these … words and images' (du Guy, 1996: 53). A key consequence of this state of affairs is that failure to achieve the goal of self-fulfilment is not associated with the possession of a false idea of what it means to be human; nor is it that individuals do not possess an essential core self which is the real and true them for all eternity. Rather, such failure is deemed to be the result of poor choices, a lack of education, or the dependency culture created by the welfare state. It is the result of learned helplessness, which in itself can be resolved with 'programmes of empowerment to enable [the individual] to assume their rightful place as self-actualizing and demanding subjects of an "advanced" liberal democracy' (Rose, 1996: 60).

A key place where this can be most readily seen is the criminal justice system. For it is here that neoliberal society deals with those who for one reason or another either do not meet, or actively seek to resist, the expectations and requirements of the neoliberal enterprise form. Indeed, over the last three decades a noticeable trend in the criminal justice system has been noted by criminologists and criminal justice workers towards the criminalisation and incarceration of people deemed for one reason or other to be dangerous, such as the young, the mentally ill, the terrorist suspect, the unemployed and so on (Goldson and Muncie, 2006; Young, 2011). A popular punitive approach to crime certainly appears prevalent within western nation-states, with some arguing that there has been a shift towards a new penology (Kelly, 2011). Underpinning much of the discussion of socially excluded and disadvantaged groups and crime is a particular set of somewhat familiar negative imagery, the origins of which lie in its lack of congruence with the productive self of the enterprise form. There is a tendency for the media, criminal justice agencies and political elites to propagate the well-worn caricature of the dangerous outsider, with all its associated transgressive discursive imagery, and this undoubtedly accounts for much of the successful folk devilling of people from a range of different groups which has occurred over the last several decades, and in doing so, has shaped much of the contemporary discourse surrounding the problem of crime and how to solve it.

Indeed, it has been argued that the last three decades in particular have witnessed the emergence of an actuarial-managerial penal policy for dealing with the problem of dangerous offenders and unruly risky populations (Garland, 2002). Here 'the management of risks and resources has displaced rehabilitation as the central organisational aim of the criminal justice system' (Garland, 2002: 177). The aim now is for criminal behaviour to be increasingly profiled and predicted, as the penal emphasis shifts to containment and control, as opposed to offender treatment and rehabilitation. Evidence for this position can be found in the prison statistics – the prison population has risen dramatically in most western countries over the last two decades. For example, in the UK in 1984 there were 43,295 individuals in prison, by 1994 it had risen slightly to 48,621, in 2004 it stood at 74,658, while by 2012 it stood at 86,812 (Ministry of Justice, 2013a). Such a dramatic increase cannot be put down to fluxes in crime rate patterns. It can only be the result of a deliberate shift in penal policy (Chamberlain, 2013).

Actuarialism and the new penology

The concept of actuarial justice was developed by Jonathon Simon (1987), and further expanded upon by Feeley and Simon (1992). They argue that a new penology has taken over from the old penal system, with its focus on due process to protect notions of human rights and social justice. Here differing social groups are increasingly being identified, classified and consequently controlled, based solely on the risk of danger they allegedly pose to society at large. As a result, actuarial justice techniques replace traditional criminal justice goals of rehabilitation, punishment, deterrence and incapacitation. Increasingly, a person is not solely punished for crimes they have committed, but for crime they might commit in the future. With this shift being based upon stereotyped (and indeed often scientised and medicalised) statistical assessments of human behaviour. The actuarialism of the new penology focuses on a kind of calculative logic which transforms crime control to a process based on prediction and pre-emption (Feeley and Simon, 1992). Hudson (2003) identifies three areas that have shifted to distinguish the old and the new penology: (1) discursive themes, (2) targets of penal strategies and (3) penal techniques. The alteration in discursive themes, for example towards tougher sentencing patterns, does not by itself constitute a change as it can be political rhetoric, but it nevertheless undoubtedly reflects changes in opinion of the government and public.

The new penology has defining characteristics that reveal it to be a more punitive form of penal strategy which employs socially divisive penal techniques. It is associated with 'identifying, classifying and managing groups assorted by levels of dangerousness' (Feeley and Simon, 1994: 180). This focus on risk and populations, instead of individuals, differentiates it from the old penology of individualism, rehabilitation and utilitarianism, as first advocated 200 years ago by the followers of Classical criminology, and which has dominated notions of justice in western societies ever since. The new penology is, according to Feeley and Simon (1994), still concerned with guilt, blame, identification of the individual and the punishment and treatment of the offender. Blaming the individual undoubtedly remains an ever present feature of the system and perhaps always will be. But what is new is an increasing reliance on an actuarialist focus on probability. It is this focus on attempting to 'manage the risk' which infringes traditional socio-legal notions of due process within the legal system – not least because, as we have already noted, under the conditions of high modernity emphasis is placed on risk assessment, displaying the legal sanction of legitimate surveillance, preventive detention and the social exclusion of certain politically unwanted groups (i.e. the protestor, the immigrant, the socially unproductive and so on). As a result, notions of rehabilitation in actuarial justice are diminished as 'objectives such as reform and rehabilitation become subsumed to mechanical functions such as measurement and classification of risk and efficient deployment of resources to minimise the threat of harm' (Smith, 2006: 93). This is partly due to the focus on groups instead of individuals, as well as ongoing debates surrounding the merit of rehabilitation, with some right-leaning neoconservative political elites in particular concluding that 'nothing works' due to consistently low statistical evidence for the success of rehabilitation, particularly over the last four decades (Easton and Piper, 2012). As a result, under the new penology, the meaning of recidivism has also changed. It was previously about analysing success or failure. Yet this focus had dropped out of the political discourse to avoid the possibility of accusations of institutional failure. But this state of affairs is not so much about avoidance. Instead it represents a fundamental change in the way neoliberal governing systems engage in self-evaluation under the conditions of high modernity. As Hudson (2003: 49) notes, 'with the new, actuarial justice, the "truth" of an assessment lies in correctly identifying the risk factors, not in whether an individual really would or would not reoffend'.

Responsibilisation and actuarial justice

The focus on aggregate groups to identify risk is called categorical suspicion: a person is seen as a criminal because of the groups they belong to rather than their behaviour (Hudson, 2003). Yet under the actuarialism of the new penology the fact that persistent offenders tend to come from deprived backgrounds is by and large ignored, or at the very least is only paid lip-service to when it comes to the day-to-day delivery of criminal justice. A significant number of offenders in the criminal justice system suffer from a range of psychological and psychiatric issues as a result of being physically and/or sexually abused as a child. They might well have alcohol and drug abuse issues in addition to poor educational qualifications and life skills. These factors undoubtedly influence and shape human thought and action, and as such, can lead to repeat offending behaviour. Yet these factors are by and large ignored by advocates of 'just desserts' punitive models of criminality, who tend to favour viewing repeat offenders (and indeed first-time offenders) as being untreatable and inherently dangerous, rather than deserving of compassion, treatment and care. Such positions can lead to governments being ever more able to justify more punitive and actuarial sanctions on offenders. This state of affairs is fed by the mass media, who, under the conditions of the risk society, constantly seek to persuade and justify to the viewing public that more punitive justice methods are needed by using high profile, dramatic crimes, which are unrepresentative of the vast majority of crime.

Actuarial justice invokes a focus on cost-effectiveness, efficiency and public protection, regardless of the cost to notions of due process and notions of individuals being innocent until proven guilty, or deserving of rehabilitation. In tune with the neoliberal ideals of the enterprise form, this shift is underpinned by an emphasis on 'responsibilisation', where 'individuals are expected to be actively engaged in their own self-governance' (Gray, 2009: 445). The new penology draws on statistical techniques and new managerialist methods to control offenders and the risk of offending, hence why it has been termed actuarial justice. It is also why we are witnessing the rise of managerialism and the narrow focus of Right Realist criminologists on reforming strategies concerned with cost-effectiveness while simultaneously advocating harsher social control mechanisms against already marginalised groups with a view to keeping them out of sight and out of mind. For 'these new forms of control are not anchored in aspirations to rehabilitate, reintegrate, retrain, provide employment, or the like' (Feeley and Simon, 1992: 457).

The introduction of actuarial techniques across the main political parties in the UK and elsewhere over the last three decades reinforces that, 'right-wing governments of the 1980s and the 1990s were neo-liberal with regard to public spending, but by no means libertarian with regard to public morals' (Hudson, 2003: 61). One of the major arguments regarding the development of the new penology is the perceived failure of rehabilitative ideals, giving rise to other, more punitive principles, which seek to reduce the opportunities to offend while enforcing incapacitating sanctions against transgressors. Actuarial justice has components such as neglecting the causes behind crime, and the subsequent focus on the control of stereotyped groups is (somewhat ironically) diametrically opposed to liberalism, which traditionally focuses on the individual and the equality of liberty (Hudson, 2003).

Yet this new actuarial-managerial penal policy is not solely concerned with containing crime through 'warehousing' a growing number of offenders, both young and old, in penal institutions. Its focus remains on managing instead of solving the problem of crime, to such a degree that western societies can be said to be in no small part governed through crime, and this has led, in turn, to a widening of the surveillance net, in part through the intensification in community-based surveillance and profiling of people deemed to be 'a risk' (Garland, 2002). Hence, the shift in emphasis to managing the problem of crime through risk profiling and assessment means that diversionary and rehabilitative programmes actually intensify rather than gradually disappear: yet they shift to emphasising surveillance and containment rather than treatment and care.

In part this is achieved through establishing a broader range of partnerships between criminal justice agencies and community stakeholders, i.e. community leaders, voluntary and charity groups, business leaders and so on. For example, in the UK criminologists have noted that the New Labour government of the mid-1990s onwards oversaw the rapid expansion of community-based interventions for youth offenders, with the 1998 Crime and Disorder Act establishing Youth Offending Teams (YOTs) in addition to Youth Justice Boards (YJBs) to oversee them. The creation of YOTs extended the responsibility of youth intervention and supervision beyond probation and social workers alone (Ministry of Justice, 2010). The result was that a wide range of criminal justice and welfare agencies – the police, the probation service, educational providers, benefit, housing and health agencies – were joined by local community voluntary groups and youth group organisations. Bound up with this was the introduction of Youth Inclusion and Support Panels (YISPs) to target young people under the age of 13 who were at risk of offending and to establish preventative strategies at a local level to tackle both offending and reoffending behaviour (Ministry of Justice, 2013b). This, in turn, led to an increase in the role of 'alternative' programmes, such as sports-based interventions, which seek to involve a range of voluntary and statutory organisations with local community groups, to tackle the problem of antisocial behaviour and youth offending (Kelly, 2011). Such developments continued after the Coalition government replaced New Labour in 2010. What we have here, then, is a long-term policy trend within the criminal justice system which arguably is heavily influenced by broader socio-cultural, technological and political changes occurring in western neoliberal societies under the fluctuating social conditions of high modernity. As already discussed, this is underpinned by a view of the individual citizen-subject as a rational enterprising self. It is the implications of this state of affairs which the final section of this chapter will turn to consider.

Box 9.2   Key summary points

- As a result of the broader social changes which have occurred due to an increasing focus on the enterprise self, the criminal justice system has become ever more punitive and increasingly emphasises the identification and risk management of dangerous offenders rather than their rehabilitation.

(Continued)

(Continued)

- Critical criminologists have highlighted that new actuarial-managerial penal polices – the new penology – are not solely concerned with containing crime through 'warehousing' a growing number of offenders, both young and old, in penal institutions. These policies also extend 'the criminal gaze' to include the law-abiding population. This has led, in turn, to a widening of the surveillance net, often using advances in new information and communication technology. There has been as a result an intensification in community-based surveillance and profiling of young people and socially excluded and disadvantaged groups, all of whom are deemed to be a potential risk to neoliberal forms of good governance.

Further reading

Feeley, M and Simon, J (1992) The new penology: notes on the emerging strategy for corrections. *Criminology* 30 (4): 449–75.

Feeley, M and Simon, J (1994) Actuarial justice: the emerging new criminal law. In Nelken, D (ed.), *The futures of criminology*. London: Sage.

Garland, D (2001) *Mass imprisonment: social causes and consequences.* London: Sage.

Hudson, B (2003) *Justice in the risk society: challenging and reaffirming justice in late modernity.* London: Sage.

Simon, J (1987) The emergence of a risk society: insurance, law and the state. *Socialist Review* 95: 6–89.

Simon, J and Feeley, M (1995) True crime: the new penology and public discourse on crime. In Blomberg, TG and Cohen, S (eds), *Punishment and social control: essay in honor of Sheldon L. Messinger.* New York: Aldine de Gruyter.

Young, J (2011) *The criminological imagination.* Cambridge: Polity Press

CONCLUSION: REFLECTING ON THEORIES OF CRIME AND THEORIES OF HUMAN NATURE

Modern individuals are not merely 'free to choose', but obliged to be free, to understand and enact their lives in terms of choice. (Rose, 1999: 87)

So where does this state of affairs leave the student of criminological theory? The possessive individualism which lies at the heart of the neoliberal enterprise self emphasises a 'positivist ego psychology, which is hostile to any notion that the self is complexly structured and differentiated' (Peterson and Bunton, 1997: 190). It is important to examine the limitations of this viewpoint when the ever changing social conditions of high modernity are taken into consideration. Indeed, given the uneven distribution of social position and personal wealth in western neoliberal societies, only a relatively few individuals have the access to the work and leisure opportunities which arguably make the enterprising self an achievable possibility (Rose, 1999). Hence crime and other social problems, such as unemployment and health inequality, are perhaps an inevitable common feature of modern neoliberal societies (Rose, 1999). However, there is a deep-seated contradiction lying at the heart of a viewpoint which, on one hand, advocates that an individual's sense of self is nowadays arguably more than ever before a product of their own making, and yet on the other hand, remains wedded to the idea of the citizen-subject as an autonomous social actor possessing a coherent core self. Furthermore, theories of crime can suffer from the same contradiction when they seek to locate the causes of crime within a concrete empirical individual in order to subject them to scientific investigation and expert manipulation to better enable social regulation and state governance of the population. Typically, this is because these focus on a person's capacity for reason and choice (in the case of Classical criminology), elements of their biological makeup (in the case of Biological criminology), or their cognitive health and functioning (in the case of Psychological criminology). As has been discussed in Chapters 7 and 8 in particular, Critical forms of criminology are by and large highly wary of positivist theories of crime which by and large remain wedded to the notion of the individual as a distinctive unity, not least because their application enables the governing state to continue to de-emphasise the role structural social inequalities and injustice play in shaping the conditions for crime in the first place (Young, 2011).

In contrast to the possessive individualism of neoliberalism, following Foucault (1991), some Critical theorists, particularly those influenced by postmodernism, firmly historicise their conception of the individual by discursively locating it within the history of western thought through critiquing the development of neoliberalism as being tied up with a post-Enlightenment conception of a rationally autonomous citizen-subject (Peters, 2001). As a result, they advocate an alternative viewpoint whereby individual subjectivities are neither fixed nor stable, but rather are constituted in and through a spiral of power/knowledge discourses – generated by political objectives, institutional regimes and expert disciplines – whose primary aim is to produce governable individuals (Deleuze, 1988). Such a conception arguably better fits the fluctuating social circumstances associated with the individual's everyday experience of life under the globalising conditions of high modernity. Furthermore, this alternative view of human nature and agency may well offer an avenue for achieving positive social change. Indeed, the presence of social inequality, difference and exclusion – on the basis of age, race and ethnicity, class and gender – remains for many Critical criminologists *the* underpinning cause for the majority of crime and *the* reason why they reject apolitical criminological discourses which claim to be value-free and objective (Young, 2011). The Chicagoan school of sociology of deviance, alongside the Critical criminological perspectives outlined from Chapter 5 onwards in this book, reinforce the need to consistently and actively challenge the normalising processes of social engineering – via social policy, welfare reform and criminal justice practice – in addition to perspectives which advocate the manipulation of human psychology and biology by chemicals, genetics or surgery – when they fail to take into account the influence of social organisation and structural inequalities in all their forms, on human behaviour. For in terms of Berlin's (2002 [1969]) famous dichotomy of 'positive' and 'negative' liberty, although liberal mentalities of rule may appear at first to promote 'negative liberty' (i.e. the personal freedom of the individual-subject to decide who they are and discover what they want to be), in reality they promote 'positive liberty' (i.e. a view of who and what a citizen-subject is and should be). It certainly can be argued that a key facet of advanced neoliberal society is its central concern with disciplining the population without recourse to direct or oppressive intervention. Yet liberal mentalities of rule seek to promote good citizenship by discursively constructing and promoting subjective positions for subject-citizens to occupy in relation to the form of the enterprise self (Rose, 1999). In doing so, it is arguable that under the guise of advocating personal freedom and minimal forms of government as the 'natural way of things', liberal mentalities of rule run the risk of promoting a highly limiting view of what it is to be a human being, let alone a good citizen, within today's increasingly complex, globally interconnected world.

As a result of such considerations we can perhaps best conclude our introduction to the world of criminological theory by saying that today's students of crime must be ever mindful that when disputing parties are at loggerheads this is often because unspoken assumptions are being made about the human condition. Certainly the historical development of criminology as an academic discipline arguably reinforces that it is all too easy to conclude that criminals are somehow psychologically or morally defective, or are just biologically different from the rest of us, when in reality the causes of their behaviour may well lie elsewhere.

SELF-STUDY TASKS

1. Write a 15-minute PowerPoint presentation explaining why the broader social conditions of late or high modernity are important to understanding current developments within the criminal justice system.
2. One important division when it comes to criminological theory is between determinists, who see human behaviour as the outcome of forces outside individual control, and others who believe that, while we often find ourselves in unwanted situations, we are always responsible for making the most of any predicament. Write 500 words outlining which of these two viewpoints is emphasised by the possessive individualism of the neoliberal enterprise self. Make sure you provide reasons for your answer.

GLOSSARY

BECCARIA

Eighteenth-century scholar regarded as the founding father of Classical criminology. Beccaria subscribed to the political philosophy of utilitarianism, which holds that politics and deeds, particularly those associated with the government, should provide the greatest good for the greatest number of people. Bound up with this viewpoint was the belief that the governing apparatus of the state should seek to minimise its influence over the freely choosing rational thinking individual. As a result, Beccaria argued that the general objective all legislative laws and legal systems should have in common is to augment the total happiness of the community

BIOLOGICAL CRIMINOLOGY

A collective term referring to approaches to the study of crime which emphasise three overlapping perspectives; namely, traditional evolutionary theories as influenced by the early thinking of Darwin, later genetic theories which focus on inherited traits, defects or deficiencies, as well as more recent biochemical theories that focus on hormonal or chemical imbalances. Although its origins stretch back much further through the work of the physiognomists and phrenologists, the historical development of modern forms of Biological criminology from the beginning of the nineteenth century onwards overlaps with the emergence of Classical criminology from the eighteenth century onwards, as well as Psychological criminology at the turn of the twentieth century. Biological criminology rejects Classical criminology and its focus on explaining human behaviour in general, and criminal behaviour in particular, as being the end product of individual's rational exercise of their free will. Instead, human behaviour is seen as being more or less determined, or at least heavily influenced by human biology acting in tandem with environmental factors such as parenting style and upbringing. Sociological forms of criminology, particularly Critical criminology, are highly critical of such approaches.

BONGER

Bonger applied Marx's insights to developing a radical Marxist form of criminology. He observed that crime rose as western societies became industrialised from the nineteenth century onwards, that capitalist societies appear to have considerably more crime than other societies, as well as that the crimes committed within them appear to be mostly committed by the working class (or the proletariat in Marx's terms). Bonger argued that this was because, under capitalism, the characteristic trait of humans is self-interest egoism: both people and business are seeking profit maximisation and social relations are class structured and geared to the economic exchange of goods and services for cash, which creates the potential for conflict. For both Marx and Bonger criminal law is principally constituted according to the will of the dominant bourgeoisie class and hardly any act is punished if it does not injure its interests.

BROKEN WINDOWS (SEE ALSO SOCIAL DISORGANISATION THEORY)

The 'Broken Windows' hypothesis emerged from Social Disorganisation Theory and the idea that visual cues of physical and social disorder within an urban living space could over time, if not dealt with, lead to further disorder and crime. This hypothesis was most famously tested in New York City in the 1990s by Police Chief William Bratton. He used an approach called 'zero tolerance policing' where all signs of disorder are quickly and punitively addressed by proactive community policing. Zero tolerance policing involves the police more strictly enforcing the law against drinking in public, subway and bus fare evasion and did indeed did lead to a year-on-year reduction in crime rates. However, zero tolerance policing has been criticised for being overly punitive and costly.

CHICAGO SCHOOL

The collective term applied to the body of work which emerged from the Department for Sociology at the University of Chicago from the 1920s onwards and in doing so established sociological criminology as an important method for examining the causes of crime and deviance.

CLASSICAL CRIMINOLOGY

Classical criminology emerged in the eighteenth century in the writings of Cesare Beccaria and Jeremy Bentham as a result of the Enlightenment, which is a social movement which stressed naturalistic as opposed to religious explanations for both physical events (i.e. the weather) and human behaviour, including behaviour labelled deviant or criminal. Classic criminology emphasised deterrence and the rationality and agency of the social actor. Indeed, ability of an individual to conduct a cost-benefit analysis of a cause of action in order to achieve a goal before actively pursuing it is held to be *the* key defining characteristics of human beings by Classical criminologists. Its influence persists to this day in contemporary criminology; for example, in situational crime prevention research, particularly routine activity theory.

CRIME

A label society attaches to particular human behaviours deemed to be socially or morally unacceptable and as a result are held to be deserving of, at the very least, stigmatisation and disapproval, at most, punishment and retribution.

CRITICAL CRIMINOLOGY

Critical criminology encompasses a range of different approaches which have different emphases and nuances, and which have been categorised under various headings, including Marxist criminology, Critical criminology, Left and Right Realism, Feminist criminology, Peacemaking criminology and Cultural criminology, amongst others. These diverse viewpoints share a concern with examining how different forms of oppression, inequality and conflict affect people in everyday life as well as through the lens of crime and law. Critical criminology rejects the idea that it is possible to follow the positivist methodology of the natural sciences and for criminology as a discipline to be 'value-free'. Many Critical criminologists also reject the idea that a crime-free society is possible. While early Critical criminology in the form of Marxist criminology emphasised the deterministic nature of social structure, later forms of Critical criminology, such as Cultural criminology, tend to emphasise what is called the 'duality of structure'. This stance acknowledges that we are clearly in no small part a product of our social environment, and our practical circumstances do act in certain situations to constrain and shape our everyday behaviour; but people nevertheless do intrinsically possess agency and free will, and furthermore, certain structures in society can actually act to enhance agency (for example, equal opportunities and human rights legislation and institutions).

CULTURAL CRIMINOLOGY

Cultural criminology is a Critical criminological perspective which emerged during the 1990s. It emphasises the powerful role the modern media and new information sharing and social networking technologies play in shaping our experience of crime, deviance and law. It also focuses on the role human emotion plays in shaping our lived experience of crime, as both victim and offender (also see Critical criminology).

DIET AND CRIME

Over the last two decades there has been an increase in focus within Biological criminology on the possible link between biochemistry, hormones and diet in influencing human behaviour, including antisocial and criminal behaviour. Evidence suggests that nutrition and diet in particular can impact on human behaviour, particularly excessive consumption of sugar, carbohydrates, processed foodstuffs and stimulants such as caffeine. However, outside of the laboratory it is difficult to conclusively link diet to aggressive and rule-breaking behaviour, particularly as a range of psychological and socio-cultural factors influence how human beings behave within social situations. See Biological criminology and Genes and crime.

DIFFERENTIAL ASSOCIATION

See Sutherland and Psychological criminology.

DUALITY OF STRUCTURE

See Critical criminology and the individual characteristic/social phenomena dichotomy.

DURKHEIM

A sociologist who along with the philosopher Mead influenced the development of the sociology of deviance and criminology through informing the work of the Chicago School. Durkheim held that society exists independently to its individual members and acts to constrain and shape their behaviour while at the same time providing a moral and cultural framework which they internalise through processes of socialisation. He also argued that crime plays an important regulative social function within a society and as such it is not possible to have a crime-free society.

EYSENCK

Hans Eysenck is a psychologist who explains the criminal personality as resulting from the interaction between three psychological traits: neuroticism (N), extroversion (E) and psychoticism (P). Eysenck argued that some people have nervous systems that are more reactive or sensitive to stimuli than others, and this makes them more excitable and less able to exercise self-control, with the result that they may be more likely to engage in risk taking and criminal behaviour. Eysenck's theory has been criticised on moral and ethical grounds for potentially providing a deterministic model of criminal behaviour whereby it is justified on the basis that a person couldn't choose to act differently given their nervous system physiology.

FEMINIST CRIMINOLOGY

Feminist criminology emerged against the background of the growth of feminism as a social movement in the mid-1960s. Highlighting the missing voice of women in criminological discourse surrounding deviance and crime, it advocated the need to address forms of gender-based violence and sexual abuse, such as domestic violence. It criticised mainstream criminology for failing to develop a theory of female offending behaviour which did not solely rely on empirical data which had emerged from studying juvenile and/or adult male offenders.

GENES AND CRIME

Since the late 1960s Biological criminologists have looked at the role of genetics in making criminal behaviour more probable through influencing human behaviours, such as impulsivity or a willingness to take risks, as well as looking at their role in influencing the production of certain enzymes which may act as a trigger for aggressive behaviour. However, no serious biologist would argue that there is a single 'criminal gene'. Indeed, most contemporary Biological criminologists argue for the need to take into consideration both biological and environmental factors when it comes to analysing the effect of genetics on human behaviour, as the available evidence indicates that neither nature (genes) nor nurture (upbringing and social environment) are sufficient in themselves to cause antisocial and criminal behaviour. See also Biological criminology.

INDIVIDUAL CHARACTERISTIC/SOCIAL PHENOMENA DICHOTOMY

The causes of crime have been theorised by criminologists in different ways. But generally speaking these can be divided into being either a result of characteristics which belong to an individual – their biology, their psychology or their ability to use their own free will to choose to act – or due to features of the society to which they belong – its social and economic inequalities, class divisions, poverty levels and so on. This is called the individual characteristic/social phenomena dichotomy.

LABELLING THEORY

A sociological theory of crime derived from the work of Lemert, Becker and Erikson and heavily influenced by the work of Durkheim and Mead. Focusing on the role of society in creating norms and values to create social order and govern human behaviour, labelling theorists argue that deviance and crime are not a quality of the act the person commits, but rather are a consequence of the application by others of rules and sanctions to an offender. Labelling Theory argues that the societal reaction to deviance – be it imprisonment or rehabilitation for the criminal – does not seem to reform the criminal, which is their manifest or announced function. Instead, it stigmatises the offender, segregates them with other deviants; and in doing so establishes and reinforces a feeling of distrust within the community towards them. As a result, it is argued that the latent function of the labelling is to provide society with a pool of offenders for defining moral boundaries and reaffirming social solidarity.

LEFT REALISM

Left Realist criminology developed in the late 1980s and early 1990s, originating in the writings of the British criminologists Jock Young and Roger Matthews, in response to the populist punitive discourse of Right Realism. It argues that Right Realism grew out of a critique of Strain Theory and Labelling Theory from the mid-1980s onwards. Two core Left Realist concepts are 'the square of crime' and 'relative deprivation'.

LIFE COURSE CRIMINOLOGY

The life course of an individual can be conceptualised as a series of events taking place in the context of life stages, turning points and pathways, all of which are embedded in social institutions, specifically, the family, the school, the workplace, the penal system and so on. Life Course criminology focuses on tracing over time the life trajectories and stories of criminals. It is viewed as an integrated theory of crime in that it seeks to incorporate both developmental biological-psychological and social factors within its analysis of the criminal career trajectory from youth delinquency to adult offending. Its primary concern is with the fact that the majority of crime in western nations is committed by youth offenders between the ages of 16 and 25 and that desistence from crime as a person ages is common to all offenders regardless of any similarities or differences in their early childhood experiences. Life Course criminologists often argue for preventive school and penal system based interventions to promote a change in the delinquent and criminal career trajectory. However, this approach is often at odds with the broader, more punitive Right Realist youth crime agenda of most western societies of the last three decades, which has seen an increase in juvenile punishment and incarceration rates worldwide.

LOMBROSO

Cesare Lombroso was an Italian doctor who was influenced by the evolutionary theory of Charles Darwin and the ideas of natural selection. Lombroso's central theory was that the criminal was a biological throwback to an earlier stage in human evolution, more ape-like than human. He called this degeneracy atavism. Atavism manifested itself, according to Lombroso, in certain physical characteristics that he called stigmata. The stigmata did not cause criminality, atavism did. But the stigmata were useful for identifying atavists, or born criminals, as Lombroso called them. The work of Lombroso established Biological criminology while his emphasis on adopting a scientific approach to studying the causes of criminology separated his work from Classical criminology and established a biological positivist form of criminology which lives on to this day in modern forms of Biological criminology (i.e. research into crime and genetics).

MARX

A philosopher who argued that the story of human history and civilisation is one determined primarily by economic factors. Marx argued that contemporary society consisted of two main classes, the bourgeoisie and the proletariat, with the former exploiting the latter and society's key governing bodies, including its legal and criminal justice institutions, being designed to serve the vested interests of the bourgeoisie. His work, along with that of Willem Bongor, influenced the development of radical Marxist forms of criminology.

MARXIST CRIMINOLOGY

A form of Critical criminology influenced by the writings of the philosopher Karl Marx, which argues for the importance of a structural sociological factor – class and class-based struggle – in determining human thought and action, including criminal behaviour. Marxist criminologists view crime and deviance as social constructs, rather than as things which somehow belong to individuals as a result of some aspect of their individual biology or psychology. They argue that people are brutalised by the conditions of capitalism, and the problem of crime therefore can only be solved by restructuring society. Furthermore, by divorcing the study of crime from the study of class domination criminologists are tacitly involved in reproducing the inequalities caused by capitalism. Marxist criminology challenges the idea that criminology can be a disinterested social science and argues that criminologists must not simply look at the law breakers, but the law makers and law keepers as well. It has been criticised for possessing an overly deterministic view of human behaviour and an over-romantic view of the working-class criminal. It has also been criticised by later Critical and Feminist criminologists who argued that certain crimes involving female victims and victims from ethnic minorities, including forms of hate crime, rape and domestic violence, are due to ideological factors relating to patriarchy or institutionalised forms of racism, rather than responses to the class-based inequality caused by capitalist systems.

MEAD

A philosopher who, along with the sociologist Durkheim, influenced the development of the sociology of deviance and criminology through informing the work of the Chicago School. Mead emphasised the role of language and symbols in constituting the world around us and our perceptions of ourselves and also argued that individual identity formation is highly influenced by important or significant others, who tend to be members of our primary groups, such as families and friends. These are sometimes referred to as reference groups because they provide the individual with a perspective, a point of reference and a comparison for their own behaviour and thinking. Therefore, for Mead, and by extension label theorists, the exercise of self-control by the individual is simultaneously the exercise of social control by the social group to which they belong. This idea has been highly influential in the development of criminology as an academic discipline more generally over the last several decades.

ONTOLOGY

The study of human nature and what it means to be human. One important ontological division for the study of crime is the division between viewing human nature as being egotistical and self-interested or seeing it as communal and altruistic. Another is between determinists, who see human behaviour as the outcome of forces outside individual control, and those who emphasise free will and believe that, while we often find ourselves in situations not of our own choosing, we are always responsible for making the most of any situation.

PHRENOLOGY

An early form of Biological criminology which argues that physical structure, or more precisely human biology, determines a person's personality and behaviour. It is the emergence in the eighteenth century of Phrenology which established the focus of Biological criminology on naturalistic as opposed to religious causes for human behaviour through experimenting with the developing medical sciences of the time; including most importantly, the emerging disciplines of anatomy and physiology. Phrenologists such as Francis Gall argued that various brain functions are localised within certain structures of the brain. That is, specific areas of the brain control particular types of behaviour and personality traits. Gall identified some 26 distinct bumps, with later phrenologists expanding this to 35 bumps, which were felt to reflect major regions or compartments of the brain and related to key aspects of human personality, including, higher intellectual reasoning, moral faculties and what were viewed as more animalistic needs such as that for sex. Although influential during its time, phrenology was gradually discredited and replaced by Lombroso's atavistic form of Biological criminology.

PHYSIOGNOMY

Physiognomy means 'nature's judge'. The idea that an individual's character can be read from their physical appearance dates back to the ancient Greeks and Romans and can be found in the writings of Zopyrus, an artist and playwright who lived in Athens during fifth century BC Athens. Practitioners studied faces, skulls and other physical features, such as hands and feet, which they believed revealed a person's natural disposition. It is an early precursor to phrenology and Lombroso's atavistic form of Biological criminology.

POSITIVISM

Positivism advocates the adoption of a scientific approach to the study of human behaviour. Emphasis is placed on identifying and systematically collecting 'the facts' through careful observation and experiment. Positivism assumes there is an objective reality that exists independently to human beings and emphasises the need for a researcher to engage in systematic observation and experiment in a value-neutral and dispassionate manner in order to discover underlying causal laws of behaviour. Positivist criminologists, be they focusing on the biological, psychological or sociological factors which contribute to the problem of crime, focus on criminals and criminal behaviour, not on crimes, as Classical criminologists did. Consequently, they reject Classical criminology and its focus on explaining human behaviour in general, and criminal behaviour in particular, as being the end product of an individual's rational exercise of their free will. Instead, human behaviour is seen as being more or less determined, or at least heavily influenced by, factors either within the makeup of an individual or their natural environment. See also the individual characteristic/social phenomena dichotomy.

POSTMODERNISM

See Realism/anti-realism.

PSYCHOLOGICAL CRIMINOLOGY

Psychological criminology covers a broad range of research into personality and cognitive development as well as psychosocial learning theories in the form of social learning and differential association theory. It also plays a key role in the identification and risk management of violent and sex offenders as well as the care and treatment of offenders diagnosed with a mental illness. Like Classical criminology and Biological criminology, Psychological criminology locates the causes of crime inside the individual, although rather than emphasising free will it is argued that our actions are to some extent determined by our psychological makeup, learned behaviour and mental health.

REALISM AND ANTI-REALISM

Realism is a philosophical stance concerning the nature of reality which underpins positivism and assumes there is an objective reality that exists independently of human beings and emphasises the need for a researcher to engage in systematic observation and experiment in a value-neutral and dispassionate manner in order to discover underlying causal laws of behaviour. Anti-realism underpins postmodernism and assumes the contingent nature of human knowledge, holding that accounts of the world are social constructions which do not exist independently of the social actor and the language they use to describe the world around them.

RIGHT REALISM

Key proponents of Right Realism were James Wilson and Richard Herrnstein, who tried to construct a biosocial approach to crime, based on the Classical criminological concept of free will and Eysenck's social-psychological theory of criminality, which argued that the biological basis for crime lies in the human nervous system. Right Realism grew out of a critique of Strain Theory and Labelling Theory, which informed much of criminal justice policy in the USA and UK during the 1970s and 1980s. These approaches, it was argued by Right Realists, ignored the victim of crime and were too closely tied up with left-wing politics and the viewpoint that an expansion of state welfare to promote equality of opportunity could reduce crime. The realist tag, which is shared by both Left and Right forms of realism, results from the view that the state should set itself clear and doable targets to deal with crime.

ROUTINE ACTIVITY THEORY

Routine activity theory holds that the probability that a crime will occur at any specific time and place is a function of the convergence of likely offenders and victims in a situation where there is an absence of capable guardians to protect the victim. Hence, there are three essential elements of a crime: (1) a motivated offender, (2) a suitable target and (3) the absence of a capable guardian. Routine activities are activities which reoccur and our everyday lives are full of them: eating, sleeping, working, keeping fit, going to the cinema, having sex, are all routine activities. So is crime. For example, we would expect that handgun crime would occur depending on the routine activities of offenders and victims and the relationship between the two. Research has shown that it certainly appears to be the case that, due to their routine activities at the day-to-day level of lived human experience, handgun crime involving relatives is likely to occur in the home and those involving strangers in the street.

SOCIAL DISORGANISATION THEORY

Influenced by Durkheim and his arguments for the value of exploring sociological explanations for deviance and crime, Park and Burgess focused on urban geographic areas and argued that social change caused social disorganisation within them. Park and Burgess identified several distinct zones in Chicago that expanded out in a pattern of concentric circles from the centre of the city. They noted that the heart of the city – zones I and II – were constantly encroached on by business, and had high concentrations of transient populations, the homeless and newly arrived immigrants, all of whom occupied street corners and run down housing. They noted that these 'zones of transition' tended to be areas with a high level of social unrest and crime. Social Disorganisation Theory and later developments, such as the Broken Windows hypothesis, are sociological theories of crime as they seek to connect the structure of urban environments with participation in criminal activity.

SOCIOLOGICAL CRIMINOLOGY

A collective term covering an array of perspectives which share in common the view that criminal and deviant behaviour should be explored and explained in terms of social structures and forces. These have been conceptualised in different ways, such as for example in terms of a society's social and economic inequalities, its class divisions, its poverty levels, its cityscapes and urban geographies, as well as its cultural norms and values and common-sense ways of doing and thinking about things.

STRAIN THEORY (ALSO KNOWN AS GENERAL STRAIN THEORY OR INSTITUTIONAL ANOMIE THEORY)

A sociological theory of crime derived from the work of Durkheim, Merton and Agnew. Sometimes referred to as General Strain Theory (Agnew) or Institutional Anomie Theory (Merton) Strain Theory recognises that a person's freedom of action is constrained by their position within the social structure of society, which can lead them to experience anomie (feelings of difference, isolation and alienation) that in turn can lead to personal feelings of strain, with the result that they might respond to this sense of strain by engaging in deviant and criminal behaviour. Therefore, for strain theorists, the causes of crime are not wholly located within an individual and their biology, their psychology, or their free will to act as they wish. Rather they are in no small part a result of negative emotions and feelings which arise from contradictions present within the organisational and ideological fabric of the everyday social worlds we inhibit as we live out our lives.

SUTHERLAND

Sutherland is a social psychologist who argued that the idea that people who break the law are psychologically different or atypical is highly problematic. In contrast, he proposed the theory of differential association, which states that we gain most insight into the causes of crime by looking at which people individuals associate with, as like any other type of behaviour criminal behaviour is socially learned in and through interaction with other people. Differential association theory has been tested repeatedly over the last 80 years and it does seem to be a key predictor of delinquent and criminal behaviour. However it does not help us to understand non-verbal cues for human behaviour and it is not known if people become delinquent because they acquire delinquent friends or acquire delinquent friends after they have themselves become delinquent.

REFERENCES

Adler, F (1975) *Sisters in crime: the rise of the new female criminal*. New York: McGraw-Hill.

Adler, PA and Adler, P (2003) *Constructions of deviance, social power, context, and interaction*. Belmont, CA: Wadsworth.

Agnew, R (2006) *Pressured into crime: an overview of general strain theory*. London: Sage.

Agnew, R and White, H (1992) An empirical test of general strain theory. *Criminology* 30 (4): 475–99.

Alexander, F and Healy, W (1935) *Roots of crime: psychoanalytic studies*. Montclair, NJ: Patterson Smith.

Andrews, J and Andrews, G (2003) Life in a secure unit: the rehabilitation of young people through the use of sport. *Social Science and Medicine* 56 (3): 531–50.

Austin, S (2001) *When the state kills: capital punishment and the American condition*. Princeton, NJ: Princeton University Press.

Bakermans-Kranenburg, MJ and van Ijzendoorn, MH (2006) Gene–environment interaction of the dopamine d4 receptor (drd4) and observed maternal insensitivity predicting externalizing behaviour in pre-schoolers. *Developmental Psychobiology* 48 (5): 406–9.

Barry, A, Osborne, T and Rose, N (eds) (1996) *Foucault and political reason*. London: University College London Press.

Bartels, L and Richards, K (2011) *Qualitative criminology*. Annandale, NSW: Federation Press.

Bartol, CR (1999) *Criminal behaviour: a psychosocial approach*. Englewood Cliffs, NJ: Prentice-Hall

Beccaria, C (1764) *On crime and punishments*. New York: Bobbs-Merril.

Beck, U (1992) *Risk society: towards a new modernity*. London: Sage.

Beck, U and Beck-Gernsheim, E (2002) *Individualization: institutionalized individualism and its social and political consequences*. London: Sage.

Becker, H (1963) *Outsiders: studies in the sociology of deviance*. New York: The Free Press.

Becker, H (1967) Whose side are we on? *Social Problems* 14 (3): 234–47.

Beirne, P (1987) Adolphe Quetelet and the origins of positivist criminology. *American Journal of Sociology* 92 (5): 1140–69.

Bennett, J (1981) *Oral history and delinquency: the rhetoric of criminology*. Chicago: University of Chicago Press.

Benson, M (2013, 2nd edn) *Crime and the life course*. London: Routledge.

Bentham, J (1789) *The principles of morals and legislation*. Oxford: Clarendon Press.

Berlin, I (2002 [1969]) Two concepts of liberty. *Four essays on liberty*. Oxford: Oxford University Press.

Bletzer, KV and Koss, MP (2006) After-rape among three populations in the southwest: a time for mourning, a time for recovery. *Violence Against Women* 12 (1): 5–29.

Blumer, H (1969) *Symbolic interactionism: perspective and method.* Englewood Cliffs, NJ: Prentice-Hall.

Bogard, W (2007) Surveillance, its simulation and hyper-control in virtual systems. In Hier, SP and Greenberg, J (eds), *The surveillance studies reader.* Milton Keynes: Open University Press.

Bonger, W (1905) *Criminality and economic conditions.* London: Sage.

Bowlby, J (1969) *Attachment and loss: volume 1. Loss.* New York: Basic Books.

Braithwaite, J (2002) *Restorative justice and responsive regulation.* Cambridge: Cambridge University Press.

Burchell, G (1993) Liberal government and techniques of the self. *Economy and Society* 22 (3): 26–82.

Burchell, G (1996) Liberal government and techniques of the self. In Barry, A, Osborne, T and Rose, N (eds), *Foucault and political reason.* London: University College London Press.

Burgess, R and Akers, RA (1966) Differential association-reinforcement theory of criminal behavior. *Social Problems* 14 (2): 128–47.

Button, TM, Scourfield J, Martin N, Purcell, S and McGuffin, P (2005) Family dysfunction interacts with genes in the causation of antisocial symptoms. *Behavioural Genetics* 35 (2): 115–20.

Carlen, P (1988) *Women, crime and poverty.* Milton Keynes: Open University Press.

Chamberlain, JM (2013) *Understanding criminological research: a guide to data analysis.* London: Sage.

Chesney-Lind, M (1987) *Girls' crime and women's place.* Honolulu: University of Hawaii Press.

Christiansen, KO (1977) Seriousness of criminality and concordance amongst Danish twins. In Hood, R (ed.), *Crime and public policy.* New York: The Free Press.

Clandinin, DJ and Connolly, FM (2000) *Narrative inquiry: experience and story in qualitative research.* San Francisco: Jossey Bass.

Cloninger, CR and Gottesman, I (1987) Genetic and environmental factors in antisocial behaviour disorder. In Mednick, SA, Moffitt, ET and Stack, SA (eds), *The causes of crime: new biological approaches.* Cambridge: Cambridge University Press.

Cohen, AK (1955) *Delinquent boys: the culture of the gang.* Glencoe, IL: The Free Press.

Cohen, E (2010) *Mass surveillance and state control.* London: Palgrave Macmillan.

Cohen, LE and Felson, M (1979) Social change and crime rate trends: a routine activity approach. *American Sociological Review* 44 (4): 588–608.

Cohen, S (1973) *Folk devils and moral panics.* St Albans: Paladin.

Cohen, S (1985) *Visions of social control: crime, punishment and classification.* Cambridge: Polity Press.

Coleman, R, Sim, J, Tombs, S and Whyte, D (2009) *State, power, crime.* London: Sage.

Connell, R (1995) *Masculinities.* Cambridge: Polity Press.

Corman, H, Dhaval MD, Reichman, N and Dhiman, D (2010) Effects of welfare reform on illicit drug use of adult women. NBER working paper 16072.

Cornish, DB (1994) The procedural analysis of offending and its relevance for situational prevention. In Clarke, RV (ed.), *Crime prevention studies, volume two.* St Louis, MO: Willow Tree Press.

Cornish, DB and Clarke, RV (1985) Modelling offenders' decisions: a framework for research and policy. *Crime and Justice* 6: 147–85.

Cornish, DB and Clarke, RV (1986) *The reasoning criminal.* New York: Springer.

Davidson, R (2004) What does the prefrontal cortex do in affect: perspectives on frontal EEG asymmetry research. *Biological Psychology* 67: 219–34.

DeFeudis, FV and Schauss, AG (1987) The role of brain monoamine metabolite concentrations in arsonists and habitually violent offenders: abnormalities of criminals or social isolation effects? *International Journal of Biosocial Research* 9 (1): 27–30.

Deflem, M (2006) *Sociological theory and criminological research: views from Europe and the United States.* London: Elsevier.

DeKeseredy, WS (2011) *Contemporary critical criminology.* London: Routledge.

Deleuze, G (1988) *Foucault.* Minneapolis: University of Minnesota Press.

du Guy, P (1996) *Consumption and identity at work.* London: Sage.

Durkheim, E (1964 [1895]) *Rules of sociological method.* New York: The Free Press.

Durkheim, E (1979 [1897]) *Suicide: a study in sociology.* London: Routledge and Kegan Paul.

Easton, S and Piper, C (2012) *Sentencing and punishment: the quest for justice.* Oxford: Oxford University Press.

Eck, JE (1994) Drug markets and drug places: a case-control study of the spatial structure of illicit drug dealing. Unpublished PhD dissertation, University of Maryland, College Park.

Elster, J (1986) *Karl Marx: A reader.* Cambridge: Cambridge University Press.

Erikson, K (1962) Notes on the sociology of deviance. *Social Problems* 9: 307–14.

Evans, T and Wallace, P (2008) A prison within a prison: the masculinity narratives of male prisoners. *Men and Masculinities* 10 (4): 484–97.

Eysenck, HJ (1952) The effects of psychotherapy: an evaluation. *Journal of Consulting Psychology* 16: 319–24.

Eysenck, HJ (1997) *Dimensions of personality.* London: Transaction Publishers.

Eysenck, HJ and Eysenck, SBG (1976) *Psychoticism as a dimension of personality.* London: Hodder and Stoughton.

Feeley, M and Simon, J (1992) The new penology: notes on the emerging strategy for corrections. *Criminology* 30 (4): 449–75.

Feeley, M and Simon, J (1994) Actuarial justice: the emerging new criminal law. In Nelken D (ed.), *The futures of criminology.* London: Sage.

Feilzer, M and Hood, R (2004) *Difference in discrimination?* London: Youth Justice Board.

Felson, M and Clarke, RV (1998) *Police research series, paper ninety-eight: Opportunity makes the thief.* London: Home Office.

Ferrell, J (2004) Boredom, crime, and criminology. *Theoretical Criminology* 8 (3): 287–302.

Ferrell, J, Hayward, K, Morrison, W and Presdee, M (eds) (2004) *Cultural criminology unleashed.* London: Cavendish/Glasshouse.

Foucault, M (1979) *Discipline and punish: the birth of the prison.* London: Allen Lane.

Foucault, M (1991) Governmentality. In Burchell, G, Gordon, C and Miller, P (eds), *The Foucault effect: studies in governmentality*. Hemel Hempstead: Harvester Wheatsheaf.

Freud, S (2012 edn) *A general introduction to psychoanalysis* (Wordsworth classics of world literature). London: Wordsworth Editions Ltd.

Fukuyama, F (1992) *The end of history and the last man*. London: Penguin.

Gall, FJ (1835) *On the functions of the brain and of each of its parts: with observations on the possibility of determining the instincts, propensities, and talents, or the moral and intellectual dispositions of men and animals, by the configuration of the brain and head*. Boston: Marsh, Capen and Lyon.

Garland, D (2001) *Mass imprisonment: social causes and consequences*. London: Sage.

Garland, D (2002) The development of British criminology. In Maguire, M, Morgan, R and Reiner, R (eds), *The Oxford handbook of criminology*, 5th edn. Oxford: Clarendon Press.

George, L and Kelling, GL (1998) *Fixing broken windows: restoring order and reducing crime in our communities*. New York: Simon and Schuster Touchstone.

Gesch, B (2002) Influence of supplementary vitamins, minerals, and essential fatty acids on the antisocial behaviour of young adult prisoners. *British Journal of Psychiatry* 181: 22–8.

Giddens, A (1990) *The consequences of modernity*. Cambridge: Polity Press.

Giddens, A (1991) *Modernity and self-identity: self and society in late modernity*. Cambridge: Polity Press.

Giddens, A (1999) Risk and responsibility. *Modern Law Review* 62: 3–10.

Goldson, B and Muncie, J (2006) *Youth crime and justice*. London: Sage.

Golomb, BA, Stattin, H and Mednick, S (2000) Low cholesterol and violent crime. *Journal of Psychiatric Research* 34 (4–5): 301–9.

Goody, J (2000) Biographical lessons for criminology. *Theoretical Criminology* 4 (4): 473–98.

Gordon, C (1996) Foucault in Britain. In Barry, A, Osborne, T and Rose, N (eds), *Foucault and political reason*. London: University College London Press.

Goring, C (1913) *The English convict: a statistical study*. London: HMSO.

Gray, P (2009) The political economy of risk and the new governance of youth crime. *Punishment and Society* 11 (4): 443–58.

Gresswell, DM and Hollin, CR (1994) Multiple murder. *British Journal of Criminology* 341: 1–44.

Gul, S (2009) An evaluation of rational choice theory in criminology. *Sociology and Applied Science* 4 (8): 36–44.

Hagan, J, Gillis, AR and Simpson, J (1990) Clarifying and extending power-control theory. *The American Journal of Sociology* 95 (4): 1024–37.

Haggerty, KD (2009) *Crime, media, culture: modern serial killer*. London: Sage.

Haggerty, KD and Ericson, RV (2006) *The new politics of surveillance and visibility*. Toronto: University of Toronto Press

Hall, S (1978) *Policing the crisis: mugging, the state and law and order*. London: Macmillan.

Hickley, EW (2010) *Serial murderers and their victims*. Belmont, CA: Wadsworth, Cengage Learning.

Hirschi, T (1969) *Causes of delinquency*. Berkeley: University of California Press.

Hirschi, T and Gottfredson, M (1995) Control theory and the life course perspective. *Studies in Crime and Crime Prevention* 4 (2): 131–42.

Hogg, R (2002) *Critical criminology: issues, debates, challenges.* London: Willan Publishing.

Holmes, WM and DeBurger, J (1985) Profiles in terror: the serial murder. *Federal Probation* 44 (3): 29–34.

Home Office (2013a) *Crime survey of England and Wales 2011/12.* London: Home Office.

Home Office (2013b) *An overview of sexual offending in England and Wales.* London: Home Office.

Hooton, EA (1939a) *The American criminal.* New York: Greenwood Press.

Hooton, EA (1939b) *Crime and man.* New York: Greenwood Press.

Hoskison, J (1998) *Inside: one man's experience of prison.* London: John Murray.

Howitt, D (2006) *Introduction to forensic and criminal psychology.* Harlow: Pearson.

Hudson, B (2003) *Justice in the risk society: challenging and reaffirming justice in late modernity.* London: Sage.

Humphreys, L (1970) *Tearoom trade: a study of homosexual encounters in public places.* London: Duckworth.

James, J (2004) American prison notebooks. *Race and Class* 45 (3) 10–20.

Katz, J (1988) *Seductions of crime.* New York: Basic Books.

Keizer, K, Lindenberg, S and Steg, L (2008) The spreading of disorder. *Science* 322 (5908): 1681–5.

Kelly, L (2011) Social inclusion through sports-based interventions? *Critical Social Policy* 31 (1): 126–50.

Kendler, KS and Baker, JH (2007) Genetic influences on measures of the environment: A systematic review. *Psychological Medicine* 37 (5): 615–26.

Kirkcaldy, BD and Brown, JM (1999) Personality, socioeconomics and crime: an international comparison. *Psychology, Crime and Law* 6 (2): 113–25.

Kleck, G, Tank, J and Bellows, JJ (2006) What methods are most frequently used in research in criminology and criminal justice? *Criminal Justice Education* 17 (2): 503–25.

Knepper, P (2007) *Criminology and social policy.* London: Sage.

Knepper, P and Ystehede, PJ (2012) *The Cesare Lombroso handbook.* London: Routledge.

Kretschmer, E (1921) *Physique and character.* New York: The Humanities Press.

Kubrin, C and Weitzer, R (2003) New directions in social disorganization theory. *Journal of Research in Crime and Delinquency* 40 (4): 374–402.

Laub, JH and Sampson, RJ (1991) The Sutherland–Glueck debate: On the sociology of criminological knowledge. *American Journal of Sociology* 96 (6): 1402–40.

Lemert, C (1951) *Social pathology.* New York: McGraw-Hill.

Lemert, E (1951) *Social psychology.* Chicago: University of Chicago Press.

Leyton, A (1986) *Compulsive killers.* New York: New York University Press.

Lombroso, C (1876, 2006 edn) *Criminal man.* Durham, NC: Duke University Press.

Lombroso, C (1895, 2006 edn) *The female offender.* Durham, NC: Duke University Press.

Lupton, D (2011, 3rd edn) *Medicine as culture.* London: Sage.

Lyng, S (1990) Edgework: A social psychological analysis of voluntary risk taking. *American Journal of Sociology* 95 (4): 851–86.

Lyon, D (1993) *The electronic eye: The rise of surveillance society: computers and social control in context.* London: Sage.

Lyon, D (2001) *Surveillance society: monitoring everyday life.* London: Sage.

Macpherson, CB (1962) *The political theory of possessive individualism.* Oxford: Clarendon Press.

Maguire, M, Morgan, R and Reiner, R (2012, 5th edn) *The Oxford handbook of criminology.* Oxford: Oxford University Press.

Matthews, R and Young, J (1992) *Rethinking criminology: the realist debate.* London: Sage.

Matthews, R and Young, J (2003) *The new politics of crime and punishment.* London: Willan Publishing.

May, T (2010) *Statistics on race and the criminal justice system.* London: Ministry of Justice.

Mead, GH (1934) *Mind, self and society.* Chicago: University of Chicago Press.

Merton, RK (1938) Social structure and anomie. *American Sociological Review* 3 (5): 672–82.

Merton, RK (1949) *Social theory and social structure.* New York: The Free Press.

Messerschmidt, JW (1986) *Capitalism, patriarchy and crime.* Totowa, NJ: Rowman and Littlefield.

Messerschmidt, JW (1997) *Crime as structured action: gender, race, class, and crime in the making.* Thousand Oaks, CA: Sage.

Messerschmidt, JW (2004) *Flesh and blood: adolescent gender diversity and violence.* Lanham, MD: Rowman and Littlefield.

Millie, A, Jacobson, J, McDonald, E and Hough, M (2005) *Anti-social behaviour strategies: finding a balance.* London: The Policy Press.

Ministry of Justice (2010) *Breaking the cycle: effective punishment, rehabilitation and sentencing of offenders.* London: HMSO.

Ministry of Justice (2013a) *Prison population statistics 2012–13.* London: HMSO.

Ministry of Justice (2013b) *Proven re-offending statistics: definitions and measurements.* London: HMSO.

Moffitt, TE (1993) Adolescence-limited and life-course persistent antisocial behaviour: a developmental taxonomy. *Psychological Review* 100 (4): 674–700.

Monachesi, E (1955) Pioneers in criminology: Cesare Beccaria. *Journal of Criminal Law, Criminology and Police Science* 46: 440–5.

Moore, K and Measham, F (2012) The silent 'G': a case study in the production of 'drugs' and 'drug problems'. *Contemporary Drug Problems* 39 (3): 565–90.

Morgan, S (1999) Prison lives: critical issues in reading prisoner autobiography. *The Howard Journal of Criminal Justice* 38 (3): 23–45.

Mullins, CW and Wright, R (2003) Gender, social networks and residential burglary. *Criminology* 41 (3): 813–40.

Mythen, G (2004) *Ulrich Beck: a critical introduction to the risk society.* London: Pluto.

Nellis, M (2002) Prose and cons: offender auto/biographies, penal reform and probation training. *The Howard Journal of Criminal Justice* 41 (5): 32–48.

Pager, D (2003) The mark of a criminal record. *American Journal of Sociology* 108 (5): 937–75.

Park, RE and Burgess, EW (1969 [1921]) *Introduction to the science of sociology.* Chicago: University of Chicago Press.

Park, RE, Burgess, EW and McKenzie, RD (1967 [1925]) *The city: suggestions for the investigation of human behaviour in the urban environment*. Chicago: University of Chicago Press.

Parssinen, TM (1974) Popular science and society: the phrenology movement in early Victorian. *Britain Journal of Social History* 8 (1): 1–20.

Paternoster, R and Bachman, R (2007) *Explaining criminals and crime: essays in contemporary criminological theory*. Oxford: Oxford University Press.

Peckham, A (1985) *A woman in custody: a personal account of one nightmare journey through the English penal system*. London: Fontana.

Pepinsky, HE and Quinney, R (1991) *Criminology as peacemaking*. Bloomington: Indiana University Press.

Peters, M (2001) *Poststructuralist, Marxism and neo-liberalism: between theory and practice*. Lanham, MD: Rowman and Littlefield.

Peterson, A and Bunton, R (eds) (1997) *Foucault health and medicine*. London: Routledge.

Plummer, K (2001, 2nd edn) *Documents of life*. London: Sage.

Pogarsky, G (2002) Identifying deferrable offenders: implications for research on deterrence. *Justice Quarterly* 19 (3): 431–532.

Polanyi, M (1967) *The great transformation*. London: Routledge.

Pollak, O (1950) *The criminality of women*. Philadelphia: University of Pennsylvania Press.

Potter, J (1996) *Representing reality: discourse, rhetoric and social construction*. London: Sage.

Presdee, M (2000) *Cultural criminology and the carnival of crime*. London: Routledge.

Quinney, R (1979) *Class, state, and crime*. London: Longman Group

Radzinowicz, L (1999) *Adventures in criminology*. London: Routledge.

Raine, A (2002) Biosocial studies of antisocial and violent behaviour in children and adults: a review. *Journal of Abnormal Child Psychology* 30 (4): 311–26.

Raine, A (2005) Neocognitive impairments in boys on the life course persistent antisocial path. *Journal of Abnormal Psychology* 114 (1): 38–49.

Raine, A (2013) *The anatomy of violence: the biological roots of crime*. New York: Pantheon.

Reiman, J and Leighton, P (2012) *The rich get richer and the poor get prison*. Harlow: Pearson.

Rose, N (1992) Governing the enterprise self. In Heelas, P and Morris, P (eds), *The values of the enterprise culture*. London: Routledge.

Rose, N (1996) Governing advanced liberal democracies. In Barry, A, Osborne, T and Rose, N (eds), *Foucault and political reason*. London: University College London Press.

Rose, N (1999) *Powers of freedom: reframing political thought*. Cambridge: Cambridge University Press.

Ross, J and Richards, S (2002) *Convict criminology*. Belmont, CA: Wadsworth.

Rowe, D (2002) *Biology and crime*. Los Angeles: Roxbury.

Sampson, RJ and Laub, JH (1990) Crime and deviance over the life course: the salience of adult social bonds. *American Sociological Review* 55 (5): 609–27.

Sampson, RJ and Laub, JH (1993) *Crime in the making: pathways and turning points through life*. Cambridge, MA: Harvard University Press.

Sarat, A (2001) *When the state kills: capital punishment and the American condition*. Princeton, NJ: Princeton University Press.

Searle, C (1999) *The quality of qualitative research*. London: Sage.

Shaw, CR and McKay, HD (1942) *Juvenile delinquency in urban areas*. Chicago: University of Chicago Press.

Sheldon, WH (1940) *The varieties of human physique*. London: Harper and Brothers.

Sherman, LW (2012) *Experimental criminology*. London: Sage.

Silverman, D (2007) *A very short and fairly interesting introduction to qualitative research*. London: Sage.

Simon, J (1987) The emergence of a risk society: insurance, law and the state. *Socialist Review* 95 (6): 6–89.

Simon, J and Feeley, M (1995) True crime: the new penology and public discourse on crime. In Blomberg, TG and Cohen, S (eds), *Punishment and social control: essay in honor of Sheldon L. Messinger*. New York: Aldine de Gruyter.

Simpson, D (2005) Phrenology and the neurosciences: contributions of F. J. Gall and J. G. Spurzheim. *Australian and New Zealand Journal of Surgery* 75 (6): 475–80.

Smart, C (1977) *Women, crime and criminology*. London: Routledge and Kegan Paul.

Smith, R (2006) Actuarialism and early intervention in contemporary youth justice. In Goldson, B and Muncie, J (eds), *Youth crime and justice: critical issues*. London: Sage.

Spitzer, S (1975) Toward a Marxian theory of deviance. *Social Problems* 12: 638–51.

Staller, KM and Nelson-Gardell, D (2005) A burden in your heart: lessons of disclosure from female preadolescent and adolescent survivors of sexual abuse. *Child Abuse and Neglect* 29 (2): 1415–1432.

Stevens, LJ, Zentall, SS and Deck, JL (1995) Essential fatty-acid metabolism in boys with attention-deficit hyperactivity disorder. *American Journal of Clinical Nutrition* 62 (4): 761–8.

Stone, MD (2001) Serial sexual homicide: biological, psychological and sociological aspects. *Journal of Personality Disorders* 15 (1): 1–18.

Sutherland, D (1939, 3rd edn) *Principles of criminology*. Chicago: University of Chicago Press.

Taylor, I, Walton, P and Young, J (1973) *The new criminology: for a social theory of deviance*. London: Routledge.

Tewksbury, R, Dabney, D and Copes, H (2010) The prominence of qualitative research in criminology and criminal justice scholarship. *Criminal Justice Education* 21 (4): 297–322.

Thalia, A (2008) *The critical criminology companion*. Sydney: Hawkins Press.

Thomas, WI (1923) *The unadjusted girl: with cases and standpoint for behaviour analysis*. Boston: Little Brown.

Venkatesh, S (2008) *Gang leader for a day*. London: Penguin.

Vold, GB and Bernard, TJ (1986, 3rd edn) *Theoretical criminology*. New York: Oxford University Press.

Walklate, S (2004, 2nd edn) *Gender, crime and criminal justice*. Cullompton: Willan Publishing.

Walklate, S (2007) *Imagining the victim of crime*. Maidenhead: McGraw-Hill and Open University Press.

Ward, T and Marshall, B (2007) Narrative identity and offender rehabilitation. *International Journal of Offender Therapy and Comparative Criminology* 51 (3): 279–97.

Warshow, R (1970) The gangster as tragic hero. *The immediate experience: movies, comics, theatre and other aspects of popular culture.* New York: Atheneum.

Webber, C (2009) *Psychology and crime.* London: Sage.

White, K (2001) *The early sociology of health.* London: Routledge.

Wilson, A (2007) *Northern soul: music, drugs and subcultural identity.* Cullompton: Willan Publishing.

Wilson, JQ and Herrnstein, RJ (1985) *Crime and human nature: the definitive study of the causes of crime.* New York: The Free Press.

Wilson, JQ and Kelling, GL (1982) Broken windows. *The Atlantic Monthly* 249 (3): 29–38.

Wolfgang, ME (1973, 2nd edn) Cesare Lombroso. In Mannheim, H (ed.), *Pioneers in criminology.* Montclair, NJ: Patterson Smith.

Wright, JP, Tibbetts, SG and Daigle, LE (2015) *Criminals in the making: criminality across the life course.* London: Sage.

Young, J (1994) *The exclusive society: social exclusion, crime and difference in late modernity.* London and Thousand Oaks, CA: Sage.

Young, J (2011) *The criminological imagination.* Cambridge: Polity Press.

Zalberg, Z (2010) Effects of nutritional supplements on aggression, rule-breaking, and psychopathology among young adult prisoners. *Aggressive Behaviour* 36 (2): 117–26.

INDEX

NOTE: page numbers in **bold type** refer to glossary entries.

Cloninger, C.R., 46
Cohen, Albert, 135–7
Cohen, S., 171–3, 174
collective consciousness, 74
commitment, and social control theory, 157
communal view of human nature, 12
community-based interventions, 181
conflict theories, 102–3, 146–7
conformity, 77
Connell, R., 132
consensus theories, 102, 146
consumption, and surveillance, 175
coping, with strain, 80
Cornish, Derek, 28–9
crime and deviance
    Chicago School and social deviance, 82
    crime definition, **187**
    deviance as societal creation, 91–2
    as feature of society, 3–4
    human nature and theories of, 10–11, 182–4
    individual or social basis of, 9, 10, 145,
        189–90
    as labels *see* labelling
    medicalised solutions to, 5–7
    primary and secondary deviance, 90–1
    as problem to solve, 4–5
    rational choice theory focus on, 28
    relationship with capitalism, 107, 108–12
    as social fact, 42–3
    social functions of, 74, 75, 93–5, 102, 145–6
    see also offending
crime prevention, 29, 159–60, 173
crime scripts, 28–9
criminal careers *see* life course criminology
criminal justice
    actuarial justice, 178–82
    issues relating to, 7–8
    and left realism, 116–17
    and neoliberal enterprise form, 177–8
    new penology, 178–82
    peacemaking view of, 113
    positivist bias within, 150–1
    pre-eighteenth century, 20
    punitive approach, 112–13, 115, 177–8
    and right realism, 115
    and stigmatisation, 91
    see also punishment
criminology
    and life course, 155–61
    'malestream', 121–6
    methodology *see* methodology in
        criminology
    social context of *see* social change
    see also biological criminology; classical
        criminology; psychological
        criminology; sociological criminology

critical criminology, **187**
    and conflict theory, 102–3
    determinism and free will in, 102, 105,
        134, 148
    and duality of structure, 104–5
    intersection of gender, class and race, 132–4
    overview of, 144–9
    rejection of positivism by, 151
    see also cultural criminology; feminist
        criminology; left realism; Marxist
        criminology; peacemaking criminology
cultural criminology, 135–41, **187**
cultural structure, 76

DeBurger, J., 68
Deflem, M., 65
degeneracy atavism, 39
delinquency
    social psychological theory of, 63–5
    see also juvenile delinquency
determinism, 36
    in Chicago School approaches, 101–2
    and free will in critical criminology, 102,
        105, 134, 148
    in Marxist criminology, 102, 111
    problems of, 61
    and voluntarism, 11
deterrence, in classical criminology, 22–4, 25–7
developmental theories *see* life course
    criminology
deviance *see* crime and deviance
diagnostic tools, 66–7
diet, 50–1, **188**
differential association theory, 62–6
disciplinary power, 169–71
discipline, dispersal of, 171–3
disintegrative shaming, 96
dizygotic (DZ) twins, 46
domestic abuse, 124–5
dopamine, 50
dual taxonomy, 155–7
duality of structure, 104–5, 147–8
Durkheim, Émile, 8, 9, 73–6, 93–4,
    145–6, **188**

ecological school, 81–6
economic marginalisation thesis, 130–1
egalitarian family, 129
ego, 56, 57
egoism, 107
emotionality of crime, 136, 138–40
Enlightenment, 19, 20–1, 164–5, 169
enterprise self, 176–8, 182–3
environment *see* social environment
Ericson, R.V., 174–5
Erikson, Kai, 93–4

eugenics, 43, 44
experienced strains, 79
experts and expert knowledge, 14–15,
    167–8, 172
external risk, 167
extroversion, 60, 61
Eysenck, Hans, 59–62, **188–9**

false consciousness, 103, 146–7
fame, and serial murder, 69
family background, 47, 57, 68, 129, 157, 159
Feeley, M., 178, 179
felicity calculus, 24
feminist criminology, **189**
    approaches within, 124
    critique of 'malestream' criminology,
        121–6
    and female victims, 124–5
    growth of female offending, 125, 128–31
    and Marxism, 126–8
    and masculinity studies, 132–4
Ferrell, J., 138, 140
Foucault, M., 169–71, 173–4
free will/agency
    in Chicago School approaches, 101–2
    in classical criminology, 18, 21
    in cultural criminology, 138
    and determinism in critical criminology,
        102, 105, 134, 148
    in neoclassical criminology, 25
    and resistance to surveillance, 173–6
    and right realism, 115
    and structure, 105, 148–9
    see also rational choice theory
Freud, Sigmund, 56–7

Gall, Francis, 38
gang delinquency, 135–7
gender
    and biological criminology, 40, 122
    and class, 127, 128–9, 130–1
    as identity and structure, 104, 147–8
    intersection with class and race, 133–4
    men and masculinity, 132–4
    and relations of production, 126–7
    see also women and crime
gender roles, 128–9
general deterrence, 24
general strain theory, 79–81
genetic solutions to crime, 5
genetic theories of crime, 46–8, **189**
Gesch, B., 51
Giddens, A., 166, 167, 168, 169
Goring, Charles, 43
Gottesman, I., 46
group autonomy, 136

Hagan, John, 128–9
Haggerty, K.D., 174–5
Hall, Stuart, 110
Healy, W., 57
hegemonic masculinity, 132–3
Herrnstein, Richard, 115
Hickley, E.W., 68
high modernity, 166
    and risk society, 166–71
Hirschi, Travis, 157–8
Hobbes, Thomas, 19
Holmes, W.M., 68
home environment, 47, 57, 68, 129,
    157, 159
homicidal protest model, 68–9
Hooton, Earnest, 43
hormones, 50
Hudson, B., 178, 179
human nature
    Durkheim's view of, 74
    in Freudian theory, 56
    individual in risk society, 166–8
    liberalism and possessive individualism,
        165–6
    rational in classical criminology, 18–19,
        21, 22–3
    theories of crime and, 10–11, 182–4
    see also determinism; free will/agency
Humphreys, Laud, 95
hypoglycaemia, 50–1

id, 56, 57
identity
    and labelling theory, 90–1, 95
    race, class and gender as, 104, 148
    role of reference groups, 89
    see also self
imprisonment
    and biological criminology, 35–6
    in capitalist states, 112
    rise in use of, 178
    and surveillance, 169–70
impulsivity, 47
individual
    agency of see free will/agency
    in classical criminology, 18
    liberal view of, 165–6
    origins of crime within, 10
    in rational choice theory, 28
    in risk society, 166–8
    theories based on see biological
        criminology; classical criminology;
        psychological criminology
individual characteristic/social phenomena
    dichotomy, 9, 10, 145, **189–90**
industrial revolution, 21, 165

inequality
  and anomie, 77
  and conflict theories, 102, 147
  and labelling theory, 93
  and liberalism, 165
  structural, 104–5
innovation, 78
institutional anomie theory, 76–9
internet, 140
involvement, and social control theory, 157
Italian School, 39

justice *see* criminal justice
juvenile delinquency
  adolescent limited offenders, 156
  gang delinquency, 135–7
  group influences on, 64
  Shaw and McKay's work, 82–4
  see also youth offending

Katz, J., 138–9, 141
Keizer, K., 84–5
Kelling, G.L., 84
Keynesian economics, 166
Kirkaldy, B.D., 61
Kretschmer, Ernst, 44

labelling
  crime as label, 4, 8–9
  in interests of state, 7–8
  and Sutherland's social learning theory, 64
labelling theory, 86–7, 146, **190**
  Becker's work, 91–3
  Braithwaite's reintegrative shaming theory, 96–7
  criticisms of, 95
  Erikson's social functions of deviance, 93–4
  and free will, 101–2
  impact of, 95, 96
  Lemert's primary and secondary deviance, 90–1
late modernity *see* high modernity
Laub, J.H., 158–9
Law of Effect, 58
law enforcement, and labelling theory, 92–3
learning *see* behaviourism; social learning theory
left realism, 102, 114, 115–16, **190**
Leighton, P., 113
Lemert, Edwin, 90–1
Leviathan, Hobbes concept of, 19
Leyton, A., 68–9
liberalism, 165–6
  see also neoliberalism
liberation opportunity thesis, 129–30
life course criminology, 155–61, **190–1**
life course persistent offenders, 156
life events, and serial killers, 67, 69

life story research, 152–3
Lombrosian criminology, 35–6, 42
Lombroso, Cesare, 39–40, 122, **191**
Lyng, S., 139
Lyon, D., 168, 174

McKay, Henry, 82–3
'malestream' criminology, 121–6
maliciousness, 136
managerialism, 180
manufactured risk, 167
Marx, Karl, 106–7, **191**
Marxist criminology, **191–2**
  crime as response to capitalism, 108–12
  criticisms of, 110–11
  determinism of, 102, 111
  and false consciousness, 103, 146–7
  and feminist criminology, 126–8
  Marx and Bonger's influence, 106–8
masculinity studies, 132–4
Matthews, Roger, 115
Mead, G.H., 87–9, **192**
means of production, 106–7
Measham, F., 140
mechanical solidarity, 74–5
media, 69, 137–8
medicalised solutions to crime, 5–7
men
  and masculinity, 132–4
  women's offending compared with, 125, 127, 128–9, 130
mental capacity, 25
mental health disorders, 66–9, 156–7
Merton, R.K., 76–9, 135
Messerschmidt, J.W., 126–7, 133–4
methodological problems of twin studies, 47
methodology in criminology
  narrative and life story research, 152–3
  positivist bias, 150–1
  see also scientific approach
modernity
  birth of, 164–5
  liberalism and possessive individualism, 165–6
  replaced by high modernity, 166
Moffitt, Terri, 155–7
Monachesi, E., 20
monozygotic (MZ) twins, 46
Moore, K., 140
moral crusaders, 92
moral order, 93–4
moral panics, 137
Mullins, C.W., 130
murder, 67–9

narrative research, 152–3
negativism, 136

neighbourhood studies, 82–3
neoclassical criminology, 24–5
  critique of, 25–7
neoliberalism, 182–3
  and actuarial justice, 178–82
  and enterprise self, 176–8
nervous system, and personality, 60, 61
neurocriminology, 49
neuropsychological deficits *see* mental
    health disorders
neuroticism, 60
neurotransmitters, 50
New Labour, 116–17
non-utilitarianism, 136
norepinephrine, 50

offenders
  categorising, 60–1, 68
  crime and emotion of, 136, 138–40
  in rational choice theory, 28
  violent and sex offenders, 67–9
offending
  growth of female, 125, 128–31
  male compared with female, 125, 127,
    128–9, 130
  over life course, 155–61
  see also crime and deviance
ontological viewpoints, 10–11, 12, **192–3**
operant conditioning, 58–9
opportunity theories, 29–31, 129–30
organic solidarity, 75

panopticon, 170, 175
Park, Robert, 82
patriarchal family, 129
patriarchy, 124
Pavlov, Ivan, 58
peacemaking criminology, 102, 112–14
penal policy, and actuarial justice, 178–82
Pepinsky, Harold, 112, 113
personality
  and body type, 44
  Eysenck's theory of, 59–62
  Freud's theory of, 56–7
perspectives, of author, 11–12
pharmacological solutions to crime, 5–6
phrenology, 38–9, **193**
physical appearance, and criminality, 37–45
physiognomy, 37, **193**
place, ecological school, 82–6
Pogarsky, G., 26
Pollak, Otto, 123
positivism, 36, **193–4**
  and biological criminology, 39, 42–3
  and critical criminology, 150–1
  and psychological criminology, 55

possessive individualism, 165–6
postmodernism, and anti-realism, 152
power
  disciplinary, 169–71
  justice and interests of, 7–8
  and labelling, 93
power/control theory, 128–9
Presdee, M., 139–40
primary deviance, 90–1
prisons *see* imprisonment
privacy, 175
private sphere, women in, 122–3, 127
profiling
  of offenders, 60–1, 68
  of risk populations, 173, 181
protest
  and false consciousness, 103
  labelled as deviant, 7–8
  see also resistance
psychological criminology, **194**
  behaviourism, 57–9
  Eysenck's personality theory, 59–62
  Freud's theory, 56–7
  and life course approach, 156
  mentally disordered offenders, 66–9
  positivist approach in, 55
  social learning theory, 62–6
psychoticism, 60
public sphere, women in, 129–30
punishment
  in classical criminology, 22, 23–4
  Foucault on surveillance and, 169–70
  functions of, 93–4
  and phrenology, 38
  see also criminal justice; imprisonment
punitive approach
  in capitalist societies, 112–13
  of neoliberalism, 177–8
  of right realism, 115
punitive deviation, 91

qualitative research, 152–3
quantitative research, 150–1
Quinney, Richard, 109–10, 112, 113

race and ethnicity
  in criminal justice system, 112, 134
  and criminality, 43–4, 83
  and duality of structure, 104, 147–8
  intersection with gender, and class, 133–4
rational choice theory
  in classical criminology, 10, 18–19,
    21, 22
  in contemporary theory, 28–9
  and situational crime prevention, 29–31
rationality, in Marxist criminology, 108–9

realism, 150, 151–2, **194**
    left realism, 102, 114, 115–16, **190**
    right realism, 114–15, 159, **195**
rebellion, 78
recidivism, 179, 180
reference groups, 89
rehabilitation, 179
Reiman, J., 113
reintegrative shaming theory, 96–7
relations of production, 107, 126–7
relative deprivation, 117
religious perspective
    move away from, 19, 21
    on phrenology, 38–9
resistance
    to surveillance, 173–6
    see also protest
responsibilisation, 180
restorative justice, 97, 113–14
retreatism, 78
right realism, 114–15, 159, **195**
risk populations, and penal policy, 178, 179
risk profiling, 173, 181
risk society
    rise of, 166–8
    as surveillance society, 168–71
ritualism, 77
role-taking, 88–9
routine activity theory, 30, **195**
rule enforcers, 92–3

Sampson, R.J., 158–9
scientific approach
    of Enlightenment, 164–5
    of Lombrosian criminology, 35–6, 39, 42
    of positivism, 36, 55, 150–1
    and social control, 173
second life, crime in, 139–40
secondary deviance, 90–1
self
    enterprise self, 176–8, 182–3
    Mead's concept of, 88
    see also identity
self-governance, 180
self-surveillance, 171, 172
serial murder, 67–9
serotonin, 50
sex crimes, 124–5
sex offenders, 66–8
shaming theory, 96–7
Shaw, Clifford, 82–4
Sheldon, William, 44
short-run hedonism, 136
Simon, J., 178, 179
situational crime prevention, 29–31
Skinner, B.F., 58

Smart, Carol, 124
social bonds, 157, 158, 159
social change
    and anomie, 75
    and approaches to crime, 20–1
    and birth of modernity, 164–5
    dispersal of discipline, 171–3
    resisting surveillance, 173–6
    and rise of risk society, 166–8
    risk society and surveillance, 168–71
social contract, 19
social control
    and dispersal of discipline, 171–3
    resistance to surveillance, 173–6
    role of social bonds, 157, 158, 159
    surveillance society, 168–71
    see also social order
social control theory (SCT), 157–8
social defiance, 26
social deviance, Chicago School
    focus on, 82
social disorganisation theory, 81–6, 101, **196**
social environment
    in biological theory, 47, 51
    in Eysenck's theory, 60
    ignored in new penology, 179–80
    in individual-based theories, 55
    in neoclassical theory, 25
    in right realism, 115
    in Sutherland's theory, 65
    see also home environment
social exclusion, 116
social facts, 42–3, 74
social functions of crime and deviance, 74, 75,
    93–5, 102, 145–6
social interaction *see* symbolic interactionism
social learning theory, 62–6
social norms and values
    and anomie, 75
    and status frustration, 136–7
social order
    and classical criminology, 19–20, 21
    and cultural criminology, 138
    and Durkheim, 74–5, 146
    see also social control
social phenomena
    crime as individual characteristic or, 9, 10,
        145, **189–90**
    origins of crime in, 10
    theories based on *see* sociological criminology
    see also social environment
social psychology, 62–6
social reformers, 165–6
social structure
    and agency, 105, 148–9
    Merton's concept of, 76